What readers are saying about *Manage It!*

As a 30+ year veteran in the growth of PM, I gained insight into things I have been doing for years. Here, process takes a backseat to context, and Johanna provides the professional with one of the finest compendiums of observations, advice, and counsel on managing projects I have come across.

▶ **Mike Dwyer**
   Sr. Manager, Strategic Initiatives, Healthways

Johanna packs a wealth of practical advice into this book. Even the most experienced project managers will find numerous nuggets and gems that they can immediately apply to their project work.

▶ **James A. Ward**
   Senior Project Management Consultant, James A. Ward and Associates, Inc.

As I was reading this book, I was picturing in my mind many similar experiences. As I thought to myself, "But what about this?" I kept finding what I was thinking of! This is one of the best IT books I have ever read, but it still shows Johanna's personality. It almost feels like she is at your elbow as you read it.

▶ **Eric Petersen**
   Senior Consultant, Emprove

Most project management stuff I've read is very cerebral and theoretical, and then sometimes it's extraordinarily specific and dictatorial but in a realm that has nothing to do with me. This book provides just what I need—specific suggestions about dealing with reality. Moreover, it suggests how to think about the problem, rather than stopping at the cookbook answer.

▶ **Peter Harris**
   Solutions Architect, Claricode, Inc.

This book is a pleasure to read and is packed with wisdom. Junior project managers will get a great introduction with some really valuable practical advice, while senior project managers will learn some new tricks and relearn some forgotten fundamentals. Project sponsors and customers should get a copy too. I pulled some classics from my shelves including DeMarco, Weinberg, Brooks, McConnell, Cockburn, McCarthy, and Humphrey. Johanna is as readable as the best of them.

► **George Hawthorne**
   Project Manager, Oblomov Consulting

I've been on the receiving end of (mostly) poor project management for nearly twenty years. I had never entertained the thought of becoming a project manager, however, until I read this book. Johanna places the art in perspective and codifies a practical, flexible approach, founded on empirical process control theory that thrives on dynamic environments—where continuous learning is essential to project success. I've implored everyone associated with project work to read it. Twice.

► **Bil Kleb**
   Aerospace Engineer

In twenty years of managing projects, there have been many new items for project managers to consider. Johanna Rothman describes many of them in *Manage It!* The chapter on meetings is worth the price of the book by itself. Read this book, and practice its principles. The people who work on your projects will think you are really smart.

► **Dwayne Phillips**
   Senior Systems Engineer

Each project is unique—which is why all project managers need to know more than one approach for managing projects. Johanna walks us through her thought process to assess the context around the project, choose a life cycle, and establish clear criteria for a project. Her advice will help you make choices that will help your project succeed.

► **Esther Derby**
   President, esther derby associates, inc.

Manage It!

Your Guide to Modern,
Pragmatic Project Management

Manage It!

Your Guide to Modern, Pragmatic Project Management

Johanna Rothman

The Pragmatic Bookshelf
Raleigh, North Carolina   Dallas, Texas

Many of the designations used by manufacturers and sellers to distinguish their products are claimed as trademarks. Where those designations appear in this book, and The Pragmatic Programmers, LLC was aware of a trademark claim, the designations have been printed in initial capital letters or in all capitals. The Pragmatic Starter Kit, The Pragmatic Programmer, Pragmatic Programming, Pragmatic Bookshelf and the linking *g* device are trademarks of The Pragmatic Programmers, LLC.

Every precaution was taken in the preparation of this book. However, the publisher assumes no responsibility for errors or omissions, or for damages that may result from the use of information (including program listings) contained herein.

Our Pragmatic courses, workshops, and other products can help you and your team create better software and have more fun. For more information, as well as the latest Pragmatic titles, please visit us at

http://www.pragmaticprogrammer.com

ISBN-10: 0-9787392-4-8

ISBN-13: 978-0-9787392-4-9

Printed on acid-free paper with 85% recycled, 30% post-consumer content.

First printing, June 2007

Version: 2007-5-8

To Ilse Rothman, the first project manager I knew who worked in timeboxes and chunks.

And for Naomi, Shaina, and Mark, who supported me whenever I descended into my "cave" to write.

Contents

Foreword

Hello, and welcome to Johanna's latest book. I'm currently a director at Yahoo! (in Berkeley) and have been in the software business for several decades. In fact, you might have heard of Digital Equipment Corporation (the foundation of the early Internet) and its Alpha system. That was a very important project for me.

I played a major role in the delivery of the Alpha software. It was a monumental task: some 2,000 engineers scattered all over the world, all working on various parts of the system. It required rigorous planning and project management, and we delivered on a four-year schedule within one month of our target date. So, as you can imagine, I thought I was a pretty good manager! But I was about to find out what an *excellent* manager is like.

In May 1996, I decided to leave DEC, and I heard about a job opening at another major software company in the Boston area. It was just the kind of challenge I relish, director of a product group—"a team living in chaos." Great, I thought. This is what I do! Coax the potential out of the chaos, and help deliver an actual working product. Now where's my white horse?

I heard that a consultant had been brought in to "triage" the development of the group's beta release. This only strengthened my conviction that they would soon find the hero they had been waiting for—in me.

But, wow! Instead, I was instantly (and progressively more and more) humbled and impressed. I understand what consultants are supposed to do. . . but when do they actually articulate situations in practical and actionable ways? This consultant had done just that. And in just a couple of months, she had managed to get all the pieces in place: a project charter, a program plan, and project plans, as well as defined roles and responsibilities, a defined development process, pertinent metrics, release criteria, beta customers. . . all the elements that are critical for a project to succeed.

But all that usually takes significant time to put in place—especially when starting from a deficit position. Yet here they were! You've probably guessed by now that this consultant was Johanna Rothman. (Johanna has a case study about our joint adventure on her website—only the names have been changed to protect the guilty!)

Over the years since I first met Johanna, I've run software development organizations in companies large and small. And on numerous occasions, I've engaged Johanna's services to help move my team to the next level. Her assessment process is rigorous and provides the solid footing that's required for effective project management. She tailors effective workshops on a multitude of topics—for me, she has done iterative project requirements, project management, and QA. I have hired her for interim management positions and for one-on-one coaching for people with varied skill sets. Johanna draws on a broad range of experience in a diversity of situations and organizations, and she always manages to provide solutions that are practical and realistic—solutions that can actually be implemented to solve key problems.

And so, this book is a real gift from Johanna.

She pulls knowledge from all her years on the front lines and presents the material in a cohesive way. The book provides you with the tools you need to analyze your own situation, build a framework and rational plan, and then execute. Johanna gives you lots of tips and examples of what works and what doesn't—and advice on how to avoid the rat holes. Even after years of project and program management experience, I learned new things when reviewing this book. And when I'm in a new or challenging situation or when I need a sounding board to help me think through a tough problem, Johanna is the one I call.

Oh, yeah—that project we worked on when I first met Johanna? We shipped the product to the beta customers, and it worked!

I know Johanna's book will help you succeed as well.

Ellen R. Salisbury (Director, Yahoo! Research Berkeley)
April 2007

Preface

You've been bombarded with a ton of techniques, practices, and unsolicited pieces of advice about how to manage projects. All of them are saying "Look at me, I'm right."

Well, many of them are right—under certain conditions. Since each project is unique, you will need to evaluate your context (the project, the project team, and the business in which you're working) and then make pragmatic choices about what will work and what won't.

Every day your projects become faster-paced, your customers grow more impatient, and there is less and less tolerance for products that don't work. What worked before might have been good enough to get you here, but the chances that it will work in the future are not good. You must take advantage of all practices and techniques to reduce your project's risk, including considering agile techniques for every project.

This book is a risk-based guide to making good decisions about how to plan and guide your projects. It will help software project managers, team members, and software managers succeed. Much of the information also applies if you are building more tangible products, such as a house or a circuit board, or if you are managing a service project.

I'm assuming you're managing a high-tech project, with at least some software component. You might have had some of the same project management experiences as I have: lots of software projects and some hardware/software combination projects. I've also managed a few service projects, such as planning and holding conferences. I've been part of some construction projects (one new house, one small remodel, and one large remodel). But the bulk of my experience is with software or software/hardware projects in some form.

It's harder to manage software projects than it is to manage projects that have a tangible deliverable. Software is ephemeral—not concrete, not material, not created out of substance—so we can't touch it, we can't directly measure it, and we can't see it. It's harder to see the product unfold, and it's harder to see and anticipate the risks—so it's much harder to deal with risks. The way we practice software product development does not always help us see where the project is or where it's heading.

When you manage tangible-product projects, you can see the product take shape. You can see the shell of the building, the finish on the walls, and all the steps in between. With service products with a tangible result, such as a conference or meeting, you can gain some insight into the project if there are interim deliverables, such as rough-draft reports or run-throughs of meetings. Both tangible-product projects and some service projects allow you to see project progress before the end of the project.

So, what do you do when you can't directly see project progress? What do you do when you suspect the project smells funny, and you think it might be headed toward disaster? How do you deal with stakeholders who don't want to make the decisions that will help you create a successful project?

This book is about providing insight into your software projects and managing the risks that arise from within the project as well as the risks with which you start your projects. From chartering to release, each chapter discusses ways you can see inside your software project, measure it, feel it, taste it, and smell it.

One thing you won't find in this book is the One True Way to manage projects. There is no One True Way that works for all projects. You also won't find best practices. I'll suggest helpful practices for each life cycle that might help you and the project team achieve your goals.

You'll notice that there are forward and backward references in this book. That's because a project is a nonlinear system. Your early decisions for your current project have implications for how you'll finish this one—and possibly how you'll start the next one. How you manage projects might affect the way you can manage the product backlog or project portfolio.

All the templates in this book are also online, at the book's home page, http://pragmaticprogrammer.com/titles/jrpm.

I thank all the people who helped me write and edit this book: Tom Ayerst, Jim Bullock, Brian Burke, Piers Cawley, Shanti Chilukuri, Esther Derby, Michael F. Dwyer, Mark Druy, Jenn Greene, Payson Hall, Peter Harris, George Hawthorne, Ron Jeffries, Bil Kleb, Michael Lee, Hal Macomber, Rob McGurrin, Andrew McKinlay, Erik Petersen, Dwayne Phillips, Frederick Ros, Ellen Salisbury, George Stepanek, Andrew Wagner, and Jim Ward. My editor, Daniel Steinberg, provided exceptionally helpful feedback. Kim Wimpsett was again a copyeditor *par excellence*. I thank Steve Peter for his typesetting wizardry. Mark Tatro of Rotate Graphics developed all the schedule game cartoons. Working with Andy Hunt and Dave Thomas was, once again, my pleasure. Any mistakes are mine.

The stories I'm telling are all true—the names, companies, and specifics have all been changed to protect the innocent and the guilty.

Let's start.

Johanna Rothman
April 2007

Chapter 1

Starting a Project

The easiest way to start a project wrong is to just start. Want at least a reasonable hope for success? That will take a bit more organizing and planning. You'll need to know what's driving your project and what *done* means for the project. And you need to write those decisions down in a charter so you can share them with the rest of the project team.

1.1 Define Projects and Project Managers

First, let's make sure we agree on what a project is.

Project:
> A novel undertaking or systematic process to create a new product or service, the delivery of which signals completion. Projects involve risk and are typically constrained by limited resources.[1]

Project managers manage those risks and resources. You need project management when you have risks across the project: the schedule is tight, it's not clear you can achieve the technical goals, quality could suffer, you don't have unlimited funds, and you might not have the people you need when you need them.

Each project has a different focus, so each project is unique. That means you'll need to plan and manage each project in a way that makes sense for *your* project. Before you initiate a project, start by gathering some ideas about what the project is supposed to accomplish.

---

1. © 2007 R. Max Wideman, http://www.maxwideman.com; reproduced with permission.

What Are We Building?
by Chris, project manager

I'm a project manager at a large company. I run software/hardware integration projects. My colleague Nikky runs events. My team builds machines, and Nikky's teams organize events—our outputs aren't similar in any way, but we're both project managers.

Our risks are completely different. Our deliverables are totally different. I need software, hardware, and some documentation. Nikky needs booths, food, or whatever else it takes to make her events successful.

One of the things we do that's the same is learn at the beginning what the focus of our project is so we can define what we're building quickly. Knowing what we're building and what *done* means helps both of us run our projects.

Every project is unique. Projects have different size teams with different capabilities. Some have internal customers, and others have external customers. Some work under substantial time pressure; others have very different risks for completion. At the center of every project is the product. Again, let's agree on the following definition.

Product:
  The set of deliverables that results from the project.

You're a successful project manager—or want to be. Take a little time to identify what's unique about *this* project. That way, you can start, manage, and end the project with a shot at success.

Now that we have defined a project and product, let's clarify what we mean by a project manager. Wideman says that a project manager "heads up the project team and is assigned the authority and responsibility for conducting the project and meeting project objectives through project management."[2] That's great as a formal definition. But here's a working definition you might find more ambiguous and, at the same time, more accurate:

Project manager:
  The person whose job it is to articulate and communicate what *done* means and to guide the project team to done. By *done*, I mean a product that meets the needs of the organization developing the product and the customers who will use the product.

---

2. © 2007 R. Max Wideman, http://www.maxwideman.com; reproduced with permission.

That business of *done* implies substantial risk. I bet your product is loaded with risks. We'll take a look at how you identify and classify some of these risks. Before you do anything else, you must understand what's driving the project.

Small or Big—Projects All Involve Risk
by Eric, experienced project manager

I've worked in big projects (several years, with a couple hundred people) and small projects (two or three of us working with a client who had two or three people, over a total of three months). There's one thing I know about projects: there's always risk in getting to the final deliverable.

Sometimes the risks depend on the team. Think of something simple like making your bed at home. To me it's just a checklist item. But to my kids, making a bed is a project full of risks. Mostly the risk is they won't finish before bedtime!

1.2 Manage Your Drivers, Constraints, and Floats

One of the biggest risks to finishing a project is understanding the project's context.

The project's context is a result of what is important to the organization. What's driving the project? Are there constraints on the project? Can you trade off any of the drivers and constraints or buy yourself some more degrees of freedom?

What's Driving This Project Is Different from My Previous Project
by Stuart, project manager

I'm managing my second project now. The first project was a point release for our flagship product. It was pretty easy to figure out what we needed to focus on—adding a few new features and making sure we fixed a bunch of defects.

But this second project—wow, this one is really different. This is an experiment for us so we can see whether we want to enter this market. We need a bunch of new features. The features have to work, but we don't have to focus on defects. And the deadline is really close. My boss told me we could have a couple of more people, but not contractors, because we need to manage the cost.

What really helped was when I identified what was driving this project. The number-one priority was the feature set. The second was date. The third was the people. I had a lot more flexibility for defects and cost to release.

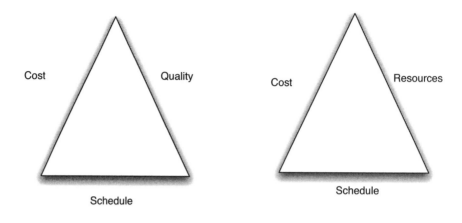

Figure 1.1: TRADITIONAL IRON TRIANGLES

You've probably heard of the *iron triangle* in projects. Two of the three sides of the triangle are cost and schedule. The third side is usually either quality or scope (see Figure 1.1). The iron triangle is too simplistic. Look at Stuart's two projects. The drivers were vastly different.

Successful project managers like Stuart trade off many more factors than what's in the iron triangle. You can't just tell your customers to choose two of the sides of the iron triangle, and then you can deliver what they want. If that was all there was to it, anyone could be a project manager.

First, write down your customers' expectations—what's driving the project from your customers' perspective [Rot98]. Your list includes what your customers expect (the feature set), when they will receive it (time to release), and how good it is (defect levels) [Gra92].

Next, write down the constraints you are under. What's your environment like? Do you have the flexibility to collocate the team? What processes are you stuck with? Who do you have? What can they do? How much money do you have? You can change these constraints (this often happens when a project is in trouble). Constraints dictate how big (or how long or how good) your project can be.

Look at your list of customers' expectations and project constraints. What jumps out as you as being required for your project's success?

Choose one item, say time to release. That is what you identify as your *driver*.

What's left on your list? You'll see things such as feature set, low defects, and cost to release. Which of the remaining items will you need to manage to make the project successful? Create a hierarchy with these concerns being a little less critical to the success of your project than the driver. Your customers' expectations and sponsors' concerns will constrain your project in one or more of those dimensions. Choose two or three of these. We will call these the *constraints* of the project.

Again, look at the remaining items. Some of these items are important to the project, but you have flexibility to manage them. We call these *floats*, and you should have at least three of them for this project.

Finally, go back to the set of items you did not select. Are any of them more important than the ones you did select? If so, you are allowed to do some juggling. If not, you have identified the driver, constraints, and floats for this project.

I've seen projects with up to three constraints succeed, but only with extraordinary effort on the part of the project team. In my experience, if you have one driver, two constraints, and three floats, you have a reasonable chance of success. The more floats you have, the easier it is to organize the project.

Ideally, you would have no more than one driver, no more than one constraint, and four floats. Most of us work on less than ideal projects, so if you have one driver, two constraints, and three floats, you can still succeed. More drivers or more constraints lead to an overconstrained project. You might be able to succeed, but you and your project team will have to select a project organization and practices that can help you get close to success—and realize you still might not achieve total success.

If you have more drivers or constraints and you feel like you have no choice but to start the project, the best thing you can do is choose something as a driver and deliver pieces of the project as often as possible to help your sponsors decide what they do want. As you start the project, keep asking context-free questions (see Section 1.5, *Use Context-Free Questions to Identify Project Drivers*, on page 10) to elicit success criteria for the project. And, define release criteria (see Section 2.3, *Release Criteria*, on page 21) so you know when you're done.

Tip: With Too Many Constraints, You Decide

Overconstrained projects will fail. Too many drivers means no one knows what the success criteria are. Too many constraints means no one in the organization is willing to make priority decisions.

If you need to, push your management into making some decisions about what's driving the project, what the constraints are, and where you have more flexibility. If that doesn't work, make the decisions yourself. Your project and the organization will benefit.

You can't create project requirements that don't fit inside the project constraints. If you try, you have the problem of a ten-pound project in a five-pound project bag. No matter what you try, you just don't have enough people, time, money, or tools to release a product when management wants it, with the features management wants, and without too many defects.

1.3 Discuss Your Project Constraints with Your Client or Sponsor

Feel free to take the initiative to understand what your sponsor wants. Here's a conversation I had with a sponsor for a recent project:

JR: *Hey Clyde, let's discuss what's really driving this project.*

Clyde: *Oh, no. Not this again. You made me do this the last time.*

JR: *Yup. And remember when you wanted to add another feature? Because you told me you wanted to squeeze in as many features as possible before the release date, I was able to add it, because of the way we had organized the project. It wasn't easy, but it was possible.*

Clyde: *Oh, yeah. I forgot. OK. But this project is different.*

JR: *Oh? Tell me more.*

Clyde: *Look, you take care of the people. And the project environment— that's your job too. Since you won't need capital equipment, I don't have to think about the cost because the cost is all salary.*

JR: *And maybe some software.*

Clyde: *Picky, picky. OK, if you need some software, let me know. But honestly, the cost is practically all salary—not something I need to manage. I really care how long this project is going to take.*

JR: *What about the feature set? Or how good it has to be? This is a small app for the finance department. You know what perfectionists they are. If I don't give them everything perfectly, Leslie blows her top.*

Clyde: *Yeah, but I'm paying for it. And what I want is to give them the smallest number of features that work well enough so that you and the team are done soon, say, in maybe ten weeks.*

JR: *If it's week eight and we don't quite have all the features and we have too many defects, what do you want to do?*

Clyde: *JR, come on. I want it all. You and your team have done this before. You can do it again.*

JR: *Clyde, you know that the project team and I will do as much as we can, assuming I understand what you really want.*

Clyde: *Fine. No half-baked features. You start it, you finish it so that Leslie likes it. Otherwise, Leslie will have my head. And I'm going to need you and the project team later to join that big program Vince has started. He says he'll be ready for more people in about ten weeks. That gives you just enough time to do something reasonable for Leslie.*

1.4 Decide on a Driver for Your Project

In my conversation with Clyde, I asked Clyde to identify what was most important to him. When Clyde said the big program was going to start in ten weeks, it was clear the date was the driver.

Early in the project, everything seems possible, especially if no one has tried to estimate anything. Your sponsor may say, "We want this project to have these five features, be done by August 1, and have no critical defects. And we want you to bring it in under a million bucks. You have these six people. OK?"

Don't say OK.

Once you estimate the work, you can see whether those six people really can do that work for the money and time. If they can, great. But more likely, it's not possible to do everything your sponsor wants in the time, for the money, with the people, and at the quality they desire, given your work environment. In that case, your sponsor needs to make some hard decisions. Make decisions based upon what's driving this project for your organization: the release date, the feature set, the cost, who's assigned and when they're assigned, and the practices and techniques you'll use.

Sponsors who don't decide what's driving their project push that decision down to the project manager. If the project manager doesn't decide, the project team will decide. But they won't decide with one mind. And they won't necessarily make the choice that the sponsor would have wanted them to make. Instead, each person—regardless of his or her role on the project—will make an individual decision. Some will optimize for the release date, throwing any concerns about low defects out the door. Some will optimize for schedule by implementing only one thing—one thing in totality with a full regression test suite—and leaving all the other features undone. Some will optimize for feature set, implementing as many stubs as possible and filling in where the testers find problems, until they run out of time. Each person will do what he or she thinks is right. Without a decision from the project sponsor (or the project manager), each person will make a different decision.

One approach is to develop a ranked list [Hal07], explaining it's like Sudoku. List the possible drivers down the left side and leave a space on the right to fill in a number.

Use a Matrix to Articulate the Project Priorities

Here's Clyde's ranked matrix.

Project Priorities	Rank
Cost to release	5
Release date	1
Feature set	2
Low defects	3
People	4
Work environment	6

In this project, the release date was the primary driver. If we had missed the release date this year, we would have lost all the value of the project.

But the features were also important—the release date without enough features was also valueless. And, given that the product was in a regulated industry, the defect levels had to be low. The people were next, because they had to be available in ten weeks for the next program. The cost of the project was less important, because the value of the project was so high. The work environment was last, because I had the flexibility to change things to finish this project on time.

Even though I had the priorities in order, we didn't have much flexibility. But knowing what was driving the project helped me define success criteria and choose a life cycle. The project team could create release criteria and use these drivers to make reasonable choices about their work. And yes, we met the requested deliverables for this project.

1.5 Manage Sponsors Who Want to Overconstrain Your Project

Most of the time, the conversation about what success looks like is not easy. You can see that I had to push Clyde to make some choices. That is typical.

I bet you've either been a project manager or worked on a project team who was told the feature set, low defects, and schedule are all the same priority—all number one. You can't add more to the project. And, the cost is fixed. And you have to use the company-mandated process, offices, or furniture, or you have some other work environment issue that makes the project work difficult to perform. Nobody can make a project like that succeed unless there's no technical or schedule risk in the project. But you have some approaches that can help you clarify those supposedly fixed constraints.

You saw the matrix of project drivers in Section 1.4, *Use a Matrix to Articulate the Project Priorities*, on the preceding page. This approach is most appropriate if the sponsor is ready to make choices. It might help a reluctant sponsor to be more decisive. You may have to rough out the rankings yourself and present them to your sponsor. For example, you might have several sponsors who don't agree on the relative ranking, or you might have a sponsor who is reluctant to decide. In this case, make the decisions and show them to your sponsor. She might be more willing to correct your rankings or sign off on them than to create her own.

You have a couple more approaches: to imagine the future and to use context-free questions to elicit what's really driving your project.

Imagine the Future

Begin by asking the sponsor to imagine that you are three weeks from the end of the project. Not all of the features are implemented. (Specifically discuss the one or two features this sponsor needs.) In addition to the missing features, there are still significant defects and too many of them. It's clear you can't finish the features and eliminate the defects before the desired release date. What would the sponsor do then?

If the sponsor says to you, "I'll have your head," it could be time to leave the organization. See Section 7.7, *Know When It's Time to Leave*, on page 134.

But it's more likely the sponsor will say something like this, "Finish the damn project. You need more people?" Follow up with, "Finish the features or the defects?" The sponsor will typically say, "Those two features and these defects." Ask, "In that order?" More often, you need to help the sponsor articulate which constraints are real constraints and which constraints are the sponsor's wishes.

A conversation including context-free questions can help you and the sponsor identify the project's drivers, constraints, and degrees of freedom.

Use Context-Free Questions to Identify Project Drivers

Project managers can identify the *project* requirements when they determine the project drivers. It makes sense to use context-free questions [GW89] to help elicit those requirements. Context-free questions are high-level questions that help elicit other people's implicit assumptions about the project. Start with these questions:

- What does success look like?
- Why are these results desirable?
- What is the solution worth to you?
- What problems does this system solve?
- What problems could this system create?

Be careful to use these questions instead of more "why" questions. The fewer "why" questions, the more you're learning about the business needs (and the less you sound like an obnoxious two-year-old). Also, "why" questions are more likely to put the other person on the defensive. Avoid "how" questions also. These sound like you're asking the sponsor to design the system.

Ask these questions out of a genuine desire to know about the project, not to put anyone on the defensive. You can use these questions to lay the groundwork for a useful collaboration with your sponsor, not a difficult relationship.

These questions address the value of the system. When you ask the sponsors these questions, keep the conversation collegial. Take notes on paper, not on a computer, so that there's no barrier between you and your sponsor. Use these questions as a starting point in the conversation. The more information you gather at the beginning about the project's value to the sponsor, the more you'll understand how to design the project.

What Does Success Look Like?
by Justin, project manager

I'm a couple of months into managing a two-to-three-year project, when my boss comes to me and says he wants to add a feature. Part of me says, "Cool, this particular feature would be great." Part of me says, "Uh-oh, we're two months into the project. If I train my boss that it's OK to ask for more features, either I need to change the way we're working or I'll be in trouble." I asked the question, "What does success look like to you?"

Imagine my surprise when I realized my boss thinks success is a completely adaptable project. He's pretty sure the requirements are going to keep evolving until the last minute—maybe a week before we release. I haven't run a project like that before! But now that I know, I can figure out how to do this.

1.6 Write a Project Charter to Share These Decisions

A project charter identifies the project requirements and constraints, and it helps a project manager decide how to design the project. The charter is the one place the entire project team and the sponsors can visit to make sure they all agree on the decisions about the project.

Start every project with a project charter to help elicit some of what this project needs to accomplish and the constraints on this project from the people who want the project. Even if you don't know everything you need to know about the project, writing the charter helps uncover some of the project issues. The project charter helps you and the project team understand what some of the risks are, what success is, and the ways you and the team can consider organizing and steering a project.

If you're managing an agile project (one using an agile life cycle, Section A.4, *Agile Life Cycles*, on page 331), your charter can be quite short. You might need only the project vision (so people involved with the project can make good decisions) and the release criteria (so you don't end up gold-plating past the time the project could end).

Here is my project charter template:

- Vision
- Requirements
- Goals
- Success criteria
- ROI estimate

The project charter is short by design. The charter helps the project team start. It doesn't say how the team members will know they are done. It doesn't say how the team will organize the project. But it's enough to get started.

Vision

There's a reason (or two or three) behind every project. What's the reason for this project? Use the vision statement to show what's valuable about this project. The easier it is for you to articulate the project's value early in the project, the more the project team is likely to tell you whether the project makes sense—or whether you're starting an impossible project. If you can't articulate the vision, chances are good that you're starting on an impossible project (because there's no way to end a project with no vision). A useful vision is compelling to the project team.

Requirements

Sometimes the only requirement of a project is to release something by some particular date. More often, the requirements are intermingled in some way: "We need the blatz feature in a major release by February 20." Think of your project drivers for this part, not the product's list of features.

Goals

Project goals are the things you'd like to accomplish with the project, but they may not be something the customer or sponsor wants to back. (For more discussion of goals, see Section 2.3, *Goals*, on page 22.)

\\// Joe Asks...

Who Writes the Project Charter?

Chartering is one early way to help a team jell. Involve as many of the team members as possible in writing the charter.

But if you don't have anyone on your project team yet, write a charter yourself. If you have some people on the project, write the charter with them. In the project kickoff meeting (see Section 10.3, *Project Kickoff Meetings*, on page 187), walk through the charter and make sure everyone understands what's in the charter and why.

Goals are not the same as requirements [DeM97]. Project goals are things the project is not *required* to deliver. If you've been doing traditional phase-gate or waterfall development, you probably have substantial technical debt (Appendix B, on page 335) in your product. Working off technical debt in the form of redesign, adding more automated tests, and developing smoke tests are all examples of possible project goals.

Sometimes, the customer has asked for something specific: "I'd love to get an electronic signature if we can do that for free within the current schedule." As a pragmatic project manager, you can say, "OK, we'll add it to the goals. That way if Shirley and Jane have some time, they can do it."

Success Criteria

Success criteria are the things that define what the customers will be able to do with the product when you are done. Success criteria are not about defects; they are about capabilities (see [Rot02b] and [Wie05]).

Here are some examples of success criteria:

- Include features 1, 2, and 3 so we can sell to that specific market.
- Improve and measure performance so we can create marketing material that compares our product to our competitor's product.
- Our customers can open the packaging and load the software without knowing how to access our site.
- Release in Q1.

Projects Start Before You Think They Do

Most of the time, projects start before the official schedule start. Maybe someone has done some prototyping. Maybe someone has estimated some features. Maybe the management team has talked to the chief architect about what's possible and what's not. That's part of the project, even if you don't think it is part of the project.

Since the project starts before you think it does, don't be worried about iterating on the project charter, the project plan, and the project schedule. As a pragmatic project manager, you spend the first part of the project trying to wrap your arms around the project while the work has already started. In the middle, you steer the project as you reevaluate the project's progress and risks. At the end, if you've been pragmatic, you have little to do except to worry.

The project team has control over success criteria. As a project manager, you'll have to guard against success criteria that only other people can fulfill (such as "Sell 50,000 units"). You and the project team have no control over what other people do; you and the project team can control only what you do. Make success criteria something in your control.

ROI

Few of my clients measure return on investment (ROI). It's too easy to manipulate the numbers. However, if your management requires it and you can estimate the benefit of the project, try calculating ROI. And check it after the project is over to see whether you achieved it.

1.7 Know What Quality Means for Your Project

Understanding the project drivers, constraints, and floats is the first step to understanding what quality means to your sponsors and customers. The sponsors are the people who are paying for the project. The customers are the people who use the product. Those people are not necessarily the same—and neither is their definition of quality. And yes, that makes life harder for you. But part of knowing what *done* means is understanding what *quality* means for your project.

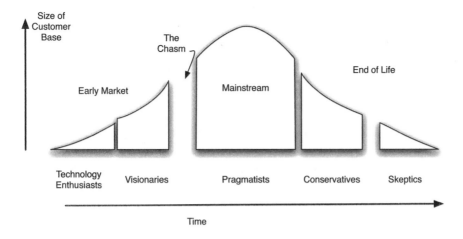

Figure 1.2: MOORE'S CHASM

Weinberg says, "Quality is value to someone" [Wei92]. This definition allows you to add more features and see how many more (and what kinds) of "someones" a feature might attract. Shortening or extending a release might attract (or not!) other "someones." As you think about your sponsors and customers, think about what they would like from your project. That will give you options to increase/reduce the time to release, the project cost, and the number of people, as well as allows you to consider whether all your "someones" need this feature. If you and the team know what these "someones" accept as quality, you can continue to work toward that as they change their minds—and you'll still be successful.

Your customers have a different definition of quality depending on where your product is in its adoption lifetime [Moo91], as shown in Figure 1.2.

At the beginning of a product's life, the size of the customer base is small, but technology enthusiasts want to see what you have, so there's substantial pressure to release. The product doesn't have to do much, or be rugged, but it needs to do something well enough to attract more customers.

Once you reach the early adopter market, each customer will have different requirements, whether you have a bazillion or three customers.

Each set of customers wants your product to do something—not necessarily what the other customers want. And all your customers want their release, with their features, fast. Your product can't be too awful to use, but these people have a problem, and only your product can solve their problem, so defects won't prevent you from selling your product.

But once your product (or products like it) has hit the mainstream, the pragmatists now care that you fix the defects in your product. If you've created technical debt (see Appendix B, on page 335) in your product in previous releases, now is the time to start paying it off. And because the pragmatists have such tremendous buying power, they will pressure your management to release often—even if not all the customers want to install the release. You don't have to add too many features in a given release, but you can't only make the software more rugged.

The conservatives will buy your product, but only under duress. And, the conservatives will take any and every opportunity to complain about your product if it does not do what it says it will or if it has too many defects. Conservatives don't want more features; they want the promised features to work. This is where you could release just fixes or a more reliable/high-performance/rugged product.

Laggards and skeptics might or might not buy your product. Sometimes, companies call products in this space *cash cows*, because they make more money on support contracts than they have to spend on support.

Although there is substantial pressure for many releases early in the product's lifetime, there is even more pressure from more customers for low defects later during the product's lifetime.

 ## Remember This

- Start every project with a charter.
- Expect to iterate on the project charter. The charter doesn't have to be perfect; it just has to exist to help the entire project team with their planning.
- Know what *quality* means and what's driving your project so you and the team can make good decisions as you proceed.

Chapter 2

Planning the Project

By now, you have a project charter. If your team wasn't available to write the charter with you, conduct a walk-through of the charter in a project kickoff meeting (see Section 10.3, *Project Kickoff Meetings*, on page 187). Once the team is familiar with the charter, you and the team are ready to do some targeted planning and just a little scheduling.

Planning and scheduling are two different activities. Planning includes writing a project plan with release criteria. Scheduling creates the sequenced description of the work.

2.1 Start the Wheels Turning

The charter helps everyone plan just a little up front to point themselves in a reasonable direction—or determine early whether there is no reasonable direction. The project plan focuses the team on the desired project results.

If you have a small enough team, say fewer than ten people, write the project plan with them as a group. Have a conversation with your team about where to head for the next couple of days or weeks, keeping the project's outcome in mind. If you have some requirements, the team can start prototyping or developing the first iteration. If you're using an agile life cycle, use the project plan as the release plan.

More likely, you have only some of the people you need, or too many people for the prototypes, or you don't really know what you have to do. In that case, ask some or all of the people to start fixing defects from a previous release. See Section 13.1, *Start People with a Mind-Set Toward Reducing Technical Debt*, on page 255.

2.2 Plan Just Enough to Start

You've got a charter, but what is your plan? Your management still wants to have an idea of when you'll deliver which features into the code base. How will you measure progress? When will the project be done?

Your plan does not have to be perfect. In fact, there's no way it can be. Your plan only has to be good enough to start the project with a chance of success. If you're working on time-pressured projects (which I do most of the time), timebox your planning activities. If you plan to replan the project, you don't need to worry about perfecting plans at the beginning.

A *timebox* is a specific amount of time in which the person or team will attempt to accomplish a specific task. As much as the person or the team can accomplish in that duration is what you bring to the next part of the project. If necessary, the person/team decreases the scope to complete the timebox.

We Timebox Our Initial Planning
by Steve, senior director of project portfolio management

We typically have somewhere between two and five big projects and an additional fifteen or so small and short projects going on at the same time. For almost all of our projects, we need to start in order to see how many people we really need and how long it will really take. Even when we do initial planning for a new project, we keep the initial planning really short.

Our most recent big program is turning out to be almost two years, with several releases. We timeboxed the initial planning to just three days. At the end of three days, we had a project charter, a project plan with release criteria for the first release, and a schedule for the first three weeks. That's it. But it was enough to start the project.

For our last couple of short projects (less than six months), we timeboxed the initial planning to one day, including organizing a two-week schedule. As the project team proceeds on those projects, we use the feedback from the initial planning to plan more, as we need.

For those projects that need to predict when specific features are available, we use those first few weeks of the project to perform an initial forecast, and then we update it through the next few weeks. By the time we're at the eight- to twelve-week mark, we have a really good idea of when we will be done with which features. We're not perfect, but we don't waste time planning without data. We plan a little, gather some data, and replan. It works like a champ.

Even if you're not working on a time-pressured project, if you take too much time trying to get to just the "right" plan, it will become a time-pressured project.

Tip: Make Your Planning Empirical, Not Predictive

Empirical planning, which means planning just a little and then gathering information on actual progress to feed back into future planning, works. *Predictive planning*, which is attempting to predict the future, doesn't work well unless you have a crystal ball. Use empirical planning and scheduling as much as possible in your projects.

You've probably heard the famous Eisenhower quote, "Plans are worthless, but planning is everything."[1] Your projects have too much uncertainty and risk to bother planning everything in advance. Plan to start and replan every few weeks, as in Section 5.6, *Using Rolling-Wave Scheduling*, on page 80. No matter what life cycle you use, assume you'll be replanning. Don't create a perfect plan; create one that works until you replace it (soon).

Tip: Start with the End in Mind [Cov91]

As you start planning, think about how much you need to write down. Release criteria (see Section 2.4, *Define Release Criteria*, on page 26) can help focus your sponsor and your project team. If you want to reduce planning time, make sure you have release criteria and a risk list. Iterate on the planning as necessary. If you're running an agile lifecycle project, you won't need any more up-front planning. [Coh06].

2.3 Develop a Project Plan Template

Organize your thoughts with a project plan, preferably one you can reuse for more projects at your organization. Here's my template for a project plan:

- Product purpose

---

1. A speech to the National Defense Executive Reserve Conference in Washington, D.C., on November 14, 1957.

- History
- Release criteria
- Goals
- Project organization
- Schedule overview
- Project staffing (staffing curve)
- Proposed schedule
- Risk list

Product Purpose

Briefly describe the product, why the organization wants to produce it, what benefits accrue to the company, and so on. What's the value of this release, if it's a follow-on release (three to four sentences)? If you have written the vision in a charter, you might be able to use that here.

Sometimes the vision from the charter isn't enough for a project. Or, the vision applies to a program (a series or group of projects; see Section 14.1, *When Your Project Is a Program*, on page 279). In those cases, make sure the purpose for this project is clear.

Years ago, before TCP/IP was built into operating systems, I managed a program for a hardware/software combination product. We included a variety of features, each of which was its own project. I had a charter for the program, where the program charter's vision was something like this: "Release this product in time for such-and-such trade show." We had about six project teams, one of which was networking team. They had a purpose for their project: "Ensure the TCP/IP works as of the first integration date and continues to work throughout the project." Their purpose was clear and was related to the program's vision but was much more specific.

Depending on the size and duration of your project (or program), each project team (or subproject team) may have its own purpose. That purpose aligns with the program charter's vision but is not the same.

History

If you're managing a follow-on release. such as Release 4.3 after Release 4.2, review the history of previous or related releases. The history can clarify any known technical debt (see Appendix B, on page 335). The data you can review is as follows: frequency of releases, number of released defects, customer-reported problems, and anything else that might affect how you determine what quality means or how you'll manage this project.

Tip: The Less You Know...

> The less you know about any part of your project, the more likely you are to be surprised. This applies to technical debt, a new architecture, a development or testing risk, or planning. Anytime you don't have previous experience with a project like this, the more surprises you'll encounter. A little planning and planning to replan will help.

If your customers are accustomed to one release a year and are not asking for more (*mainstream customers* in Moore's language, as in Figure 1.2, on page 15), you have several alternatives. The first alternative is to resist senior management's request for more frequent releases. Instead of resisting, consider a different alternative: either use release trains (see Section 14.3, *Organize Multiple Releases of a Product into Release Trains*, on page 283) or use an agile life cycle to allow for more-frequent releases. If you're trying to open a new market or move into a new market, organize the project so that you can push for even more frequent releases.

Review the number and type of released defects so you understand the level and kind of technical debt (Appendix B, on page 335) you are starting with in the code base.

If the customers are reporting a large number of problems in one area, review that to see whether it's a documentation issue or a code issue (or some other kind of issue). The more about the incoming technical debt you know, the more opportunity you have to manage it early.

Release Criteria

Itemize the key product deliverables from the project. A good way to identify these is to ask, "If we don't do that, do we still have a release?" Include functionality, performance, and quality requirements. See Section 2.4, *Define Release Criteria*, on page 26 for more specifics.

Goals

You might have known about some of the goals as you wrote the project charter. By the time you're ready to write a project plan, you probably know more about the goals. If you didn't know about any goals when you wrote the charter, this is a good time to think about them.

You might have goals that fit in the following categories—product goals, project goals, team goals, or organization goals:

- Product goals might be the ranked requirements that have not been committed for this release. You might keep this list in a product backlog (see Section 16.6, *Build a Product Backlog*, on page 313).
- Project goals could be something such as a performance standard that's better than the requirement, or "Decrease the open defect list at ship time from 50 open defects to 40 open defects." Especially if you're running a program, the goals for each subproject may be specific to that project's area. There may be specific technical debt a project team wants to pay off.
- Team goals could be " Increase the percentage of automated smoke tests for the product." A team might also want to improve a specific feature's performance or reliability.
- Organization goals could be "Reduce the overall duration of projects to improve our organizational agility."[2]

If your goals are detailed in your project charter document, you don't need them in your project plan. Choose one place or the other to specify the goals.

Project Organization

Articulate how you expect the team will work on the project. Address how you'll organize the project's work with a life cycle, some of the key practices, and whether there are any decision makers who can decide something about this project. If you know (or suspect) you need some prototyping, explain that here. "Steve and Jenny will prototype the architecture for that feature set. Bill will concurrently test. Because of the time pressure, the project team will select techniques that allow us continuous review of the code."

---

2. I thank Bill Ramos for this example.

Describe the general approach to the project, including such issues as ramping up with the entire project team at the project start, hiring new people, developing complete features including code and documentation, writing all the code and seeing what you can document in the time, and the like.

The actual details of what you will include here depend on the life cycle of the project and structure of the team. If you have one product owner who makes all the product decisions, decide whether you need to name that person. If you have multiple decision makers deciding about features and trade-offs, list those decision makers and their areas of responsibility.

If you're using timeboxed iterations, explain how long each timebox will be. Or, if you're using release trains, explain how long the duration of each train is.

Schedule Overview

Create a schedule overview with the major milestones and what people can expect at those milestones. If you're using iterations or increments, explain how long the iterations (or increments) are and what you expect at the end of each one. Don't put in a work breakdown structure, but if you have one, include a pointer to it for people who want more detail. No matter what life cycle you're using, if there's a beta test or an early release to the customer, show those milestones.

Work breakdown structure:
> The work breakdown structure (WBS) is the organization of tasks, showing their dependencies, durations, and owner. The higher level the WBS (and the earlier in the project), the less you know. Expect to evolve the WBS as you proceed.

Schedule Overview Makes the Project Real to My Managers
by Terry, project manager

I'm managing my second project now. My managers didn't believe that this one requires much more customer interaction than the last one did. I developed a project overview with milestones to explain it to them. Here's what it looked like:

Date	Milestone
July 1	Project initiation.
July 15	Show Lucinda the prototypes for the web interface. (cont.)

Date	Milestone
July 30	Show Lucinda and kitchen staff prototypes for the kitchen interface.
August 15	Deliver the web and kitchen interfaces internally.
August 30	Deliver early release to Lucinda's five hand-picked customers (beta test).
September 1	Start beta test.
September 30	End beta test.
October 30	Launch site including all customer orders and kitchen interface.

Once my management could see what I was doing, they realized why I asked for the time, people, and customer access I had requested.

For more complex projects, if you think the schedule is at risk before you even start, consider offering several alternatives for the project so your sponsors can see their choices. Figure 2.1, on the facing page is based on an organization where people are matrixed into a project.

Make sure you understand the value, not just the cost of each alternative. If you deliver a product that doesn't meet the release criteria, that's not an alternative with sufficient value.

Project Staffing

Many project managers do not have control over who is assigned to their project. If you acquire all the people for your project on the first day of the project, don't bother with a staffing curve. If you need to request people from other groups or teams, this is the place to explain how many of which people you'll need when. See Chapter 7, *Creating a Great Project Team*, on page 121 for how to do this.

Proposed Schedule

Outline the major milestones, as much as you understand them. If you have a Gantt chart that reflects the original scheduling, provide a pointer here. Of course, you'll need to keep a working Gantt chart that shows the current reality as you replan. Keep the working Gantt chart separate from the project plan so it's easy to update.

I tend to schedule with yellow stickies, so I rarely have a full Gantt chart for my projects. I've been known to say, "See the wall in the project room for the most current WBS." (If you don't have a project room to post the Gantt, make sure you use a public area so everyone can see the schedule. That way, the project team can alert you early to schedule problems.)

Alternative	Calendar Duration	Architecture Time	Development Time	Test Time	Doc Time
Features 1 and 2	2 months	1 person-month	6 person-months	6 person-months	2 person-months
Features 1, 2, 3	4 months	2 person-months	10 person-months	10 person-months	3 person-months
Features 1, 2, 3, 4, 5, 6	12 months	6 person-months	60 person-months	50 person-months	8 person-months

Figure 2.1: PROJECT ALTERNATIVES WITH A MATRIXED TEAM

The more you use rolling-wave planning (see Section 5.6, *Using Rolling-Wave Scheduling*, on page 80), the less detail you need to insert past the first wave.

Tip: Beware of Early Detailed Schedules

Iterate on your schedules, building detail as you proceed. See Chapter 4, *Scheduling the Project*, on page 49 for more discussion. The earlier in the project you provide a detailed schedule to your sponsors, the more likely they are to think that there is little or no risk in your project. They will see the projected end date and believe it's the Real End Date for your project.

Develop a Project Risk List

Keep at least the top-ten risks in your project plan. Monitor them frequently, and update the list when appropriate. If you're not sure you have ten risks in your project, take the time to brainstorm risks with your project team [DL03].

Numbered Risk	Risk Description	Probability	Severity	Exposure	Trigger Date	Mitigation Plan
Number each risk	Name the risk with a phrase or sentence	Probability the risk will occur	The severity if the risk occurs	Multiply the probability times severity	Date by which you need to act	Plan to deal with the risk
1	We don't know if the algorithm will be fast enough until too late in the project	50-50 (Medium)	High	(M, H)	July 14	Add test developers to work with alg. developers to test the algorithm alone
2	Booting takes longer than 2 minutes	Low	High	(L, H)	Aug 21	Monitor booting with each build

Figure 2.2: RISK LIST

It's never too early to start identifying and managing risks. Figure 2.2 is the risk table I use to start and examples from a real project.

As you proceed through the project, update the risk list. Use the practices in Chapter 8, *Steering the Project*, on page 143 and Chapter 9, *Maintaining Project Rhythm*, on page 167 to help reduce the risks.

2.4 Define Release Criteria

Release criteria tell you what *done* means ([Rot02a] and [BWe01]). Some project managers release software when some senior manager says so, when the testers "approve" it, or when people feel it is right. The problem is everyone has a different opinion of what *done* means.

Release criteria are not about shifting blame from one group to another; they exist to provide some objective measurement about when a product is ready to release. Release criteria allows the sponsor/customer to make a reasonable business decision about the quality and risks of the product.

When you develop release criteria, first decide what's critically important to this specific project. For example, why is the company doing this project? Why would the customers buy this product?

Release criteria can also help you build whole-product responsibility into the product release. For example, can the salespeople sell the product that meets these criteria? Can the support staff support the product? Can the trainers develop and deliver training? When you work with people across the organization to define what success looks like, they realize not only are they accountable for their part but also that they're pointing you toward project success as well.

Once you know what success means, you can define what's most important for this project—the release criteria.

Use these steps for defining and using release criteria:

1. Define what's important for this release so you can monitor release criteria throughout the project.
2. Draft release criteria.
3. Make release criteria SMART: Specific, Measurable, Attainable, Relevant, and Trackable. See Section 2.4, *3. Make Release Criteria SMART*, on page 30.
4. Gain agreement from the project team and senior management.

1. Define What's Important for This Project

What's critically important to this project is a combination of what the organization needs and what the customers need. Customers don't buy products based on the number or lack of defects. They buy products because they solve some problem the customer needs solved. When you develop release criteria, keep defects or defect levels in mind—but make sure your release criteria deal with more than defects. Think about the problems you're solving for your customers—whether those customers are outside or inside your organization.

Sometimes the release date is most important. Sometimes, it's a particular feature or set of functionality. More often, it's a combination of schedule, features, and few defects. It all depends on your customers and their expectations, as in Section 1.2, *Manage Your Drivers, Constraints, and Floats*, on page 3.

Rita worked at a start-up company driven by cash flow. The company was not fully funded, so it had a tremendous incentive to ship products early in order to obtain enough cash flow to continue the company's existence. For the first three releases, the only release criterion was the date the release had to go to customers so the company could legally recognize revenue. Once the company made it past the first couple of years and was adequately funded, the company developed other criteria including defect counts, test progress, and the states of *code freeze* (the times when developers would stop working on the release).

Rita described it this way: "When we were a start-up, we just needed to keep our heads above water. Our initial customers wanted pretty much what we gave them but were willing to work with us. We were all blown away, though, with last year's release. All of a sudden, the customers cared about defects, more than they ever had before. My management demanded to know what kind of a test group I was running, and I felt completely besieged. The only thing that saved my sanity was knowing that I had checked with the entire project team and senior management in advance to know that the release criteria we chose were what we needed. Unfortunately, we didn't realize how much demand we would have for this product, and we now realize we can't use only the date or some defect or test numbers to assess the state of the release. We need a much bigger picture to know when we're ready to release the software."

2. Draft Release Criteria

You may find it useful to draft a set of strawman release criteria so you have a vehicle to start the discussion. (If you have a test manager working with you on the project, you can work with the test manager or ask the test manager to draft the strawman release criteria.) Make sure you create a balanced representation of time to market and what your customers want, along with defect, performance, and reliability levels, if that's appropriate. You don't have to guess all the criteria correctly the first time; you just need to have something you can discuss as a group.

If you do draft criteria, make sure you stamp "DRAFT" somewhere on the page. You want the project team and the sponsor to know these are draft criteria for discussion, not a promise already made to someone.

Rita first drafted a set of release criteria as a starting place to discuss the release with the project manager and the rest of the project team. These were Rita's draft criteria:

- All code must compile and build for all platforms.
- Zero high-priority bugs.
- For all open bugs, workarounds documented in the release notes.
- All planned tests run, at least 98% pass.

- Number of open defects decreasing for last three weeks.
- Feature X unit tested by developers, system tested by the Test group, and verified with customers A and B before release.
- Ready to release by June 1.
- All open defects evaluated by cross-functional team.

However, once she started talking to the project manager (PM), Rita realized that her initial criteria were not exactly what the customers or the company needed. Yes, the customers were concerned with defects, but not to the same extent that Rita was. In fact, if a couple of the major customers were satisfied with the release, then chances were good that it was good enough for the rest of the customers.

Initially, Rita's PM was surprised that she had tried to look at the whole release from the customers' perspective and come up with a balanced idea of what would make a complete release. He'd expected that Rita would be much more concerned with a traditional test manager's perspective on quality: low defects. But, Rita knew from her previous projects at the company that low defects were just part of the story when making a release decision.

Rita, along with the PM and the rest of the project team, revised the release criteria:

- All code must compile and build for all platforms.
- Zero high-priority bugs.
- For all open bugs, workarounds documented in the release notes.
- All planned tests run, at least 90% pass.
- Number of open defects decreasing for last three weeks.
- Feature x unit tested by developers, system tested by the Test group, and verified with customers A and B before release.
- Ready to release by June 1.

These criteria don't address everything for Rita's release, but they cover what's critically important for this release: release date, good-enough software, and a specific feature tested and found working by two specific customers. Rita was disappointed that only 90% of the planned test group's tests had to pass—she thought there was too much risk with such a low passing number. But, after hearing what everyone else said, she was willing to go along with the rest of the criteria because the release date was so critical. Rita was also concerned about removing the criterion about the cross-functional team evaluating the open defects at the end of the release. However, the product manager reassured Rita that he had discussed the issues with the PM and that the PM could speak for the marketing and support staff.

3. Make Release Criteria SMART

When you draft the release criteria, make sure they can be answered by anyone on the project team in the same way. I've adapted the SMART acronym—Specific, Measurable, Attainable, Relevant, Trackable—to test that I have reasonable and objective criteria. The *T* for Trackable helps the entire project team realize that when we create release criteria, we need to be able to evaluate them throughout the project.

Each criterion should be specific for this product now for this project. When you make a criterion measurable, you're ensuring that you can evaluate the software against the criteria. Release criteria are not the place for stretch goals, so make each criterion attainable. Make sure your criteria are relevant by evaluating this product against what the customer wants and what management wants. When you make criteria trackable, you can evaluate the state of the criteria during the project, not just during the last week of the project.

"Search must return the first set of results within five seconds" is an objective and measurable criterion. You can test that. "All open defects reviewed by cross-functional team" is another example of an objective and measurable criterion. Either the cross-functional team reviewed the open defects or the team didn't.

"Fast performance" is an ambiguous criterion. To change this into an objective and measurable criterion, make it something like this: "Performance scenario A (corresponding to Use Case A) to complete in less than ten seconds." Name the specific scenario so people can refer to it, and provide a measurement that will allow the project team to know whether they met that performance.

4. Gain Consensus on Release Criteria

Once you have reasonable release criteria, it's time to gain consensus on what you've developed. If people react negatively to your draft criteria ("No, we couldn't possibly do that"), learn why they are concerned. Generating release criteria reveals assumptions and fears about the project and the product. Try these questions when generating or gaining consensus on release criteria:

- Must we meet this criterion before the release date?

- What happens if we do not meet this criterion before the release date?
- Do we put our product or company at risk by not meeting this criterion? Do we jeopardize people's safety if we don't meet this criterion?

These questions help the entire project team stay focused on what's needed for this release.

Gain consensus on release criteria with any of these ways: drafting the release criteria, discussing them, and coming to an agreement at a project team meeting; drafting the criteria with the entire team; or drafting them with the matrix managers involved with the project team. Once you have draft criteria, make the discussion of them an item for a project team meeting. I prefer generating release criteria with the entire project team, because then the team owns the release criteria, not just the managers or me. However, if you're working on a large project or have never used release criteria before and want people to understand what they're working toward, try generating strawman release criteria in advance of a project team meeting.

Once you've gained consensus, you can use the release criteria to monitor the project.

2.5 Use Release Criteria

Release criteria are either met or not met. You aren't partway to meeting a criterion—you haven't met it. You'll find that this binary approach helps you when you're discussing the state of the software with senior management. If you say you're partway there, they hear that you're done. If you say you haven't met the criterion, they hear you're still working.

With your team, discuss progress toward release criteria during your project team meetings. Combining this with a look at the project dashboard (see Chapter 11, *Creating and Using a Project Dashboard*, on page 201) lets the entire team assess the project's state of doneness during the entire project. If you have a formal system test phase, use the criteria as part of the testing status report.

You may find that release criteria are an early warning sign that the project team is not going to make the release. Manny, a project manager, was halfway through a six-month project. Manny looked at the progress to date and was concerned that the team was not going to make the ship date. He decided to make the release more real to the project team by generating release criteria with them.

Manny then used the release criteria each week during the project team meeting to verify the project was making progress. It worked for a couple of weeks until one week during the release criteria evaluation, one of the engineers said, "I'm not going to make it. I've tried and tried, and I'm just not going to make that criterion for our ship date." Manny said, "OK, I need to go back to management and see what we need to do. Before I do that, does anyone else think they're going to have problems meeting any of the release criteria?" Another engineer said, "I can't get performance that good between now and the time we have to release. When we discussed the release criteria, I thought it was possible, but now I realize it's not going to happen."

Manny was able to ascertain early data about his project's progress with release criteria. For this team, realizing they weren't going to meet the release criteria two-thirds of the way through the project instead of at the end was a relief. The PM knew what the project reality was and could work with management to see which trade-offs made the most sense. In this case, Manny was able to renegotiate the release date so that the product could meet the release criteria.

If all goes well, you'll evaluate the release criteria as you proceed, and you'll meet the criteria when the project is supposed to end. However, projects don't always go well, and you won't always be able to meet the release criteria. When that happens, make sure you're honest about what's happening.

Change Release Criteria When Necessary

Release criteria help avoid the problem of a moving target of *done*. However, there are circumstances when you can consider changing release criteria: when you learn more about what *done* means for this project and if you realize you can't meet all the release criteria by the desired release date.

If you learn more about what *done* means, ask yourself the earlier questions about the release criteria: Must we meet this criterion? What happens if we don't meet the criterion? See Section 2.4, *4. Gain Consensus on Release Criteria*, on page 30.

If you're working on a project and can't meet the release criteria, say so. First, verify with your team why you can't meet the criteria. Next, explain to your management why you can't meet the criteria. Have your management explain the situation to the project team like this: "We thought these other criteria were important, but we realize now that the date is even more important than we thought. We're going to release the product, even though we haven't met all the release criteria." If this is true, you can have them add, "We're going to determine what prevented us from meeting our criteria this time and create the next project so that we don't miss our release criteria." If you don't explain the reasoning to the project team, the project team feels as if they are playing the schedule game discussed in Section 6.1, *Bring Me a Rock*, on page 87.

 Remember This

- Project planning is ongoing; this is just a way to start.

- Develop release criteria to define *done* for the project team, the sponsors, and you.

- Your project plan doesn't have to be perfect; it has to exist.

Chapter 3

Using Life Cycles to Design Your Project

Imagine you're ready to start a daylong car trip to attend a reunion of friends. You planned your trip in advance, marking where you want to go on your maps. But just as you get in the car, one of your friends calls to explain there's a washed-out road and construction you need to drive around. You still arrive at your destination—safely and in time for the dinner—but you've taken a different route.

That's how you can think about choosing life cycles. No life cycle is perfect once you take it out on the road. You might have to stretch it a bit or modify it here and there. A life cycle is an idealized approach to organizing your project. Some life cycles will fit better with your team (and the project) than others. Make sure your life cycle allows you to change when the road is washed out or you encounter obstacles.

3.1 Understanding Project Life Cycles

A life cycle is the way you and the project team organize the work of product development—it's when you choose to define requirements, design, develop, and test, as well as how concurrently. You might have phases with gates or iterations. You could plan for a formal design phase or choose to evolve the architecture and high-level design. You could choose to integrate the testing as you proceed or have all the testing at the end. You might choose to prototype for a while and then engineer the features, or you could implement by feature and see how the architecture evolves.

When you organize the overall project, don't idealize your situation. If you've seen issues such as incomplete requirements in your projects before, don't plan for complete requirements up front this time. Choose a life cycle that helps you uncover requirements as you proceed. Be pragmatic—be aware of your project's risks, and choose a life cycle that meets the risks of your project and helps you deliver a successful product.

Projects rarely proceed in a straight line from requirements through release. Projects tend to go off track more than they stay on track. Although you might be most familiar with stage-gate and waterfall life cycles, they are not the only approaches to organizing a project. As you think about planning your project, see whether the life cycle you've chosen addresses your project's risks. If your project's risks don't match the life cycle, stop trying to make it fit, and choose another one.

You can't just think about internal project risks as you consider life cycles. Your customers and their expectations are part of your risks. As you think about how to organize your project, also think about your customers. What are their needs? What is their experience? How much are they willing to work with you? (See Section 1.7, *Know What Quality Means for Your Project*, on page 14.)

It would be lovely if you could plan on only one kind of customer with one driver for quality—but you rarely can. You'll need to figure out which risks are most important to your customer. Choose a life cycle that optimizes for those risks whether it be date to release, defects, features, or cost—and manage the other risks with the practices and people you choose for your project.

3.2 Overview of Life Cycles

Different life cycles optimize for risk differently. There are four major kinds of life cycles: serial; iterative; incremental; and iterative/incremental, which I'll call *agile* from here on. (In truth, you don't need to follow the agile values as in the Agile Manifesto[1] to use an iterative/incremental life cycle. But it's darn close to impossible to make the agile life cycles work unless you follow the agile values.) See Figure 3.1, on the next page, to see how life cycles manage the possible risks in projects.

---

1. See http://www.agilemanifesto.org.

Lifecycle Type	Examples of This Kind of Lifecycle	Strengths and Necessary Conditions for Success	Project Priorities	Prognosis for Success
Serial	Waterfall, phase-gate	Manages cost risk (if management uses the phase gates) Known and agreed-upon requirements Well-understood system architecture Requirements stable over the project Project team stable over the project	1. Features set 2. Low defects 3. Time to release	Successful with feedback
Iterative	Spiral, evolutionary prototyping	Manages technical risk Ever-evolving requirements	1. Features set 2. Low defects 3. Time to release	Successful assuming the finishing parts are planned and occur
Incremental	Design to schedule, staged delivery	Manages schedule risk Can absorb small requirements changes but not enough changes that affect the architecture	1. Time to release 2. Low defects 3. Feature set	Successful
Iterative/ incremental	Agile (such as Scrum, XP)	Manages both schedule and technical risk Difficult to do well without a colocated integrated team	1. Time to release 2. Feature set 3. Low defects	Successful
Ad hoc	Code and fix		1. Time to release 2. Feature set 3. Low defects	Unsuccessful

Figure 3.1: HOW LIFE CYCLES MANAGE RISK

If you're not sure of which life cycle is which, Figure 3.2, on the following page, is a picture of what the different life cycles look like if you were to look at them as if you were building a Gantt chart.

In a serial life cycle, the team is supposed to be able to first obtain all the requirements. Based on the requirements, the team moves into analysis and design to determine the big picture of the system. Once everyone agrees on the big picture, the team starts developing. After all the development, the team integrates all the pieces, and then the final test starts. In reality, one phase doesn't need to finish before the next phase begins, but the one-phase-at-a-time mentality is real in a serial life cycle.

Serial life cycles take longer because they are supposed to be able to predict how long it will take to implement features or find and fix defects or integrate pieces of the system or manage requirements changes—things are inherently unpredictable. Unless you have a working crystal ball, it's impossible to forecast everything you need to know about the future. In a serial life cycle, you have to allow for extra time, such as a final system test at the end of the project to make up for risks and problems you could not have known about during the project.

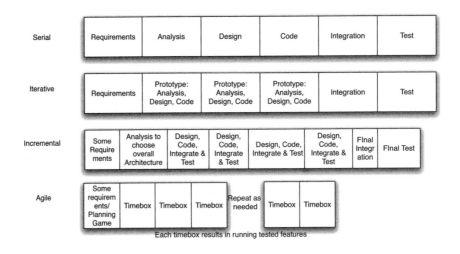

Figure 3.2: A GANTT-LIKE LOOK AT LIFE CYCLES

Iterative life cycles try to manage some of that prediction problem by helping the project team see prototypes of pieces of the system as they are created. In an iterative life cycle, the project team develops pieces of the product in each pass (iteration). Most of the iterative life cycles do not require that you have finished pieces of the product at the end of each iteration. Iterative life cycles do not require concurrent testing and integration. (When you build prototypes of the architecture, you can't predict the future well until you start building and integrating features.)

Incremental life cycles look like a bit like serial life cycles for the requirements and analysis phases, although successful teams timebox the requirements and analysis phases. They soon break into feature-based teams. The teams build one feature, test it, integrate it, and then work on another feature. Projects that use incremental life cycles have the prediction problem until they move into the increments. Once they move into increments, they can use feedback about their ability to build features to determine where the project is headed.

Agile life cycles are a hybrid of the iterative and incremental life cycles, but with small iterations and small increments. Agile life cycles start a project with a little bit of planning—just enough to get started and have an idea about what the product owner would like to finish for the release. The product owner might even specify which features they want to slot into which iteration. But the teams don't spend much time on release planning. Instead, they move into planning a time-boxed iteration's (one to four weeks) worth of work. As the team works in these timeboxes, implementing the most valuable features first, they collect data about how quickly they can work, fix problems, understand requirements, and so on. As they proceed, the team solicits feedback from the product owner about how the features look and work. The team replans for the next iteration based on their velocity and their changed circumstances. Because the team actively seeks feedback on their work and work process, this life cycle best incorporates feedback about true project status, the rate of development, the rate of finding and fixing defects, and the team's assumptions.

Unless your project team actively plans to develop, test, and integrate by feature (as in concurrent engineering or in agile), they use a design-code-test-debug loop, as in Figure 3.4, on page 41. First the developer designs the product, then codes it, then tests it, and then debugs it. That work can take weeks or even months. Get a bunch of developers together working on a product, and you can see how long it could take before some code is tested with other code.

Tip: Code and Fix Is Never a Useful Life Cycle

Never use "code and fix" as your life cycle. Never, never, never. Well-meaning people start with code and fix because they think it's faster than doing a planning game, prototyping to know what you could do, or gathering some requirements. It's not. No matter what life cycle you choose, make sure you plan at least a little at the beginning of the project. Dilbert summed this life cycle up nicely. The Pointy Haired Boss says, "You guys start coding; I'll get the requirements."

You don't need to know all of the requirements to start. Implement by feature, timebox the iterations, and work with your customer to make sure you're developing what the customer wants. But don't fall into the trap that you can start developing without having a customer or start a project without planning. You can, but the chances of project success plummet.

Initial pass at require ments.	Prototype what we do know about. Get feedback. Select an architecture.	Fully implement 3 features, integrating as we go.	Test architecture. Demo what we have.	Keep implementing, integrating as we go.	FInal test.

Figure 3.3: A COMBINATION OF ITERATIVE AND INCREMENTAL LIFE CYCLE

Life cycles are an idealized approach to organizing a project. Just because you choose one life cycle doesn't mean you have to follow it slavishly. You can integrate pieces of another life cycle to deal with your project's risks.

For example, if you've ever had to manage the risk of choosing an architecture early, when you know you don't know all the requirements (and you can't use an agile life cycle), Figure 3.3 might help. This combination allows the project team to prototype a little using iterations. Once the team knows enough, the team moves into incremental development, implementing, testing, and integrating as they proceed.

Figure 3.3 is a combination life cycle that uses parts of the iterative life cycle (the prototyping), part of the incremental life cycle (the three feature full implementation and continued development), some of the ideas from the agile community (initial pass at requirements and iterating on requirements as the project proceeds), and a final test to manage risk at the end of the project.

3.3 Seeing Feedback in the Project

The first time developers receive feedback on their code is during some test of that code. And, if testing has not been integrated into the project, that feedback arrives very late in the project.

Without feedback to the developers, you cannot easily assess your remaining project risks, assess the project's state, or assess how quickly the team can produce working software. You can't know whether work is actually done. This lack of feedback is why the serial life cycles especially are predictive or forecasting life cycles. The serial life cycles

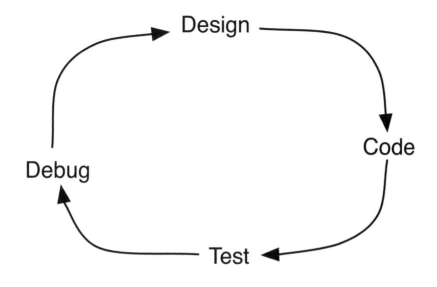

Figure 3.4: DESIGN-CODE-TEST-DEBUG LOOP

predict the future, without having sufficient data to check that the future can be accomplished based on current work. Anything that the team does to obtain feedback early about the product (not the descriptions of the product, although that is helpful) makes the prediction easier.

If you just look at a Gantt-like picture of the agile life cycles, you can't see the feedback loop the agile life cycle provides. Inside each timebox are two feedback loops. The constant feedback is Figure 3.5, on the following page. Developers test as they code, so feedback is immediate. The daily and iteration-based feedback looks like Figure 3.6, on page 43. This constant feedback to the developers and the project manager is at the heart of why the agile life cycles work.

3.4 Larger Projects Might Have Multiple Combinations of Life Cycles

No single life cycle meets everyone's needs. On projects with larger teams or multisite projects, you might find that each team uses its own

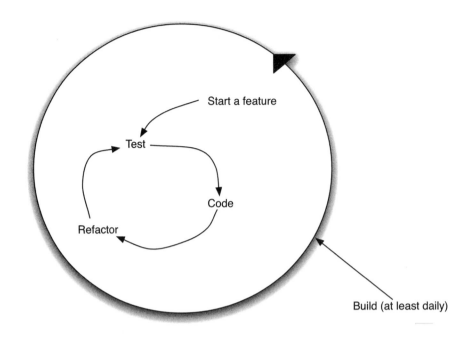

Figure 3.5: TEST-CODE-REFACTOR LOOP

life cycle. (See Chapter 12, *Managing Multisite Projects*, on page 235 for more information.) On one project with about sixty developers and twenty testers, the project life cycle looked like Figure 3.7, on page 44.

The developers used an incremental life cycle. The testers used an iterative life cycle. The testers chose to develop their tests this way so they were working from breadth-first to assess the system state. The developers worked to finish each feature, integrating as they proceeded in case the management team mandated an earlier ship date.

I've also seen multisite projects use a combination of life cycles. In one case, developers in one site used evolutionary prototyping, while the developers in another site used staged delivery. They agreed at the beginning and at each quarter during the eighteen-month project what their next deliverables would be and the criteria for those deliverables.

In another case, for a three-country project, the developers in one site used two-week iterations, developers at the second site used staged delivery, and developers at the third site used four-week iterations.

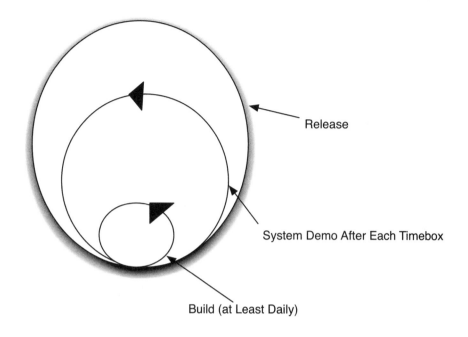

Release

System Demo After Each Timebox

Build (at Least Daily)

Figure 3.6: HOW AGILE LIFE CYCLES INCORPORATE FEEDBACK

They also defined their deliverables and criteria every month, not just at the beginning of the project. The key with multisite projects is to define what the handoffs will be and when those handoffs need to occur. See Section 12.4, *Define the Milestones and Handoffs for Each Team*, on page 243.

When Your Project Includes Hardware

If your project is to develop a new generation chip or board (new product development), your company will have a set of ambitious requirements that the hardware team might not be able to fulfill in the time allotted. You'll need to wait until the hardware has gone to fabrication before knowing precisely what can be done in hardware and what will need to be done in software. You can often fix a small issue in software with a software update. Hardware doesn't have this luxury, so the time and costs constraints might be different, and the costs of fixing hardware after it ships means that software might have to accommodate the hardware schedule. You can implement by feature while you're waiting by using a staged delivery or agile life cycle and by possibly

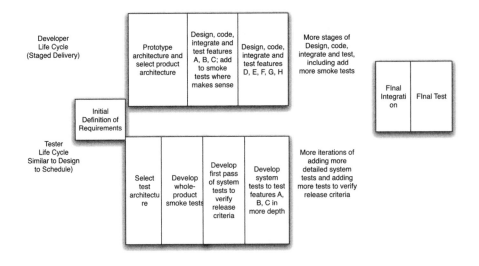

Figure 3.7: One large project's life cycle: a combination of life cycles

using stubs. When you know what the hardware can or cannot do, you might need to replace some of those stubs with hardware/driver calls or with software. You don't need to wait until the hardware is done, but you will have a "serialness" to your project until the hardware is complete enough to know which low-level features will be implemented where. A successful hardware/software combination project requires a combination of life cycles.

You can treat firmware as software or as hardware depending on the context. If you're building firmware as something to plug/download into a system externally, you can probably treat that as software. If you're building firmware that's embedded into a system and it's not easily changed, treat that as hardware.

If you're integrating a system that includes other vendors' components, you will definitely need a combination of life cycles and a regular way to manage risks during the project. For example, say you want to build a state-of-the-art refrigerator that can order groceries for you online and can assess the state of some of the perishable items.

You might buy the milk analyzer from Acme Analysis. But you buy the meat analyzer from Meats-R-Us and the vegetable analyzer from Veggies for Life Systems. In the low-end refrigerator, you include only the milk analyzer. And in the high-end refrigerator, you also include the meat and vegetable analyzers. You would run different projects as part of one program (see Chapter 14, *Managing Programs*, on page 279) for the low- and high-end refrigerators.

Before you agree to a date, or even think about a life cycle, negotiate interim deliverables from your vendors. System integration from various vendors is highly risky. Managing the risk means more than just selecting a life cycle; it means planning for integration as you proceed through the project. If your analyzer vendors have to deliver monthly releases (even if they're not releasable to your customers), you can easily use iterations and agile approaches to manage the risks.

If you find that you're managing a systems integration project and your company has not negotiated interim deliverables, you can try to negotiate those deliverables now. But even if you can't get your vendors to agree, you can still use incremental and iterative approaches to your project.

To manage the tricky part of the integration, I strongly recommend you build incrementally, using either timeboxed iterations (the best way to manage risk), such as in Figure A.6, on page 332, or using an incremental life cycle, such as in Figure A.5, on page 331. Do not use a serial life cycle—you can't see the technical risk as you proceed through the project. You will be able to see problems only at the end.

3.5 Managing Architectural Risk

No life cycle fully addresses a product's architectural risks—that is the risk that the architecture your project team has selected will be sufficient for your needs. Until the code that represents the architecture is written and integrated, it's impossible to tell whether the architecture works. I've worked with many project teams who chose a serial (waterfall or phase-gate) life cycle because they were convinced that the serial life cycle addressed the architectural risks. Unfortunately, it does not. And because final integration and testing occur last in a waterfall life cycle, the waterfall or stage-gate is actually the riskiest for managing architectural risks.

If you really want to know about the architectural risks early and you are constrained to a serial life cycle, you have several options:

- Iterate on prototypes that are close to "final" as early as possible in the project. Include testing of those prototypes. If you try only quick-and-dirty prototypes (as in a spiral life cycle), you won't know whether the performance or reliability of your proposed architecture is sufficient.

- Implement several features that will stress the architecture as early in the project as possible. I prefer to use a timebox of no more than three weeks to implement these features. See what kind of architecture emerges from those features. Also note the kinds of risks the feature teams encountered so you can see whether you need to select another life cycle.

  Let's assume you try a three-week timebox to implement four features in order to see whether a proposed architecture works. At the end of the three weeks, the team realized it can implement only two features easily. The team guessed wrong on their estimates for what they could do in a three-week iteration. You might want to continue using time-boxed iterations, or you might want to repeat that three-week timebox with a different architecture to see whether a different architecture changes the risk or the speed of development.

  The more you experiment in the beginning of a serial life cycle (even though the life cycle doesn't call for experimentation), the fewer architectural and design risks you will encounter later in the project.

- Timebox the entire architecture effort. Challenge the architects and developers to develop at least three options for the architecture and tell you (the project manager) what works with each option and what's still at risk with each option.

The only way to really manage architectural risk is to implement something and test it. Any Microsoft PowerPoint architecture [SH06b] (where the implementation is only in PowerPoint) is window dressing[2] to give a favorable impression and not worth the time.

---

2. Thanks to Jerry Aubin who suggested this term.

You might be working in an organization where the sponsors, senior management, or PMO wants to see the architecture (or a picture of the architecture) before you start on the project or where the risk of not doing an architectural review is too high. In that case, I still recommend you completely prototype a few features so that you have experience with the architecture before you bet the project on it.

Be aware that during the project, you will need to address the risk of the architecture not meeting your needs—and you want to do that earlier rather than later. If you don't, it can sink the whole project.

3.6 Paddling Your Way Out of a Waterfall

If you're stuck with a serial lifeycle, here's how to make it less waterfallish and more flexible so you can adapt to reality:

- Plan to iterate on everything, including planning, requirements, and prototyping.

- Prototype and show your customer/customer surrogate as much as possible as early in the project as you can. The more feedback you incorporate from people who are your customers or who represent your customers, the better off you are.

- Integrate testing into the project from the beginning. Work with the testers to provide feedback before an entire system is available.

- Implement by feature, integrating and testing as you proceed.

- If you must deliver documents (the typical milestones at the end of a stage in a serial life cycle), make sure the documents are not your only deliverable. Exploring prototypes with the customer and delivering working product will help provide the project team with valuable feedback.

These approaches are not traditional serial approaches. But they work. Don't lie to your sponsors about how you're managing the project; tell them you're managing the various risks. You can treat the project internals like the sausage makers. You don't have to provide the gory details about the insides of your project; they don't show you how they make sausage.

3.7 My Favorite Life Cycles

I have a strong preference toward delivering pieces of functionality into the code base sooner rather than later. In my experience, it's not possible to design the definitive architecture until after the project team writes, tests, and integrates several features. I prefer evolving the architecture and delivering features using Scrum [Sch04] as the project management framework to take advantage of the visibility, inspection, and adaptation it provides. Where possible, I add the eXtreme Programming (XP) (see [BF01] and [JAH02]) practices, or I estimate the architecture and then deliver some features with an incremental life cycle such as staged delivery.

If the project team is capable and interested in collaborating[3] the way an agile project requires, then an agile life cycle is my first choice. However, if the team can't get enough attention from the customer or if the team is not composed of people who are interested in collaborating the way an agile project requires, I tend toward a staged-delivery life cycle, timeboxing the requirements and architecture phases. (Any project without enough customer involvement will suffer. Agile helps make that problem visible earlier than other life cycles.)

I rarely use a waterfall, even on short, straightforward projects. If I use a spiral life cycle, I push the team toward something that looks more like staged delivery so I have finished work, instead of pieces of incomplete work.

 Remember This

- Design your project using any life cycle or combination of life cycles to make the project successful.

- Don't be afraid to create your own life cycle to reflect your reality. The "perfect" life cycles are models. You live in the real world.

- Use a stage-gate or waterfall life cycle only when you think you can make it successful, not by default.

---

3. See http://www.stsc.hill.af.mil/crosstalk/2007/04/0704Derby.html and http://alistair.cockburn.us/index.php/Agile_software_development:_the_people_factor.

Chapter 4

Scheduling the Project

Planning and scheduling are two separate activities. In Chapter 2, *Planning the Project*, on page 17, you started the project planning. Here, you'll think about scheduling and estimating the project. As you organize the schedule—and when you reestimate the work—you might have to modify the plan. That's fine. Your original plan is just good enough to start. Expect to refine the plan as you schedule (and reschedule). And, don't be afraid to refine the schedule as you replan.

4.1 Pragmatic Approaches to Project Scheduling

You planned just enough to start the project already. You need to schedule enough to start the project. There's no point to scheduling the whole darn project when you know the project is going to evolve. If you're working with a customer who wants to see a project schedule before they will sign a contract, be clear that the initial schedule is your best first guess. It will change. And, have that customer read about accuracy and precision of schedules in the tip *Estimates Need Accuracy, Not Precision*, on page 71.

A few years ago, I had a conversation with a project manager at a conference. I said it took me anywhere from about half a day to a couple of days to get started on a project schedule, and I wanted to shorten the two days down to half a day.

The other project manager stood there with her mouth open. She absolutely didn't believe that I could schedule a project in half a day. I explained that I didn't try to schedule everything, just the next week or so, and then I would build up the major milestones and the rolling-wave schedule (see Appendix B, on page 335) over the next few weeks.

"How do you know the end date?" she asked.

"I don't, at least not precisely. But if I tried to plan forward to see where the end date would be that early in the project without any data, I'd be wrong. Why take the time to schedule in detail when you know you'll be wrong?"

She said, "Gee, I never thought of it that way."

There are many ways to schedule a project. I think top-down, so I create a first draft of the plan because that helps me create a first-draft schedule. Other project managers start with a schedule draft first. Do what feels most comfortable to you and appropriate for the project. But don't neglect either the plan or the schedule. Every project needs both.

Tip: Projects Require Both Plans and Schedules

As the pragmatic project manager, your job is to start the project with just enough planning and to continue to plan (and replan) as you proceed. Whatever you do, don't ignore either the plan, especially the release criteria, or the schedule. You might not need a fancy schmancy Gantt chart for a schedule; yellow stickies on the wall are fine for many projects. But you do need to both plan and schedule.

Your schedule will bear some resemblance to the life cycle you choose. But remember, a life cycle is a *model* of how the project could look. When it's time to create the schedule, use the life cycle as a guideline, and make sure you've addressed the risks inherent in your life cycle, no matter how you need to do that. You might add timeboxed iterations and increments to phase-gate project schedules—as well as planning to replan—because those actions made sense for the particular project. Remember that a life cycle is a guide, not a straightjacket.

Scheduling and estimating are two different activities. Scheduling is ordering and showing the interdependencies of tasks. Estimating is guessing how many effort-hours a particular task will take. They are linked, because how you organize the schedule might depend on a given task's estimate of the effort-hours and specific people required.

I wish I could wave my magic wand and say, "Here is the One Right Way to schedule and estimate your project." But I can't. We generally need to estimate things we've never done before.

Estimation of the unknown is still an art. On the other hand, if you know what life cycle you're using, organizing the schedule is easier.

Tip: Timebox Initial Planning

> Spend as little time as possible on up-front planning, especially if your project team is already assigned to your project. Take just enough time to plan so your project team can start. Timebox the charter to one hour. Timebox the project plan to another hour. Timebox the first draft of the schedule to an hour. The timeboxing will focus everyone on the few vital pieces they need to start. Once people know what they have to work on for the next week or two, you can return to the plans and schedule and see what else you need to write.

4.2 Select from These Scheduling Techniques

I select from among these scheduling techniques when laying out the project: top-down, bottom-up, and inside out, Hudson Bay Start, and a short iteration.

Top-Down Scheduling

Top-down scheduling generally starts with milestones. Serial life cycles tend to start with top-down scheduling, because the phases are so clear. (Hint: if you must use a serial life cycle, make sure you use deliverable-based planning as a technique to generate your milestones, as discussed in Section 4.3, *Deliverable-Based Planning*, on page 60.)

Organize the project schedule into phases, iterations, or chunks. Lay them out on a whiteboard or on stickies on a wall. Dwayne Phillips recommends cards on a wall as another low-tech scheduling technique. When you schedule with cards on the wall, each person creates cards with the tasks they think they need to do. Then link the cards with string [Phi04]. This technique is particularly helpful if you don't know where to start.

The team starts organizing the schedule from the highest-level milestones and develops the tasks to support those milestones. As one or more team members understand more about what each milestone means, they break the milestone down into its component tasks.

The smaller the task at the bottom level, the easier it is to estimate how long the task will take.

Bottom-up Scheduling

Bottom-up scheduling starts with specific tasks. If you're using an incremental life cycle, it might make sense to start with bottom-up scheduling. "We know we need to do this feature first, then do those features, and then have a go/no-go decision. . . ."

The project team members, working alone or in cross-functional teams, develop the milestones from the tasks. As the project manager, you can ask questions about how things fit together. (The more technical you are, the more you can help. If you don't have domain expertise in the product, don't interfere.)

Inside-out Scheduling

Inside-out scheduling works best with people who think they need to be completely adaptable. At one of my project management workshops, one PM said, "First I make a mind-map [BB96] of everything I know about the project. I might know some go/no-go review points. I might know about certain features. But I don't know about everything at the same level, so I want to see everything before I start scheduling."

Your mind-map might be crystal clear to you. But it might not be clear to others on the project. Mind-maps communicate much more to those present when it was created than to those who are just shown the results later. If you and your project team are using inside-out scheduling, make sure the team works together to generate the tasks and milestones.

Hudson Bay Start

Imagine you're managing a project that's completely new to you and the entire project team. You have no idea whether the environment you have will support the tools. You don't know how to estimate the project. Consider a short iteration, such as a *Hudson Bay Start*.

The Hudson Bay Start approach was originated by the Hudson Bay Company in the 1600–1700s in northeastern Canada. The Hudson Bay Company outfitted fur traders. To make sure the traders hadn't forgotten anything they needed, they left Hudson Bay and camped just a few miles away. By making camp just a few miles away, the traders ensured they hadn't forgotten any tools or supplies—before they abandoned civilization. With just a short start to their journey, they had a better idea about their ability to endure the winter.

A Hudson Bay Start is a technique that allows the project team to push something through the project's environment. You want this to be as small a thing as possible. (A "Hello World" program might be just fine.) The idea is for the project team to see what it would be like to start working in this environment with this product domain.

If you and the team can't figure out what it would take to estimate any piece, timebox a Hudson Bay Start. Start something you can complete in four hours or less. (This thing doesn't have to be real functionality.) After the team has created *something*, debrief the activity. The team will know more about how to estimate the tasks needed. If the team knows only a little more, start with a short iteration, and then decide what to do.

A Hudson Bay Start helps in several ways. First, the team gains some confidence that they can accomplish *something*. Finishing something helps them gain some insight when it comes to estimating. In addition, the team has a little insight into how to organize some tasks. "Oh, if we want to do those features in parallel, we're going to have to make another branch and merge back in. Yikes, that means staging integration. That will take longer than working on the mainline."

When you hear conversations like this, where people articulate the risks, then you can capture them in a *parking lot* (see Appendix B, on page 335) to deal with later or as you schedule.

Start with a Short Iteration

Use a short timeboxed iteration when the team understands the environment but isn't sure how to estimate the tasks. A short iteration helps people see how much they can accomplish in one or two weeks, so their follow-on estimates are more accurate. You can use a short iteration after a Hudson Bay Start, once the team understands how to use the environment.

Timebox a short iteration (no more than two weeks—one week is even better), and see what the team can accomplish in that time. By the end of the iteration, the team and you will have a better idea about the requirements, the risks, and what they don't know.

If you combine a short iteration with a short retrospective, the entire team will learn more about what it takes to schedule this project.

4.3 Start Scheduling with a Low-Tech Tool

Back in the Stone Age, when I started managing projects, we didn't have electronic scheduling tools. We had blackboards, paper, and flowchart templates. I used a blackboard to lay out the schedule for projects. Blackboards worked well—if I made a mistake, I erased the sequence and inserted it where I needed it.

But blackboards can become messy if you have to erase and rewrite information. Even when I moved to whiteboards in the Neolithic Age, the whiteboard can be hard to see—sometimes the old information is still visible under the new drawings.

When yellow stickies came out in the Modern Age, I moved to yellow stickies.[1] It's easy to write a task on a sticky, put the sticky up on the wall, and discuss with the rest of the project team—sometimes quite loudly—the sequence of tasks or who will do them or what the risks are. And, if the task is in the wrong place—because the team sees another way to organize the project—it's easy to move the sticky from one place to another.

Yellow stickies involve the whole team in scheduling. The team will explain the risk as they proceed, providing you with valuable information you can use for steering the project.

High-Tech vs. Low-Tech Scheduling
by Sandy, seasoned project manager

I've been managing projects for about fifteen years. I started when we had scheduling tools, and I became an expert at the best-known tool. Sure, it had problems originally rolling up subprojects, but I knew how to get around that. And, we had a little problem with trying to track the details, but I got good at figuring out how to outwit the tool. I had a little problem with earned value calculations, but we moved to implementing by feature, and that helped (see Section 11.2, *Earned Value for Software Projects Makes Little Sense*, on page 207).

---

1. For those of you who are wondering why I didn't move to an electronic scheduling tool, the answer is easy—one didn't exist for the operating systems I was using. Since it didn't exist, I couldn't use it.

Then I started managing a really large program a couple of years ago, including about 300 people in six sites. I'm no dummy, so I brought all the project managers for an initial planning meeting. I had my computer hooked up to the projector, and we started developing the schedule. Everyone was yelling at me, trying to make me see where tasks belonged. I was a little stressed but was getting there. Then the power died.

Bob, one of the subproject managers, said, "Don't go anywhere. I'll be right back, and we can continue." He came back in about five minutes with pads of yellow stickies and pens. He explained how we would schedule and then everyone started writing their stickies. In about ten minutes, we started posting the stickies on the wall and discussed what each one meant and where we had issues.

We had an initial schedule in less than an hour. We took pictures of it, in case the power stayed off and my computer ran out of juice.

At the end of the meeting, every subproject manager congratulated me on how quickly we developed a schedule. Me! I gave all the credit to Bob. That schedule was good for a couple of months, and when we had to update it, we gathered the subproject managers together and did the same thing.

I was amazed by how well it worked. I still use scheduling tools, but I always start with low-tech scheduling, and if we need a major replan, I use low-tech scheduling now.

Many project managers prefer to start scheduling with an electronic scheduling tool. If you need to lay out many tasks at once and you think the sequence of those tasks are not going to change, maybe an electronic scheduling tool works at the beginning of the project. But it doesn't involve the entire team in the scheduling activity. Using a tool to generate a schedule shortcuts the discussion and doesn't expose silent dependencies and risks.

The project manager can type only one task at a time—and only the project manager can create tasks. The scheduling tool can show you only one page of information at a time, and the team might lose context if they can't see the whole schedule.

If you're not using rolling-wave planning, then an electronic scheduling tool might be OK once you and the team create the initial project schedule. (You will lose the benefit of a Big Visible Chart or Information Radiator; see Chapter 11, *Creating and Using a Project Dashboard*, on page 201.) But starting with a tool says to the team, "I'm in charge of the schedule; you're not."

If the project team owns the schedule, they will stay committed to it. If you own the schedule, you're likely to micromanage the team, not manage the interdependencies of their tasks.

I hope I've convinced you to start with stickies or cards on the wall. If you're not sure how to do that, here are several techniques I've used for different projects.

Basic Sticky Scheduling

Gather the entire project team together in a room with a long wall or a long whiteboard. Hand everyone a pad of yellow stickies and a medium or bold black pen. (I prefer to use three-inch by five-inch stickies so they're big enough to read and a felt-tip black pen.) If you know you're using a serial, iterative, or incremental life cycle, post the major milestones on the wall so people can see the structure of the project. Ask everyone to write all their tasks down on a sticky, one task per sticky. As the team members write down tasks, they post them on the wall. (You can see examples of this in Figure 4.1, on the next page, as well as in Figure 4.2, on page 58.)

Assign one part of the wall as the parking lot (Appendix B, on page 335), the place where the team will collect questions and assumptions that you'll need to resolve as part of the scheduling. I use flip chart paper for the parking lot, so if I need to take the parking lot back to my office to resolve, it's easily transportable.

Now stand back, out of the way. The project team members will start collaborating about the sequence of events, any prerequisites, assumptions, and questions.

As developers start writing their tasks, they will have questions for requirements analysts, writers, and testers—who will have questions for the developers. The project team starts to bond in a cross-functional way before the project "starts." (In reality, the project has already started—see the sidebar on page 14—there just are no other artifacts at this time.) You can see what a short project might look like in Figure 4.1, on the next page.

Once the team has written down as much as they can and resolved the issues, it's time for you to be involved. Expect to see these issues in the schedule:

- The team has scheduled only the first few weeks of their work. They can't see much more detail than a few weeks out, so that's

Figure 4.1: ONE PROJECT'S YELLOW STICKY SCHEDULE

all they've scheduled. That's OK, because you can use rolling-wave planning (Section 5.6, *Using Rolling-Wave Scheduling*, on page 80) to iterate on the schedule. And, it's OK because you don't want people to provide detail that isn't based in reality. More detail is a waste of time.

- You might see long sequences of serial tasks. Expect this in a serial life cycle. But if you're seeing this in an iterative or incremental life cycle, ask the team whether something is preventing them from working more in parallel. See Figure 4.2, on the next page, to see exactly the same project as Figure 4.1—except organized in a more serial way.

- You might see long sequences of many parallel tasks. You have to worry about this only in a serial life cycle, which does not—by its nature—lend itself to parallelism. However, it's a risk to the project in any life cycle other than agile. The risk is that people will fall out of sync and extend the critical path where you did not expect the critical path to be.

Once the team has created the schedule, the team is ready to estimate how long each task will take.

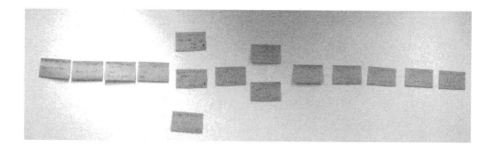

Figure 4.2: ANOTHER PROJECT'S YELLOW STICKY SCHEDULE

Sticky Scheduling with Arrows

One of my clients starts with yellow-sticky scheduling as described here, but once the schedule is "set," they draw arrows from one sticky to another. The arrows help them in several ways. The first is that if a sticky falls down, they know where to put it back. The second is that after they do the initial yellow-sticky scheduling, they transition to an electronic scheduling tool. A project coordinator transcribes each sticky into a task into the tool, and the arrows help them keep track of dependencies.

Sticky Scheduling for Each Group

If you're stuck with a phase-gate schedule and can't create a cross-functional team to implement by feature, you might need the help of a schedule to convince your management that there are other options. I've used sticky scheduling for a week-by-week look at the schedule to help management understand that organizing by functional team slows the project down.

On a large whiteboard or on paper taped to the wall, draw vertical lines down, one for each week. Use different colored stickies to show when different people in different functional organizations are working on the project.

Don't forget to show the end of the project. The end of functionally organized projects tends to be difficult. Because management thinks the developers are free to start another project, they are less dedicated to the project at the time the project needs them most—when it's time to fix defects.

Sticky Scheduling for Features

Recently, I've started using sticky scheduling to show how each feature will integrate with the others. If you are working on complex projects where you have dependencies during the project for integration, you might find it useful to plan an iteration's worth of work with stickies.

Generate a sticky for each deliverable. Sometimes, a single feature will have several interim deliverables. Put the stickies up on the wall. Ask the project team to organize when they need which deliverable delivered into the code base. Ask the team to add any hard dates; "If you don't deliver that piece then, we can't finish before the end of the iteration."

Especially if you're working in short iterations, you don't need to transcribe the stickies into a Gantt chart. If you're working in an incremental life cycle, you might need to tape the stickies up for a longer project or use a Gantt to manage the dependencies.

Benefits of Using Sticky Scheduling

If you use sticky scheduling, you will not have a beautiful Gantt chart that can show you the critical path. That's good, because the critical path for a software project runs through the tasks, the people, and sometimes the equipment. And, I bet your critical path changes day by day, depending on what people finished. Even if your critical path doesn't change daily, it changes weekly. If you don't have a line on the Gantt chart that purports to show you the critical path, you and the team will have to think about it. Thinking about it more consciously will help everyone to manage it.

In addition, a yellow-sticky schedule will not show you the end date. That's because you should never estimate a single-point end date [DL03]. But since a scheduling tool does calculate the end date (and it's the earliest possible end date you can't prove the project won't be complete by), people—especially senior management—believes that end date.

If you're running a multisite project, you can still use sticky scheduling. If each team is responsible for a complete deliverable (a set of tested implemented features; see Section 12.3, *Make Sure Each Site Has Complete Deliverables to the Project*, on page 238), each team does its own day-to-day scheduling. You gather the team leads or project managers together to make sure they understand who is delivering what to whom and when. Since you're dealing with major milestones, you can use videoconferencing or webconferencing to use the equivalent of sticky scheduling.

Deliverable-Based Planning

Yellow-sticky planning lends itself well to deliverable-based planning. As people think about what they have to deliver to the rest of the project, they develop milestones based on deliverables, not on the ending of phases.

Phase-based planning or functional-based planning assumes that teams of people from a particular function are responsible for a piece of the project. And you can assume a phase of the project is done when those people say they are done. If you've ever worked on a project that had a milestone such "requirements freeze" or "code freeze," you've worked on a phase-planned project.

The problem is that although those people try hard to complete their deliverables, the freezes are rarely frozen, and the completes are mostly incomplete. You end up with slushy milestones. The way to avoid slushy milestones is to plan for the milestone as a rollup of the tasks before it. If you know you have several areas of requirements, the milestone "requirements freeze" is a rollup of "requirement 1 written and reviewed," "requirement 2 written and reviewed," "requirement 3 written and reviewed," and so on, until all the requirements are in the rollup.

You can use deliverable-based planning in any life cycle. Especially if you must use a serial life cycle, use deliverable-based planning to obtain feedback early about the project's progress. If you can't meet requirements freeze, how can you know you'll meet any of the later milestones?

Tip: Late Projects Don't Make Up Time; They Get Later

If you realize at the beginning of the project that the team is not making the progress you want to see, decide what to do differently. Late projects never make up time. They get later and later and later....

If you do think the project will make up time, you will find yourself in the schedule game discussed in Section 6.15, *We'll Go Faster Now*, on page 117.

Remember This

- Start scheduling with low-tech tools. If you really need a scheduling tool, transfer the data later. Be aware of the costs associated with losing the Big Visible Chart or Information Radiator.

- Schedule by deliverables, not by functions.

- Plan to iterate the schedule. A write-once schedule is not worth the time you spent generating it.

Chapter 5

Estimating the Work

You've arranged your schedule. It's time to estimate how long each task will take. You don't have to settle for a SWAG;[1] you have other options. Choose the option that provides you the best estimate you need—not the most precise estimate.

5.1 Pragmatic Approaches to Project Estimation

I have successfully used these estimation techniques: historical data, Delphi, wideband Delphi, relative ranking and sizing, and spikes to gather some data before estimating. I have not successfully used any counting or computing techniques. See McConnell [McC06] for more information about counting and computing techniques.

Historical Comparison for Estimates

If you're managing a follow-on release similar to the previous one, you might be able to estimate the duration of the project. "Well, the last time, it took us eight people for six months. This looks about the same size, so my first estimate is the same." Just remember that projects are not linear. If this project looks even just a little bit bigger than the previous one, your historical comparison could be way off. Historical data is even more useful with either Delphi or wideband Delphi.

---

1. A SWAG is a Scientific Wild Tush Guess.

Delphi and Wideband Delphi Estimation

In Delphi estimation, the project manager gathers the team in one room and explains the project. The teams asks questions, and then each person repairs to his/her office to write their task list and time estimates, also noting their assumptions [Wie00].

The team then gathers together and reviews the task lists, seeing where tasks can be parallelized. The project manager adds up the estimates, and that's the project estimate.

If you don't have access to the people who will be doing the work—the real project team—wideband Delphi might be a useful choice. A small group of experts takes the place of the project team. They generate task lists and estimates. When they gather after generating their estimates, they surface their task lists, assumptions, and risks.

Both forms of Delphi are better than the project manager attempting to estimate the project. However, they both suffer from the same problem—that each person takes responsibility for estimating one piece of the project, most often by architecture. You may have the same problems I've had with either Delphi technique—that the estimate is too low. The only way I know how to manage that estimation problem is to separate sizing and duration during estimation (see Section 5.1, *Separate Sizing and Duration During Estimation*, on page 71).

When You Don't Trust the Team's Estimate

Not everyone is a great estimator. Some people are overoptimistic [Bro95] and underestimate by as much as 50% for any task. Some people are pessimistic and add buffers for every single task. Some people estimate small tasks up to three or four days well but can't estimate anything that's longer than a week in duration. What's a project manager to do?

First, know your team. Decide how much feedback you want to give each person about estimation when in the project. You don't have to solve all these estimation problems the first week of the project.

Next, eliminate any extra time buffers on each task. Ask each person whether he or she has estimated with or without buffers. Explain that you're not trying to reduce the task time but that you want to make sure you have the most accurate estimate.

If you're using a serial or iterative life cycle, consider using Theory of Constraints (TOC) [Gol04] to deal with the estimates. In TOC, everyone is supposed to provide you with a reasonable estimate for the task. You take the 50% mark and make the task that long in the Gantt, adding 25% of that original estimate into the buffer [Gol97]. When a task in the critical path requires more time, you take time from the buffer to add to that longer task. Then start managing your buffers. By measuring your buffers as the team completes the tasks, you can tell whether your overall estimate is good.

In an incremental life cycle or an agile life cycle, you'll be gathering data about what it takes to accomplish finished pieces of work. You can compare those actuals to the estimate and learn as you proceed.

In general, don't add more slack time to a task estimate. Do provide a range of dates (see Section 5.1, *Use Date Ranges for Estimates*, on page 69), a percentage confidence (see Section 5.1, *Use Confidence Ranges for Estimates*, on page 67), or even three dates: best case, likely, and the Murphy date (see Section 5.1, *Use Three Dates: Best Case, Likely, Murphy's Date*, on page 70).

Avoid the Serial Life Cycle Estimation Trap

Too often, project managers who use serial life cycles are supposed to estimate and schedule the whole project at the beginning. It takes them (and the project team members who are available) several weeks to understand enough of the requirements and the system architecture to make reasonable estimates. And depending on how new to the organization the project is, their estimates tend to be off. I've seen estimates be off from 100% to 400%.

The trap is trying to estimate the entire project at the beginning. If you're stuck with a serial life cycle, you can't estimate the project with any degree of accuracy. What you can do is start the project team doing something, measure how long it takes to finish that piece, see how many more pieces like that you have, and iterate on the estimation.

Especially if you're working in a serial life cycle, use confidence ranges (see Section 5.1, *Use Confidence Ranges for Estimates*, on page 67) and date ranges (see Section 5.1, *Use Date Ranges for Estimates*, on page 69) so other people understand how uncertain your estimates are.

Joe Asks...
When Should I Add More Slack Time to an Estimate?

People tend to be optimistic and underestimate the time required for a task. It may seem like the best solution is to routinely pad these estimates. The problem with padding estimates is Parkinson's law: work expands to fill the time allotted.

Suppose your lead developer is very optimistic. When he estimates sixteen hours, it's not thirty, and it's not twenty. But it is somewhere in between. What do you do?

First, help the developer separate size from duration when he estimates. See Section 5.1, *Separate Sizing and Duration During Estimation*, on page 71. If his tasks tend to be large, ask your developer to break the task into inch-pebbles (see Appendix B, on page 335). He might say, "Oh, this task is sixteen hours; that's two days." If he could really do eight hours of work in a day, it might be. But he is interrupted more than anyone on the project, so he doesn't do eight hours of technical work in a day. I estimate lead developers can accomplish about four to five hours of technical work a day, depending on the environment. That makes his sixteen-hour task take three to four days of calendar time.

If inch-pebbles don't work, try a spike (see Section 5.1, *Use a Spike to Gather Data Before Estimating*, on page 73). A spike helps everyone see what the task will really take.

Ask the underestimator to use three dates (see Section 5.1, *Use Three Dates: Best Case, Likely, Murphy's Date*, on page 70) to provide you with an estimate. That way the developer obtains feedback about his estimations without feedback from you.

Talk to chronic underestimators, and help them realize that what they can accomplish in calendar time is less than what they estimate. To protect the project, consider using buffers or moving to iterations.

Because iterations are short, everyone receives feedback on their estimates within a few weeks of making the estimate. The team will correct the other members of the team. "Last iteration, you said that feature was a size of 3. It turned out to be a size of 8. Tell me more about why you think this feature, which looks a lot like that one is a 3."

Joe Asks (cont.)...

When Should I Add More Slack Time to an Estimate?

Pad estimates as a last resort. Work with people to define an EQF (see Section 11.2, *Track Your Original Estimate with EQF*, on page 209), and monitor it for their tasks. Move to timeboxed iterations so people have less to estimate and the pieces are smaller. Provide feedback about estimates—either from you or from the team. But if you pad estimates, you run the risk of inviting Parkinson onto your project or initiating Student Syndrome. When people remain in blissful ignorance of their estimates, they never learn to become great estimators.

Tip: The Schedule Is the One Way the Project Will Not Proceed

The entire project team collaboratively developed the schedule. Everyone has confidence in the schedule. And then something happens.

Don't worry. The schedule is the team's best guess *today* about how the project will unfold. As soon as something happens, generally the day or two after the schedule is "complete," the original schedule is toast. That's why I try to do just enough scheduling and expect to use rolling-wave planning, so I can easily update the schedule as circumstances change.

Use Confidence Ranges for Estimates

How sure are you of your estimates? At the beginning of the project, I'm not sure at all. The only thing I know is that the project won't follow the schedule we've developed. Something will change. And that something (or somethings) will change the estimate. Instead of using a single-point estimate of the end date, try confidence ranges.

A confidence range chart looks like Figure 5.1, on the following page. The range of probabilities provides you with a level of confidence. At the beginning of the project, there is a 0 probability that the project will be done.

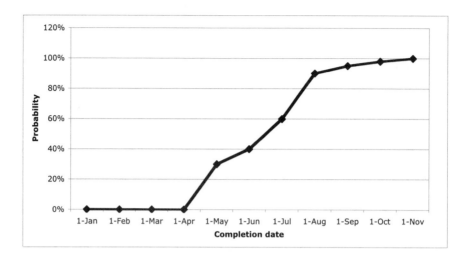

Figure 5.1: CONFIDENCE RANGE CHART

At the 60% mark, July 1 is the earliest possible date that the project might complete. That's the earliest possible date you can't prove the project won't be done.

The 80% date is mid-July, which is a more likely date at the beginning of the project. Note how the slope of the line becomes shallower. It's close to impossible to pick an absolute release date at the beginning of the project, which is why the probabilities for September, October, and November are all in the 90–100% range.

But using a chart like this allows you to have a discussion with your sponsor. "I have only 50% confidence that we can meet June 15 as a release date. I know you want it then, but that's not even my earliest possible date I can't prove we won't finish." And you can explain why you have such low confidence in that date.

Especially if you're using a serial life cycle, consider using a Cone of Uncertainty, as shown in Figure 5.2, on the next page. The cone helps explain why your estimate is not accurate at the beginning and when you can make it more accurate. The Cone of Uncertainty reestimation and improved accuracy depend on the project's ability to meet the phase milestones at separate times.

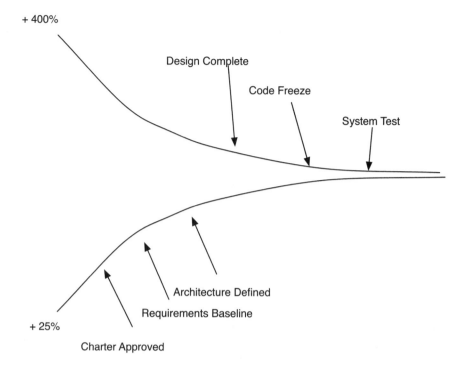

Figure 5.2: CONE OF UNCERTAINTY

If you have the early milestones, such as requirements freeze, design freeze, and code freeze at the same time, the first time you can evaluate the cone is at code freeze. You won't be able to update your estimate early enough.

If you're using an iterative or incremental life cycle, you can also use the cone. The more incremental your life cycle, the faster and the more accurate you can be about your estimates because you have real data to use to update your estimate.

If you're using an agile life cycle, you don't need the cone. You need to measure only velocity and the rate of requirements change to predict the release date.

Use Date Ranges for Estimates

If you're asked to generate a gross estimate for a project and no one on the project team can help you estimate, try using a range of dates with an explanation of when you can refine the estimate. Here's how I've used date ranges for a project: "Well, based on the three minutes of information you've told me about this project, it looks like we could deliver something in Q3. Since it's now January 10 and I won't get the project staff for another week, let me do some iterations and planning with the team and give you a better estimate February 1."

After the team had started and we had learned what we could accomplish in a two-week iteration, we had more information. Here's what I told my manager. "We learned that Q3 was too optimistic. But sometime in the October–early December time frame looks doable." In April, I updated my manager again. "Looks like late November to early December. I'll know more in a couple more months." In July, my update was this, "Still looks like November 15 to December 1. When do you need a more precise date?"

Using the date ranges helped save the project from a too-early promise of an impossible date. However, if you say, "October to December" and you work with managers who hear "October," you're better off with explaining confidence levels. Or, you could use an agile life cycle, continuing to manage the backlog so that you could release as early as management desires.

Use Three Dates: Best Case, Likely, Murphy's Date

Some managers don't like to hear an evolving date from their project managers. In that case, you can use the three-date [DL03] technique: best case, likely, and Murphy's date.

The best case is the first date you can't guarantee the project won't be done. When you generate a Gantt chart, the best case is the end date the tool provides. Even if you're managing buffers or have some contingency, you're sure something is bound to happen to make that date impossible. But you can't prove you can't meet that date. That's what makes it the best-case date.

The likely date is the date that you derive when you add your fudge factor or your buffers or however else you mush the estimate. You have more confidence in this date, but maybe only an 80–90% confidence.

Murphy's date is the date you expect if Murphy's law[2] happens to your project over and over and over again. This is when the freak snow

---

2. Murphy's law is this: whatever can go wrong will, at the worst possible time.

storms hit Florida, a typhoon destroys the data center in Southeast Asia, or the power company has a transformer meltdown in the middle of the last week before everyone goes on vacation. Those problems are all fixable, within a few days to a week. Murphy's date is not a complete disaster, such as losing all the sources or your project team all quitting on the same day.

To generate a Murphy's date, you take your likely date and add some fudge factor to it. Only you know how much of a fudge factor to add.

Tip: Estimates Need Accuracy, Not Precision

Each of these techniques so far stress accuracy of the estimate by showing how imprecise the estimate is. Early in the project, it's impossible to know what date the project will release—unless the project team is free to define what they will release and how good it is.

Precision is the exactness of the measurement, the number of decimal places.[3] Accuracy is how close you are to the estimate. What you care about for scheduling is accuracy—how close your prediction of the task durations or schedule is, not which hour of the day a task will complete or the project will end.

Don't be worried about how precise your estimate is; be more worried about how accurate it is.

Separate Sizing and Duration During Estimation

People are not good at estimating tasks they've never done before. How could they be? To manage the chronic underestimation problem, separate the sizing of the task from the task duration.

Sizing is how big the task is. A gross sizing estimate says a task is small, medium, or big. But gross estimation is inadequate for most projects; you need a finer-grained estimate. And, you need to turn a gross estimate into a duration for a task.

Cohn, in [Coh06], suggests using a Fibonacci series to generate a gross estimate for a task. A task is of size 1, 2, 3, 5, 8, 13, 21, 34, 55, 89, and so on. If your team has a good track record estimating, use the series

---

3. See http://www.ayeconference.com/Articles/Estimateprecisionaccuracy.html.

up to 21, and add 40, 60, 80, and 100. The team will need to schedule some pretask work (a *spike*; see Appendix B, on page 335) to determine the real size. (With teams who have trouble estimating how large a large thing is, use 21, 40, and 100 and not the intermediate numbers. Then use a spike to break apart the task into smaller pieces.)

Once you have a relative size, using the Fibonacci series (or whatever you choose), take the tasks estimated as "2." Do all the "2" tasks look like they're about the same size? If so, now estimate duration for the "2" tasks. If you think all the "2" tasks will take about ten person-hours, you now know how long the "2" tasks will take. Divide the duration for the "2" task by 2 to derive the duration for the "1" tasks. In this example, our "1" tasks would take five hours. Ask yourself whether that makes sense. If so, you now have the factor to use to multiply against all the other relative sizings.

If your team doesn't have much confidence in their larger relative sizings, you know how much uncertainty there is in the duration and therefore your schedule. (The more large tasks you have, the more uncertainty you have.) And, if your team estimates all tasks as "13" or greater, the team has not yet broken down the tasks into smaller pieces—a significant risk to your overall schedule.

You'll notice I suggested you estimate in person-hours, not ideal days. That's because everyone's ideal day is different. A senior person who spends lots of time coaching other people will achieve less (personally) in a day than more junior developers who understand their parts of the system but have many fewer interruptions.

Planning Poker

You want everyone on the team involved in estimating. And your team has never received feedback on their estimates. How do you start? Planning poker [Coh06].

As a team, everyone determines the relative sizing for a feature in the backlog (see Section 16.6, *Build a Product Backlog*, on page 313). You might say, "OK, the feature is to add security to ordering." Everyone thinks for a few seconds, and then each person estimates how big that task is by showing a number on paper. If there are six people on your team, and everyone thinks it's a 5, you're OK. You write "5" as the size of the feature. Instead, imagine one person thinks it's a 13. Don't take the average; ask the person to explain their concerns. You might hear, "The last time I did something like that, we found a bunch of exceptions

Joe Asks...

Should We Estimate in Person-Hours or Person-Days?

Many people prefer to estimate in person-days, also known as ideal days, and not person-hours.

But people do not finish eight hours of work in a workday. The best I've seen is six hours of technical work in a workday. Some of my colleagues report that with all their meetings and interruptions, the best they can do is up to four hours of work—and that's on a good day. Sit back and look at your project team and your environment. Your team might be only able to accomplish closer to two to three hours of technical work a day.

All too often, when you and the project team estimate in ideal days, you assume more hours in a day than you actually have—setting you up for estimation failure.

we hadn't understood at the beginning." Ask for a show of cards again, and see whether you accomplish limited consensus. (You need everyone to merely live with a number, not perfect agreement.) If several people think it's an 8 and the rest think it's a 13, ask for the number everyone can live with. If you can't agree, determine a spike task, do that, and then reestimate.

Planning poker combines the best of Delphi and relative sizing. It involves the whole team and allows a team to estimate the relative size of a backlog quickly.

Use a Spike to Gather Data Before Estimating

Sometimes, you know the task is big. But you don't know how big. And you really don't have any idea how to estimate it. "Big" is not a good-enough estimate. In that case, try a spike (see Appendix B, on page 335).

Here's an example. Let's say you're part of the team working on improving performance for some part of your product. No one on the team knows exactly what to do, so no one can tell you how long it will take.

The team can use a short timebox—here maybe a day or so—to investigate the actual tasks required. At the end of that timebox, the team should have a good idea of what the initial tasks are for performance improvement. The team may not know everything about improving performance. They might need another spike for that.

Spikes can be shorter—if someone on the team is trying to estimate the pieces of a task that looks as if it's close to sixty hours, that person might be able to spend just two or three hours (maybe with one other person) to refine the large task and break the sixty-hour task into smaller chunks of four to six hours each.

If your staff is unaccustomed to thinking in small chunks, spikes might help them learn to break tasks into the smallest possible pieces.

Tips to Make Estimation Easier

Here are approaches that will make estimation and reporting your estimates easier:

- Remember that an estimate is an approximation—a guess. The bigger the guess, the more error you will have. Make sure when you provide an estimation of the project completion "date," you provide a range of dates so your audience understands that your estimate is a guess.
- Many software people are optimistic. They are trained to be optimistic in school, where every project can be completed in one semester (with a sufficient number of all-nighters). That training will persist unless they learn to estimate small pieces and receive feedback on their estimation.
- Tasks will take longer than you think they will.
- It's easier to estimate smaller chunks of work.
- Decide how everyone on the team will estimate: in person-days or hours. I recommend person-hours.
- You and your project team need to practice estimation and receive feedback about estimation. Estimation without feedback is write-only estimation[4]—it makes you feel good, but it doesn't produce long-term results and is ultimately rendered worthless.
- Plan to iterate on the estimates. If you realize partway through the project that your estimates are too optimistic, take the time to

---

4. I thank Keith Ray for this phrase.

Don't Waste Time Estimating When You Have a Tight Deadline

Dan, the CIO, was clear. "We need this project *done* by April 11." April 12 was a Big Demo day, and Dan wanted to show off his prize project. Cecile, the project manager, was accustomed to working on projects that weren't bound by time but required a certain number of features before release. Cecile normally started projects by estimating prototype and feedback time. She was sure that approach was not going to work here.

Cecile decided that the project team could still work implementing by feature but that she didn't need good estimates about how long each feature was going to take. What she did need was the order in which the features needed to be implemented so that even if they didn't finish everything for the Big Demo, they would deliver the most important features.

Cecile and the project team performed a gross estimation on each feature but did not drill down to obtain detailed estimates. They didn't finish everything Dan wanted by April 11, but they were close. And, they had only fully completed features—not everything halfway done but most things all done.

Cecile and her team didn't waste time estimating any more than they had to estimate. They estimated the entire feature list in about an hour. Cecile tracked how long each feature actually took to complete, so she would be able to predict how much the team could complete before April 11. But she didn't waste the time they had for the project on estimation, when she knew the deadline.

---

reestimate and replan the rest of the project. Late projects don't make up time; they get later. Even if your project doesn't appear to be late, take the time to reestimate.

- If you've been given a project deadline, you don't need to estimate anything at all. Rank the features so you implement features by priority. For this case, I strongly recommend you use an agile life cycle so that you can implement and get feedback quickly. If you can't use an agile life cycle, consider an incremental life cycle, implementing by feature as you proceed.
- Timebox phases and tasks if you have an overconstrained project.
- Consider a spike if the task is too big (too much technical risk) to estimate well.

5.2 Milestones Define Your Project's Chunks

If you're trying to estimate a project bigger than a couple of people for a couple of weeks, define some milestones so you and the team can understand what you're trying to estimate. Use milestones that are deliverables, not functional activities.

If you're using a serial life cycle, remember to make sure that the end of a phase is a rollup of all the deliverables that comprise that phase.

Tip: Use Deliverable-Based Planning for Tasks

Deliverable-based planning means you and the project team create a schedule of deliverables, not functional activities. If you're developing a system that requires an architectural prototype, you might have these deliverable-based milestones: develop three alternatives for the architecture, review alternatives, select one architecture to prototype, and architecture prototype complete (as the final milestone). An alternative plan might be to implement feature 1, implement feature 2, implement feature 3, evaluate current architecture, decide on architecture for project, and architecture prototype complete. Both of these plans have a rolled-up milestone called *architecture prototype complete* based on deliverables to the rest of the project team.

When is a phase or task "complete"? Your team can't deliver on a milestone such as "architecture prototype complete" without some deliverables to understand how to complete the milestone. Either of the earlier alternatives would help the project team accomplish "architecture prototype complete," and each accomplishes it differently. (The first alternative is for iterative life cycles. The second alternative is for incremental life cycles. Agile life cycles would also implement several features before deciding on a "final" architecture.)

Use low-tech solutions to start a project schedule, especially if you're managing a project that seems to be short of time. The more time-constrained the project, the more the project team needs to develop a schedule each person can live with and attempt to meet.

Spending a few hours with the team in a conference room scheduling with yellow stickies helps everyone see the implicit constraints.

Tip: Schedule Milestones (or Iterations) Midweek

It's tempting to line up major (and minor) milestones to complete on a Friday. That way, everyone can go home knowing they've finished a major portion of work. But somehow, life rarely works out like that.

The more serial your life cycle, the more dangerous a Monday start and a Friday end are. A Friday end means that no one will check when the finishing occurred until Monday morning. That gives people permission to work crazy hours over the weekend to meet the Friday date. And, the more serial the life cycle, the less you (or the team) can tell whether the work is actually done, until you get to the testing phase, at the very end of the project.

It's a similar problem with iterations. If an iteration is supposed to end on a Friday afternoon, but the product demo isn't until Monday morning, the team will often think, "Oh, we can finish/fix this one thing over the weekend." Especially when transitioning to agile development, the team will not be as accurate with their estimates, which means they will have unfinished work at the end of the earlier iterations. You want to know what the team can do in a reasonable amount of time—not overtime. If you end an iteration on a Friday, you unwittingly allow the team the weekend to finish.

When you schedule milestones or iterations to end midweek, the amount of unfinished work is obvious (which is what you want). You can steer the project because you can see what's done or not done. But if you can't see what's not done, your options for steering narrow.

Choose Tuesdays or Wednesdays for major milestones or for beginning/ending iterations. You'll see true progress (or lack thereof), you'll reduce overtime, and you'll be able to steer the project, not be surprised by disaster at the end of the project.

5.3   How Little Can You Do?

Too often, project teams think about how much they can do. They think the project should be built around the mind-set of "How much can we fit into this project?" Instead, consider the mind-set of "How little can we do?"

How-much thinking carries these assumptions:

- People are not a scarce resource. We should put all of them to use immediately, working like mad on the project.
- Schedule really doesn't matter.
- Cost of development is not a driving factor.

How-little thinking carries these assumptions:

- Understanding the requirements is a scarce resource. We should focus our energies on delivering something that shows we understand the specific requirement and the value it has to our customer.
- Schedule is critical, and we don't have time to do it again or build technical debt (see Appendix B, on page 335).
- Project cost is important, and we need to manage it.

Too often, project managers (and their senior managers) say that the characteristics of how-little thinking are important, but they manage according to how-much. The next time you or your management asks how much, maybe you can ask how little. If nothing else, you can help clarify everyone's assumptions.

5.4   Estimating with Multitasking

Some of the members of your project team are not just assigned to your project but to other projects too. How do you estimate how long their work will take?

You don't. You can't. Don't even try.

Multitasking is a guarantee that your project will be late. You can't tell by how much the project will be late, because you can't know how much time every person can spend on your project, and you can't tell whether the people who need to be on the project at the same time will actually be there.

You cannot estimate the schedule if you have multiproject, multitasked people. (Multitasking can waste anywhere from 20–90% of your time; see [RG05] and [Wei92].) In my work, multitasking[5] is the single biggest contributor to late projects, projects that don't deliver what they need, and projects that don't work as well as they need to work.

What you can do is talk to your sponsors. Explain, "If I don't have the people I need at the time I need them, I can't deliver what you want, in the time you want it, with the quality you want. Let's talk about how little you need." (See Section 5.3, *How Little Can You Do?*, on the facing page.)

If your sponsors won't budge (they want everything now, perfect, at no cost), you get to say no—in a politically correct way, of course. See Section 16.7, *How to Say No to Multitasking*, on page 319 for ideas.

5.5 Scheduling People to Multitask by Design

Maybe you've got some people who you need for your project but not full-time. Say you need a DBA or a GUI designer, or someone else who you need some of but not all of. Or, maybe you have several small projects that require some developers and testers, but none of those projects is really a full-time project. What do you do?

You can choose to have people multitask by design. For the people you need a little time from over the course of the project, assign them on a weekly basis to one project or another. Or, maybe your team members normally pair. You could assign one pair to two projects. Now you have people work in one-week iterations, starting an iteration on a Monday and ending it on a Friday. Yes, this violates the idea of scheduling milestones midweek (see the tip *Schedule Milestones (or Iterations) Midweek*, on page 77). This works only if everyone takes the weekend off for their necessary downtime and for the inevitable context switching.

You'll pay a price—the people who multitask by design will take longer to finish their jobs. That might be cheaper than hiring more people. Just make sure they context-switch only over a weekend, not during the week.

---

5. See the costs cited at http://www.umich.edu/~bcalab/multitasking.html.

5.6 Using Rolling-Wave Scheduling

Don't try to plan the whole darn project at the beginning. You'll be wrong, and you'll be wasting time you could be spending removing obstacles so the project team can find their rhythm. Use *rolling-wave planning* (see Appendix B, on page 335) to make the most of your initial and ongoing scheduling and replanning activities.

If you're accustomed to trying to schedule an entire project, rolling-wave planning might feel strange to you. You won't generate an entire Gantt chart or know exactly what you'll be doing three months from now. But honestly, how good are you at predicting the schedule that far out anyway? I'm not that good—things happen in a project. The further out the milestone, the less you know about *exactly* how you'll get there. Because no matter how good the project team's estimate was, some events will prevent them from completing the project the way they originally estimated.

A rolling-wave plan is a continuous detailed schedule that's only a few weeks long. As you complete one week of detailed schedule, you add another week to the end of the schedule. With a four-week rolling-wave schedule, you never have less than four weeks of detailed schedule, and you never have more than four weeks of detailed schedule. You don't waste time trying to schedule something you can't know enough about.

I choose a four-week rolling-wave schedule for two reasons. If I'm not managing a project with defined two-week iterations, less than two weeks is not enough detail for me to foresee risks. A schedule that's more than four weeks long tends to be wrong the further out we schedule, so I don't bother trying. You may find that your predictability is even less than four weeks—that's OK. Start the detailed task planning where you know enough, and don't bother trying to schedule more than that.

If you've never tried rolling-wave scheduling, here's how to start. Find a large-enough room to organize the schedule on the wall or on a whiteboard. Lay out your major milestones on yellow stickies, moving from left to right, because time moves from left to right. Then ask the project team to join you in the room.

Explain to the team that instead of trying to develop the entire project schedule in detail all at once, you've identified when you want to reach the major milestones, as noted by the yellow stickies on the wall.

Ask the question for the first milestone: "What will it take us to reach this milestone?" Then ask the project staff to write down their tasks and interdependencies on stickies, one task to a sticky.

Ask people to plan in inch-pebbles (see Appendix B, on page 335). Since the project manager doesn't assign inch-pebbles to people, each member of the project staff has to understand his or her own tasks in detail and develop inch-pebbles to complete those tasks.

If the project staff isn't able to plan in inch-pebbles, ask them to tell you how you will understand their progress. Thinking in inch-pebbles is not easy for some people, and they will need time to learn how to break their work into smaller pieces.

If you must make a Gantt chart, copy the contents of each sticky into your favorite project scheduling tool. Each week, as you meet with each person on the project team, you can ask them to tell you their next set of tasks, and you can update the schedule. If the people need help with their interdependencies, bring everyone together again.

As long as you keep each milestone in mind as you proceed, you'll find that the schedule is easier to maintain and that you spend less time with the schedule, enabling you to spend more time with the project team, seeing their progress and removing obstacles.

Rolling-wave planning isn't a panacea for understanding the true state of the project and planning how to achieve the next milestone, but it's a great way to start.

5.7 Deciding on an Iteration Duration

You've decided to manage the project using timeboxed iterations. But how long do you make the iteration?

Make the iteration's duration as much time as you can afford to waste. If you can afford to waste a whole project, then you can use a serial life cycle. If you can't afford waste, then choose an iteration duration of somewhere between one and four weeks. The shorter the iteration, the easier it will be to rerank requirements and adapt to changes as they occur. The longer the iteration, the larger the chunks people can accomplish.

I don't recommend iteration durations of longer than four weeks. It's too easy for the team to fall into Student Syndrome (see the tip *Help*

\\// **Joe Asks. . .**
:f
~   **How Can I Fit Large Tasks into Short Iterations?**

Complex projects have large tasks. And breaking them into tasks that team members can complete in four weeks or less is challenging. But it's worth doing.

When a team member tells me something will take more than a few days to do, I ask what the deliverables are into the code base. I want to know whether the team member is planning on designing—and for how long—or whether the team member will prototype. If Eric plans on designing first, I ask him how he will know the design is done. If Eric is prototyping, I ask him how he plans to evaluate the prototype.

More often, people tell me it's just a really big piece of code. That's easy—they'll deliver pieces of the feature into the code base, so I work with the team member(s) to discuss which completed parts of the overall feature they'll deliver first.

If you're changing architectural infrastructure, make sure that the team is continuously integrating as they proceed, and select the iteration in which they'll integrate the whole darn thing. Be aware that you'll look as if you're losing velocity until that team integrates with the whole project. (See the *Joe Asks. . .* on page 208.)

Project Team Members Avoid Student Syndrome, on page 159) and for the team to leave large chunks of work that they can't easily estimate or break apart into smaller, deliverable chunks. Iterations longer than four weeks allow the team to avoid continuous integration (see Section 9.1, *Adopt or Adapt Continuous Integration for Your Project*, on page 167), which will make it difficult to see completed work as the team proceeds.

An iteration needs a minimum duration. If you can't plan for an iteration in under two days, don't bother with anything under a three-week iteration. You're spending too much time planning and not enough time doing. Make sure planning time isn't too long for your iteration duration.

5.8 Estimating Using Inch-Pebbles Wherever Possible

Inch-pebbles Appendix B, on page 335 are the breakdown of each task into very small pieces, no more than two days in duration, generally only one day long (see [Rot99] and [McC96]). If you're familiar with XP, inch-pebbles are user stories. Inch-pebbles are either done or not done; they are not some percentage complete. Collections of inch-pebbles are the multiple-day or multiple-week tasks that teams normally create when they define tasks in a schedule. In reality, inch-pebbles are a way to define tasks that fit into small timeboxes—one or two days in duration.

Every project can use inch-pebbles at some point to estimate tasks and monitor progress. Inch-pebbles are especially useful if you have project team members who forget tasks when they estimate. Creating inch-pebbles pushes team members to remember all the steps they need to take. Some of the most common forgotten tasks are managing the software configuration management system and rework.

Especially in a serial life cycle, it's easy to underestimate the amount of rework required. Or a developer might forget about developer testing when performing a SWAG estimate. Or a tester might forget the time needed to set up the test environment.

Forgetting any of those things causes the project to either miss the release date or miss the defect levels or feature set you wanted in this release. Using inch-pebbles can help you avoid such problems.

Inch-pebbles are commonly used in agile life cycles (how else could a team accomplish useful work in one week?). But in other projects, especially serial lifecycle projects, inch-pebbles are not commonly used. One reason is that it makes no sense to develop inch-pebbles for the entire project at the beginning. It makes sense to use inch-pebbles only as the day-to-day and week-to-week planning, not as entire-project planning.

Inch-pebbles are useful when you know what you have to do. For many of the project's tasks, you know what to do. But what happens when you don't know what to do? What do you do then?

Creating and Using Inch-Pebbles When Tasks Are Unclear

If you're managing new product development (a product that has never existed in any way before) or a research project, you'll need to adapt the way you use inch-pebbles.

Instead of having timeboxes, use questions to know when a task is complete. Whether you have a research project or new product development, each kind of project has questions that need to be answered. The project team or the people working on those tasks need to generate specific questions and know how they will find the answers. Once the team can answer those questions and the problem is not what to do but how to get it done, the team can generate inch-pebbles for the rest of the tasks.

How to Define Inch-Pebbles

Every person on the project defines his or her own inch-pebbles—each person has personal responsibility for their contribution to the project. The project manager does not define the pebbles. The technical lead does not define the pepples. If the project manager, technical lead, or architect tries to define inch-pebbles, the technical staff will resist using them. That's because the people defining inch-pebbles for others are micromanaging. It's not appropriate to micromanage people. It's fine to coach them if they don't know how to generate the inch-pebbles, but it's not OK to tell people how to spend their time.

Tip: Avoid Micromanaging with Inch-Pebbles

No one likes to be micromanaged. After all, we're professionals. It's hard to believe at first, but inch-pebbles can actually free you from micromanagement. Because the project team defines their tasks in small increments and a task is either complete or not, there is no need for continual status and task checking—for micromanagement. Project status is obvious at any time in the project. (If you're working with a project manager or senior manager who inflicts help, inch-pebbles can't save you—but then nothing can.)

Why Use Inch-Pebbles?

The more serial your life cycle or the longer the tasks, the more inch-pebbles can help. When you ask the team to schedule in inch-pebbles, everyone understands the tasks and the interdependencies with the tasks. In addition, inch-pebbles can expose dependencies. When a project team uses inch-pebbles, they can take advantage of schedule advances, those rare times that people are done with their work early.

And, inch-pebbles help create a more accurate schedule—at least for the duration that people use inch-pebbles to develop a schedule.

All of these benefits reduce schedule risk.

Remember This

- Never provide a single-point date for an end date.
- The smaller the task, the easier it is to estimate.
- Look for estimate accuracy, not precision.

Chapter 6

Recognizing and Avoiding Schedule Games

Even if you've tried to do a good job estimating, planning, and scheduling, you will still encounter sponsors, managers, and team members who will game the schedule. Your job is to bring those game players back to reality. But first you need to recognize the schedule games.

All sponsors and managers will push back against your schedule at some point. These games occur even when you've created a reasonable project schedule. Many of the ways in which they push back fall into easily recognized patterns. The better you are at recognizing the game they are playing, the better able you will be to steer the project to a reasonable outcome.

6.1 Bring Me a Rock

Cliff worked with his project team for a week developing a schedule. They'd completed a Hudson Bay Start (see Section 4.2, *Hudson Bay Start*, on page 52) and were sure they had identified the major technical risks. He explained the risks and the schedule to Norm, his boss. "Can't you bring it in earlier?" Cliff trudged off back to the team.

After another week reworking the schedule with the team, Cliff had another date. He walked into Norm's office and said, "If you give me a couple more people here and here," he pointed to specific milestones, "I can take a month off the project." Norm frowned, "Not good enough. I need this project done earlier." Cliff sighed and returned to the project team.

Figure 6.1: BRING ME A ROCK

The next week, Cliff brought another schedule to Norm, "OK, this is the best we can do," Cliff said.

Norm barely looked at the schedule before saying, "But it's still not good enough."

Cliff explodes, "What DO YOU WANT?"

Bring Me a Rock (see Figure 6.1, on the facing page) is the game where, regardless of the schedule you develop, your sponsor wants the project done in less time. All you know is that every date you suggest is not a date your sponsor wants—your date is too far out [BWe01].

The Bring Me a Rock schedule game occurs when "they" want it faster but don't tell you when or why. If they told you when, you could tell them what you can do. If they told you why, you and the project team could probably develop some creative solutions to meet their desires.

The pragmatic manager has alternatives, including the negotiating strategy that Cliff tried. But when negotiation fails—or looks like it will never succeed—try these possibilities:

- Ask some questions before attempting to fetch more rocks: Would you prefer a short schedule or a longer one? More people or fewer? How about fewer features? Learning what's important first will guide you to a reasonable solution. Or, it will prepare you for a negotiation.
- Discover the reasons for the desired date. Elicit the strategic reasons for this project, and learn what success means.
- Make sure your sponsor understands the options you've selected and why. It's possible your sponsor has something easier and faster in mind.
- Explain your confidence range for the date you provide. It's possible your management doesn't understand what your estimate means, and it's possible you don't understand what they're asking.
- Include release criteria with your date so you can ask specific questions about how good/full the release has to be. What if we implemented this feature with incredible performance, and ignored that feature? Can our users live with more defects?

Bring Me a Rock doesn't occur just once in an organization. More often, it occurs with every project. If you keep encountering Bring Me a Rock, consider adopting these practices:

- Develop a ranked product backlog. See Section 16.6, *Build a Product Backlog*, on page 313.
- Implement by feature. The more specific progress your sponsors can see, the less likely they are to muck around with the date.
- Use short timeboxes (less than four weeks duration) so your sponsor can see progress. If you can show valuable progress every couple of weeks, the date becomes much less important. You start to discuss which features to implement when and how good they have to be.

6.2 Hope Is Our Most Important Strategy

A few years ago, a senior manager called me and said, "We have a project in trouble. We started off hopeful, but now it looks impossible." I asked a few questions and discovered they had never done a project like this before. The project was bigger, in a different programming language, on a new platform, and with a shorter schedule than any they had ever done before.

The entire future of their company depended on a successful completion of this project that was bigger and more demanding than any they had tackled in the past. Their only strategy was Hope (see Figure 6.2, on the facing page).

They hadn't arranged for any training in the product domain or in the language or for the new operating system. They had never managed to release any substantial project in the time frame they were hoping they could for this project.

Hope is not enough to deliver a successful project.[1]

Here's what a pragmatic project manager can do:

- Recognize and write down where you have risks. You might have technical risks (new language, new platform), schedule risks (shorter schedule, too few people), or, most likely, both.
- Choose any life cycle other than waterfall. Why? Because you don't have any data that would allow you to be successful with the up-front planning that waterfall requires. If you've never done anything like this before, iterate on some prototypes, or iterate on a few features, to see where your work takes you.

---

1. I first heard of this game from Esther Derby.

Figure 6.2: HOPE IS OUR MOST IMPORTANT STRATEGY

- Consider a Hudson Bay Start (see Section 4.2, *Hudson Bay Start*, on page 52) to see whether you can create anything. This is especially good when you have new technology such as a language, operating system, database, and the like. A Hudson Bay Start will show you what you're hoping for and will expose some of the currently unknown risks.
- Make sure that people have the technical functional skills and solution-space domain expertise [Rot04b]. If necessary, train people. It's cheaper to train everyone on the project in a new language than waste time.
- Plan to iterate on everything, especially planning and scheduling.

- Solicit help and information in areas where you might lack experience or expertise. Check with the project team about how to make their status visible.
- Develop milestone criteria (your milestones can be iterations). Review those criteria at management review meetings. Even if management or your sponsors don't want management reviews, you can conduct those meetings. Reviewing your progress regularly against milestones will help if you aren't sure how to make this project work.

Hoping for a good outcome is not enough.

As a PM, your job is to plan, replan, and work to make the best outcome occur. One way to do that is to adopt these practices:

- Use timeboxed iterations so you and everyone else can see project progress.
- Chart the project's progress in a velocity chart. You want to make the progress (or lack thereof) as clear to everyone as possible. That way, especially if you think you need to ask for help, you have data to use.

6.3 Queen of Denial

Some bosses just won't face up to reality. You can tell them, "We can't meet your schedule."

They will look at you as if you haven't said a word and tell you, "I'm sure if you just put your mind to it, you'll meet the date." While you sit there with your mouth open not knowing what to say, they will walk away as happy as can be that their schedule will be met. You have met Queen of Denial (see Figure 6.3, on the facing page).[2]

Denial occurs for a few possible reasons. The most common one I've seen is when the manager in question wants to encourage the project team. Sometimes, people are in denial because they fear the project won't meet its deadline. They ignore what you're saying; it's the ostrich effect. Sometimes, senior managers believe that when they set ambitious/impossible dates, the project team will deliver sooner than they thought they could.

---

2. I first heard of Queen of Denial from Benson Margulies.

Figure 6.3: QUEEN OF DENIAL

Some possibilities to deal with denial are as follows:

- Investigate why your manager is in denial. Try some context-free questions (see Section 1.5, *Use Context-Free Questions to Identify Project Drivers*, on page 10) to understand the reasons behind the project. For example, you could ask, "For this project, what does success look like?"

- Write down your project's risks and their potential impact. Use High, Medium, and Low to discuss severity and exposure, not numbers. The people who are gaming your schedule will game your risk numbers.

- Show what you can do and measure the velocity (see Section 11.2, *Use Velocity Charts to Track Schedule Progress*, on page 204) you actually have on the project. Yes, iterations are your friend here. And velocity charts might help explain what's really happening.
- Make sure people on the project have the solution-space domain expertise to perform the work.

If your manager thinks that denial is the way to encourage the project team, suggest alternative encouragement techniques. Usually, that means encouraging the manager to go do something else that would either benefit the project team (negotiate a smaller list of requirements for example) or move that manager's attention to some other project. The managers who think that encouraging the project team by denying problems or potential problems tend to get in the way. Focusing their attention on some *other* project is a useful technique for moving their attention off your project.

Queen of Denial doesn't have to be a disaster, as long as the PM isn't the one in denial.

One project team tried to convince the PM of the project's reality. After several failures, they gave up. They decided they would self-organize and ignore the PM. They stopped attending project team meetings and ignored everything the PM said. They built pieces of the project and developed some data (but not velocity charts). After a few months, when it was clear the project was not where the PM said it was, the PM was fired. But the project team had lost so much time by that point, they had many fewer opportunities to manage what they could deliver when.

Inevitably, reality comes face to face with denial at some point, which is why Queen of Denial isn't always a disaster so much as it is a schedule game. When the manager does see reality, make sure you have some part of the product working and some data to show that manager so you can discuss what to do next. This is a good time to consider how little can you do (see Section 5.3, *How Little Can You Do?*, on page 78) so you can complete this project and plan better for the next one.

If you persistently encounter the Queen of Denial, integrate these approaches into your project management so people see what's actually happening:

- Use timboxed iterations, so you and everyone else can see project progress.

Figure 6.4: SWEEP UNDER THE RUG

- Develop a ranked product backlog. See Section 16.6, *Build a Product Backlog*, on page 313. That will allow the team to implement by feature in value order. When your sponsor wakes up and realizes you aren't going to make the impossible date, your team will have completed features in rank order, so you'll have something valuable.

6.4 Sweep Under the Rug

A few years ago, I received a call to help a project in trouble. I started in the middle of a release cycle and worked with the team to identify what they could and should deliver and what should be postponed. The project team was able to finish their list of deliverables.

Following the release, I suggested the team hold a retrospective to learn what to do differently the next time. The VP didn't think anyone would learn from a retrospective.

He forgot why I helped in the first place and focused on only our success. He said, "But the team did a great job. They did everything we wanted in this release."

That's sweeping the problems—especially the changes in priority—all under the rug; see Figure 6.4, on the previous page.[3] No one on the team believed they had done a good job. The VP was no longer credible. The project team was frustrated and tired. If they had known at the beginning that not everything was necessary for this release, the developers would have worked only on what was necessary.

Here are some ideas to avoid this game:

- Rank the features to implement for a specific release. (Ranking means 1, 2, 3, 4, 5, 6, and so on.) See Section 8.3, *Rank the Requirements*, on page 145.
- Implement by feature. Implementing by architecture begs for too much partially completed work, none of which is all done. And architecture evolves more during the project than most managers realize. See Section 9.3, *Implement by Feature, Not by Architecture*, on page 170.
- Develop release criteria so you have the conversation at the beginning of the project about what is needed for release. See Section 2.3, *Release Criteria*, on page 21.

If Sweep Under the Rug is a persistent problem for you, try these approaches:

- Use a product backlog so your features are ranked by value. That way you're always finishing the most valuable—and therefore most important—work first.
- Use timeboxed iterations, and implement by feature. You and team will see progress, as well as providing the most valuable features first.

These avoidance strategies all require conversations at the beginning of the project with the project stakeholders. Those conversations are difficult. But the payoff is that no one has to pretend the project was successful when it didn't deliver everything. Instead, the project can focus on what's required for success and do that—and only that.

---

3. I first heard of Sweep Under the Rug from Elisabeth Hendrickson.

Figure 6.5: HAPPY DATE

6.5 Happy Date

Sometimes, I work with organizations where there's an implicit agree-ment *not* to discuss the schedule. I've seen this most often when man-agement demands a date, and the project team says, "Sure, no problem. Christmas it is!" But they don't say which Christmas.

Eventually, when some Christmas comes around, or enough dates have been missed, people start discussing the schedule—but not until the project team has missed many milestones, possibly even the first few desired end-of-project dates.

I worked with a project team once who hadn't met a milestone or any-thing else on their project schedules in more than five years. They would repeatedly develop optimistic schedules with no confidence ranges. Finally, after a senior management change, they were called into a senior management meeting to explain the schedule.

It wasn't until one manager said, "Look, I want to know when something will be done. Let's just start with one thing and go from there." That was when the project team realized they needed to change.

I have to admit, I have a difficult time understanding how people fall into this schedule game for very long. At some point, no one can miss the reality of the project. But, I certainly have seen persuasive managers intimidate, cajole, or use political pressure to "convince" a project manager or team that they could meet the Happy Date (see Figure 6.5, on the previous page) the date the manager wants. Combine that persuasiveness with a culture of not discussing difficult topics, and you're ripe for the Dream Time/Happy Date schedule game.[4]

Happy Date is related to, but not the same as, Queen of Denial. With Happy Date, some people in the organization (the project team or project manager) placate other people (the stakeholders). In a sense, both sets of people are in denial about the need to talk about the schedule. The project team wants to placate the stakeholders. The stakeholders are willing to be placated. In Queen of Denial, the stakeholders would like to be placated, but the project team insists on explaining reality.

To prevent this schedule game, you need to work at the project level and with the organization. For the project, do the following:

- Explain schedule ranges (see Section 5.1, *Use Date Ranges for Estimates*, on page 69), especially if you're not using an iterative life cycle.
- Use an iterative life cycle, and explain what you'll implement with confidence ranges; see Section 5.1, *Use Confidence Ranges for Estimates*, on page 67. ("We can do these ten features and maybe these other three in the next month. We'll let you know before the end of the month.")
- Use an agile life cycle with a ranked product backlog; see Section 16.6, *Build a Product Backlog*, on page 313.
- Use short timeboxes, even in a staged-delivery life cycle, to help people make progress, and make that progress visible.
- Measure more than just the milestone dates for the project. Single-dimension measurements (as discussed in Section 11.1, *Measurements Can Be Dangerous*, on page 201) are poison to seeing the true project status. Use velocity charts so everyone can see progress.

---

4. I first heard of Happy Date from Tim Lister.

Figure 6.6: PANTS ON FIRE

But there's just so much a project manager can do alone. This game reflects an incongruent organization—one where everyone is willing to placate one another and avoid conflict [Wei94]. Constructive discussion (a.k.a. constructive conflict) can make an organization stronger. Avoiding conflict and the necessary discussions makes an organization weaker.

6.6 Pants on Fire

One day you arrive at work to an urgent email message from the Big Cheese. Big Cheese says, "Stop working on that project. Start on this one!"

You can be sure that if this happens once, it'll happen several times. Either you and the project team will bounce among several projects or back and forth between two projects. Whatever the circumstances, you're multiproject multitasking, and so are all the people on your project team. You know you're not making progress on anything, and the urgency of all the projects keeps going up and up and up. . . .

Pants on Fire (see Figure 6.6, on the preceding page) occurs when management is afraid or unable to choose to focus on one thing at a time. It has several possible causes: the technical staff has a track record of being late, there's no corporate strategy, or the corporate strategy hasn't been broken down into sufficiently detailed tactics.[5]

Here are some actions you can take:

- Plan for short timeboxed iterations, and start something new on an iteration boundary. To make this work, the iterations have to be short enough to start something new, such as one or two weeks.
- If you can't manage iterations, implement by feature, and use staged delivery.
- Communicate the costs of this strategy to management so they can weigh the benefit of satisfying the crisis of the day vs. the assumed additional costs. Refer to Section 16.7, *Managing Multiproject Multitasking*, on page 316 to see how to help your management calculate cost and benefit.
- Help test the tactics against the strategy. Explain, "With this strategy, we would have these results/consequences. Is that what we want?"
- Modify your current estimation techniques so the project team is more likely to meet their original estimated dates. If the team can't meet their estimated dates, management may think they have no choice but to start working on something else. Make sure people use inch-pepples (see Section 5.8, *Estimating Using Inch-Pebbles Wherever Possible*, on page 83), and try continuous integration (Section 9.1, *Adopt or Adapt Continuous Integration for Your Project*, on page 167) so the team has a chance to finish things.
- Sometimes, Pants on Fire occurs when the customer decides he or she doesn't need the product just yet. Management doesn't want the team to finish the product, so they want to move the team or most of the team to another project. In that case, make sure you work in short iterations and know at the beginning of the project whether there could be a reason to postpone work. And, make sure your management developed and is managing the project portfolio; see Chapter 16, *Managing the Project Portfolio*, on page 307.

---

5. Tim Lister named this game in conversation with Elisabeth Hendrickson.

Figure 6.7: Split Focus

Pants on Fire wastes everyone's time. But sometimes, management either cannot change their management style or cannot believe that multiprojecting wastes time. If you're in a situation like that, consider how you can create a projectwide environment that allows you and your project team to work successfully.

6.7 Split Focus

One of my managers actually said this to me. "I'd like you to spend 50% of your time on Project A, 30% of your time on Project B, and 20% of your time on Project C. In your spare time, can you look over the report for the Big Cheese?" I said, "What spare time?"

Split Focus (see Figure 6.7) is the multiproject multitasking game. It occurs when the management team is unable to commit to a project/program strategy. Instead of just saying yes or no or "when?" to each project, they say yes to all projects.

Here are some actions you can take:

- Together with the program team, try some of the approaches in Section 16.7, *Managing Multiproject Multitasking*, on page 316, especially anything that helps the program team or the management team make decisions about what to do first, second, and third.

- If your management persists in wanting you and your project team to work on several projects at the same time, move to one-week iterations for each project, making sure you have releasable product at the end of an iteration. I use one-week iterations so people stay focused on the one project for a week at a time. At the end of the week, when it's time for the weekend and people will change their focus anyway, people can stop thinking about the current project and start on the next project.

- If you can't manage iterations, implement by feature, and use staged delivery. Make sure you have release criteria for each project so you can finish the minimum work on each project.

- As before with Pants on Fire, communicate the costs of this strategy to management so they can weigh the benefit of satisfying the crisis of the day vs. the assumed additional costs. See Section 16.7, *Managing Multiproject Multitasking*, on page 316 to see how to help your management calculate cost and benefit.

- Make sure you've ranked the requirements, and finish something quickly. Sometimes Split Focus occurs because some of your stakeholders can't believe you'll finish anything quickly enough for them. They think hedging their bets by having you work on several things will help them get something faster. They're wrong, but they don't realize that.

If you work for an organization addicted to Split Focus, plan to work in one-week iterations. Yes, it's hard. You will have to work with your project team to break apart the requirements into small enough pieces that they can make progress in one week. If you can't help the team move to short chunks of work in short periods of time, you and they will never finish anything. The team slips constantly, as in the sidebar on page 294. As the project manager, you can act to help people finish— and help your management from falling into Split Focus.

Focus Means a Single Focus

I once worked for a company that decided after a several-day offsite strategy meeting that we were going to "focus on five."

That isn't focus.

Focus means to center all of the attention toward something. Five strategic areas are four too many.

Unfortunately, it's all too common for companies to spread themselves too thin in order to be all things to all possible customers. If that's the problem where you work, move to short iterations as quickly as possible so you can say to your management, "OK, we can start that next week, because we'll be finishing this in two days." Even better, make sure your iterations start and end in the middle of the week, such as a Wednesday. That way if your managers have "a-ha" ideas over the weekend, they'll probably give you a couple of days to finish what you were doing.

Your team will thank you for maintaining focus.

6.8 Schedule Equals Commitment

You and I know that the schedule is an estimate, a guess if you will. The project schedule is your best guess about when the project team will reach which milestones and when the project may complete. A schedule is not a prediction; it is a guess. But some project managers have sponsors who want that guess to be a commitment (see Figure 6.8, on the next page).

If you are facing the commitment problem, ask these two questions:

- Do you care what the project team delivers?
- Do you care how good the product is?

A reasonable schedule discussion requires discussing the rest of the project drivers, constraints, and floats: at a minimum the feature set desired in that time and how good the feature set will be at that time. If the people involved aren't ready to discuss the schedule, the feature set, and the defect levels, then any discussion of schedule being a commitment is premature.

Figure 6.8: SCHEDULE EQUALS COMMITMENT

One approach I like to use when senior managers demand a commitment is to provide them with confidence levels. "I have a 90% confidence level in August 1 as a release date. I have a 100% confidence level in October 1 as a release date." Explaining what has to happen during that time, between the 90% and 100% confidence dates, helps me explain what a commitment to the schedule means to me.

Another technique I like to use is the date-for-a-date discussion. "I can tell you we'll be able to release in the last half of the year. I can narrow it down to a quarter at this time (and specify a date), and I can narrow it down to a month here (another date) and then (at a later date) will be able to provide you a final release date."

But the best technique I know is to use timeboxed iterations (of between two to four weeks—not longer) along with a ranked product backlog. That way, you can release virtually at any time. You know that the contents of each iteration works. You know you've implemented the most important requirements first. And it's OK if management wants to release—because the product is ready. No one needs a commitment from the developers; you need a commitment from the people who decide on the requirements that they are telling you which requirements are needed when.

If someone demands you commit to a date, consider how you'll organize the project. Try iterations. Or, try date-for-a-date. Or, try confidence levels with a date estimate. But don't just commit to a date. That's inviting Murphy to hang out on your project. You'll commit to a date, but something will happen, and you won't meet the date.

6.9 We'll Know Where We Are When We Get There

A VP claimed he had Attention Deficit Disorder. He didn't demand different dates. Instead, he kept changing the project's goal. First, the goal was a specific feature set. The velocity charts proved the team wasn't going to meet the date. He changed the goal to performance for some specific features. But the performance was difficult to achieve. A few weeks later, he changed his mind to focus on reliability.

Here's what I found humorous: he didn't have this problem when he was a project manager. Nope, he made sure that each project he managed had a goal. And he watched for any senior manager who wanted to change that goal. But when he moved into senior management, he had trouble allowing the projects to finish, staying focused on one goal.

Figure 6.9: We'll Know Where We Are When We Get There

This schedule game occurs when senior managers change the goals of a project or have a great idea that changes what the project is supposed to deliver or when someone derails the project. I've seen unseasoned project managers derail the project in the same way that a senior manager does. "Oh, look over there. Doesn't that look like a great idea? Let's do that." (See Figure 6.9.)

This game is different from Bring Me a Rock. In Bring Me a Rock, the project goals don't change over time; the sponsor wants a shorter schedule. In We'll Know Where We Are When We Get There, the sponsor doesn't change the date but changes the goal of the project.

This schedule game is sometimes called Chasing Skirts, a particularly unpolitically correct name. It occurs when management can't or won't decide on a product.

They're like a guy who is always waiting for the next pretty girl to come along. He will date this pretty girl for a while, but if another pretty girl comes along, he will drop the first one and move on to the next one.

No matter what you call this schedule game, the effect is the same. The project team doesn't stay focused on a product the team could deliver. The project changes focus. The last time I consulted on a project like this, one of the senior managers said to me soothingly, "We'll know where we are when we get there."

Not in my experience. Keeping a project focused on its goal(s) is the fastest way to finish a project. Allowing a project to lose focus will prevent it from finishing for a very long time, possibly forever.

Here are some ideas to consider:

- Make sure you have written a project vision, project goals, and release criteria. Gain consensus on the vision, goals, and release criteria. You know where you're headed, what more you might be able to do, and when you're done. So does the rest of the organization.
- If your management won't define the vision, you define it. Publish it. Stick to it. If you can't, finish the project immediately, and start a new project with the new goals.
- If the project is "too long," organize the project into iterations. Evaluate where you are after each iteration. If you've accomplished enough of the goals, end this project and start another. Use shorter (no more than four-week) iterations.

Sometimes, none of these possibilities will help because management interferes with the PM, working around the PM to assign other work to the project staff. If that has happened to you, talk to your managers, and explain how you will benefit them. If they don't listen, or can't stop their behavior, remember you don't have to stay there. See Section 7.7, *Know When It's Time to Leave*, on page 134.

Projects need crisp goals. The entire project team needs to stay focused on those goals. Don't let anyone allow your project to drift. You won't know when you get there. All you'll know is that you're not anywhere.

6.10 The Schedule Tool Is Always Right, or Schedule Dream Time

Barney was a PM in an organization where the execs understood only the waterfall life cycle. They thought iterating was a waste of time. They

Figure 6.10: SCHEDULE DREAM TIME

expected to see a Gantt chart the first week of the project, that the PM would manage to the chart, and that everything would be fine. And, inevitably, if Barney had to report that the project was not on track, some helpful senior manager would say something like, "Well, it says on the schedule that you'll be here. What's wrong with you that you're not on schedule?"

The execs didn't understand projects where people had to think and react to what they had learned. They were convinced that the critical path would never change and that the tasks would stay in roughly the same order.

Here's why: the execs were accustomed to reports of already completed work/sales figures/whatever—data that reflected what had happened in the *past*. But the schedule is a guess about how things will happen in the *future*. This schedule game is also called Schedule Dream Time; see Figure 6.10, on the facing page.[6]

That variation is when the beauty of the Gantt chart blinds people to the fact the schedule is just a guess (see Section 5.1, *Tips to Make Estimation Easier*, on page 74). The Gantt chart lulls people into believing the schedule and not checking on reality.

If you're faced with these kinds of managers, consider these alternatives:

- Develop a rolling-wave schedule (Section 5.6, *Using Rolling-Wave Scheduling*, on page 80), where you've developed only the first few weeks of detail plus the major milestones. When you don't provide detail past the first few weeks, people are more likely to believe you can't predict the future. Deliver a new and updated schedule with completed tasks and the next rolling wave and updated milestones every month. That way you can explain what has occurred and still not be tied into a huge plan that can't work.
- Use a low-tech scheduling technique, such as yellow-sticky scheduling (see Section 4.3, *Basic Sticky Scheduling*, on page 56) or cards on the wall. Invite the execs in to review the schedule.
- Provide estimates with confidence levels (see Section 5.1, *Use Confidence Ranges for Estimates*, on page 67) instead of a Gantt chart.
- Use timeboxed iterations, and schedule only one iteration's worth of work at a time. Measure your velocity. After three iterations, you might know enough about your velocity to predict the rest of the schedule.

The problem with the belief that the scheduling tool is always right is that it assumes the estimated schedule is accurate. The problem is that few schedules are accurate. Many are precise—"We'll release Wednesday, at 3:32 p.m."—but not accurate. That's because the schedule is an estimate. Making it look pretty doesn't change that the schedule is an estimate and has some margin of error.

This game isn't the fault of a scheduling tool—the problem is in the belief system of the people who use the tool. As a PM, you'll need to

---

6. Esther Derby and I named this in a conversation.

Figure 6.11: WE GOTTA HAVE IT; WE'RE TOAST WITHOUT IT

determine the most effective techniques for scheduling your project and for explaining that schedule to other people. It's fine to use a scheduling tool, if that works for you. Just don't believe it because it happens to make pretty charts.

6.11 We Gotta Have It; We're Toast Without It

The boss calls Manny, the project manager: "Manny, we have to talk about your project." Manny responds, "Sure, what's up?" "Well, if we don't add this one feature, we're toast. Big Customer won't buy this release." Manny sighs and says, "Let me talk to the project team—I'll get back to you."

Manny hunkers down with the project team. They agree to fit this one extra feature into the release, even though they have no hope of meeting the schedule—which hasn't changed.

Everyone here wants the project to succeed: the boss, the project manager, and the project team. But without discussing trade-offs for the project, they remove any hope of meeting the schedule. The project (and the team) are toast.[7]

If you're faced with well-meaning management and project teams, try these alternatives:

- Negotiate for a different feature set. You can ask the question, "What don't you want in this release so I can see whether I can find a way to fit this in?"
- Negotiate for more time. "If you're willing to extend the release, we can add this feature."
- Negotiate for more money. "I see why you want it, but this additional feature will take two weeks longer to build than the other features. We can't just take one feature out and put this one in; we need to rethink the entire release. Do you want me to do that now? It's going to take the team some time to estimate and replan the release. Let's make sure that is what you want."

There's a way to prevent We Gotta Have It. If you implement by feature and regularly have the product available for release, you and your management can rerank the features for the next release. Preventing this game works best with timeboxed iterations of no more than four weeks in duration. With a four-week timebox, the longest anyone has to wait is eight weeks.

If you use quarterly releases, such as release trains, the longest anyone has to wait for a new feature is six months. That can feel like a long time to many managers. And, if you release only every six to nine months, the longest waiting period could be a year or more.

If you've seen We Gotta Have It in your organization, move to timeboxed iterations so you can manage the demand. Or, consider release trains (see Section 14.3, *Making Release Trains Work for You*, on page 284). See Section 16.6, *Build a Product Backlog*, on page 313 for ideas about how to use a backlog to manage the demand for more features and avoid We Gotta Have It.

---

7. See http://www.stickyminds.com/s.asp?F=S11829_COL_2.

Figure 6.12: WE CAN'T SAY NO

Let's agree that you have a reasonable schedule. But then things happen, and not everyone can accomplish what they said they could. In the previous section, you saw the games that sponsors and managers play. Here are the schedule games I've seen team members play. Again, your job is to bring the team member back to reality.

6.12 We Can't Say No

As the project manager, your management wants you to fit just one more feature into the release. They're playing "We gotta have it." And as a responsible project manager, you bring the request to the team. You've told your management the team will assess the request and you'll return with a new date or cost for the new feature.

But as you start discussing the feature and the trade-offs with the team, the team isn't willing to say "no," "not yet," or "here's what it will take." Instead, the team blindly accepts the extra work, without discussing the cost in reference to time and money and the impact on current work (see Figure 6.12, on the preceding page). Sometimes the team does this out of a feeling of guilt and sometimes out of lack of understanding of the actual time required to do the work.[8]

If you're managing a team who can't say no, you need to help them learn to say no. But just saying no to upper management (or marketing, or whomever is requesting more work in the same time) is not enough. You can say no all you want. If people are determined to try to do the extra work, consider these approaches to helping people manage the additional work:

- Ask people on the team whether they can create a plan to make adding this extra functionality work. Use yellow-sticky scheduling and relative sizing to see how to make it work. If they can develop a plan everyone can believe, then your job is to help make that plan happen.
- Sometimes, the project team says, "We'll suck it up and work overtime." If they want to work overtime, suggest timeboxing their overtime and measuring the results. You could say, "OK, we'll split work into one-week iterations. We'll work overtime for one week and measure our velocity to see how much more we can do and how tired we are. After that first week, we'll have a normal week and measure our velocity. Then we'll compare velocities and any open issues, such as additional changes or defects. If we don't like what we have, we'll go to normal workweeks and we'll see whether there's anything else we can do."
- Sometimes, you can add people to do more work. (Not always.) If other people in the organization have domain expertise and are able to fit into this project team and the existing project team wants those people, you can try adding those people to the team. Do not add people who don't know the product or the team already—that invokes Brooks' law. (See Section 7.5, *Know When to Add More People*, on page 131 for more discussion.)

If none of those alternatives works, you need to help the team say no. You may be able to counter the team's guilt or the desire to do what the company needs with data. Velocity charts and iteration-content charts are especially helpful here. If you don't help the team learn to say no, you're all headed for a death march [You99] project. And no one wants that.

---

8. See http://www.stickyminds.com/s.asp?F=S11829_COL_2.

Figure 6.13: SCHEDULE CHICKEN

6.13 Schedule Chicken

Schedule Chicken most often occurs in a serial status meeting.[9] The project manager asks each person how they're doing. Everyone says that they are right on schedule. In reality, no one is. Everyone is waiting for someone else to blink and admit that he or she is not on schedule. And rarely does anyone admit that he or she is not on schedule until it's too late.

A pragmatic project manager has several options:

- Avoid serial status meetings (see Section 10.1, *Never Conduct Public Serial Status Meetings*, on page 185). Instead, use the ideas in Section 10.5, *Determining Project Status*, on page 188 to determine the real status.
- Break the tasks into smaller pieces so that everyone has a deliverable every day, two at the most. (See Section 5.8, *Estimating Using Inch-Pebbles Wherever Possible*, on page 83.)

---

9. I first discussed Schedule Chicken with Dave Smith and Jerry Weinberg.

- Implement by feature. The more people are focused on a deliverable piece that they can see once it's done, the easier it is to see how much progress they're making. Sometimes people play Schedule Chicken because they started late (see Student Syndrome in the tip *Help Project Team Members Avoid Student Syndrome*, on page 159). Seeing pieces of the product come together periodically helps everyone see the project's progress, which in turn helps them see when they aren't making progress.

- Consider moving to iterations, especially in an agile life cycle. Short iterations remove the need for weekly sitdown group serial status meetings (which you should never have anyway). With daily standup meetings, people can't hide their real status.

6.14   90% Done

Too many knowledge workers—especially technical people—have never been taught to estimate. Or if they've tried estimating, they're too optimistic, so they underestimate the work involved for a task. Or they've received no feedback on their estimates, so they don't know their estimates are off. Or they didn't anticipate all the subtasks involved in this task, such as organizing the environment for testing or checking in the code. In any case, 90% Done occurs when the team member thinks he or she has accomplished 90% of the work but still has 90% of the work left to finish (see Figure 6.14, on the next page).

I fell victim to 90% Done early in my career. I was writing a conversion tool to convert a database from one format to another. I thought the data was clean. It wasn't. I thought I knew the formats for each field. I didn't. I thought I knew a lot about the requirements, but as I proceeded, one record at a time through the database, I encountered more special cases, each of which changed the requirements.

I finally smartened up and developed a set of test cases that I could run as I changed the code and made some progress in the conversion. (For a more contemporary approach, you can read more about behavior-driven development.[10]) When my manager asked me what was taking so long, I showed him my status and explained about all the cases we didn't know about at the beginning.

---

10. See http://behaviour-driven.org/.

Figure 6.14: 90% DONE

You'll need to coach [RD05] a bit as a project manager to eliminate 90% Done:

- Help the person develop their inch-pebbles. You may have to sit with the person to say, "What will it take to finish this? What are all the pieces that go into this week of work?"

- Ask the person to make their status visible to you. That might mean showing you all the cases their code is covering (as it was in my example), a list of risks, a list of test cases, or some interim version of the code that they can show you as they add to it.

- Coach the person how to track their estimate and see how well they estimated at the beginning. See Section 11.2, *Track Your Original Estimate with EQF*, on page 209.

Sometimes, people fall into 90% Done because they're implementing across the architecture. If you shift people to implementing by feature and have them work in short iterations, they start trying to estimate and complete smaller chunks of work. Their estimates will be more accurate, and they are more likely to finish the work.

6.15 We'll Go Faster Now

Imagine you're managing an agile project, a staged-delivery project, or some other life cycle that allows you to incrementally build the system. You've been measuring velocity (or the features implemented), and you're not progressing as quickly as you'd like. And, for some reason, the team is still optimistic about the release date (see Figure 6.15, on the next page).

As a pragmatic project manager, you don't want to be the voice of pessimism or cynicism. You do want to be the voice of reality and help the project team discover the real status. After all, maybe they really can pick up the speed. Approaches to manage unbridled optimism include the following:

- Discuss the project velocity with the people on the project. Ask for data: What have they seen or heard that leads them to believe they'll make more progress than they did before?

- Measure the estimation quality factor (see Section 11.2, *Track Your Original Estimate with EQF*, on page 209). Pay special attention to the reasons people think they are on or ahead of schedule.

Figure 6.15: We'll Go Faster Now

- Measure everything the project team is doing. Make sure every person is working on this project and on the tasks necessary for the deliverable date. If anyone is working on any other project or on tasks that are scheduled for a later release or for another project, stop that now.

- If you have a hardware component to the project, measure earned value (see Section 11.2, *Earned Value for Software Projects Makes Little Sense*, on page 207) for that piece, and see whether that component is on schedule. If that part isn't on schedule (the earned value is less than what it should be), replan the entire project.

- As long as you're measuring velocity, you can keep an open mind about overall project velocity until the team has completed the third iteration. By that time, they are most likely at their typical velocity.

Figure 6.16: SCHEDULE TRANCE

6.16 Schedule Trance

The Big Cheese from headquarters is coming to visit next Tuesday. Or you have a trade show in ten weeks. No matter what, you have an immovable date and an ambitious or impossible feature set to complete before that date. Maybe the team has been measuring velocity, maybe not. You don't see how the team can meet the date with the entire feature set. It seems as if the team is in a trance about the date (see Figure 6.16). Sometimes, this is a team's response to Happy Date.

First create your project dashboard (see Chapter 11, *Creating and Using a Project Dashboard*, on page 201), and measure your progress, starting with velocity. Then consider these options:

- If you're not using iterations now, break the rest of the project into iterations, the shorter the better. If you have ten weeks before the immovable date, break the project into no fewer than five iterations, preferably ten. One iteration a week will help you continually reprioritize what to do when. The goal of an iteration is completed work on a feature or features, that is, completed development, documentation, testing, and anything else your product requires to make it complete. If your trade show requires online help, the feature isn't complete until the online help is done.

- Maintain focus within an iteration. Daily standup meetings may help with this. The goal for the project team has to be on finishing pieces. When you finish enough pieces, you've got a feature or a product. Don't let people on the team distract themselves with other projects, future work, or technical debt (see Appendix B, on page 335), unless that debt will prevent this iteration's work from completing.

- Start implementing by feature if you haven't already. Even if this leaves you with partially implemented architecture, don't worry. If a feature requires that piece of the architecture, the team will finish it. If the feature doesn't require it, no one will use it.

You can fix many of the schedule games with a "guerilla-agile" approach. If you organize the project into no more than four-week time-boxes, implement by feature, integrate as you proceed, and measure velocity, you can stop the gaming. And if you keep managing this way, you will avoid most of the games entirely.

 Remember This

- Schedule games will happen. Your job is to recognize them and manage the project so you can still make the project succeed.

- Most of the time, people don't play the games with malicious intent.

- Even without malicious intent, schedule games can drag your project to a standstill.

Chapter 7

Creating a Great Project Team

You know what *done* means, and you're working on organizing the people and tasks to get to done. To accomplish that, you need the right people on your team, and you need them to work well with each other. You need to create a great project team.

There are two parts to creating a great project team: the first is to hire or attract all the necessary people and talents, and the second is to facilitate their ability to work together as a high-performing team.

7.1 Recruit the People You Need

You might not have the ability to hire new people.[1] But you do have the ability to specify the talents and skills you need on a team. Consider these roles for your project team:

Typical Name	Role on the Project
Architect	Organizes and guides the entire system development, including the test system
Developer	Designs and writes product code
Tester	Designs and writes tests, including test code
Writer	Designs and writes product documentation
Business Analyst	Gathers and writes requirements
Release Engineer	Designs, writes, and maintains the build system and any other scripts associated with the build system
Project Manager	Organizes the project's work

---

1. If you can hire, take a look at [Rot04b].

Your project may need additional roles, such as UI designer or firmware developer. You need to know enough about the technical risks of the project (see the sidebar on page 135) to know which roles are necessary.

Not all of these roles need to be different people. For example, your architect might also be a developer as well as your test system architect. Or, one of the testers might also be a test system architect.

Not all roles are as clear as you might like. Maybe you're organizing the development part of the project, but not the testing or the documentation parts of the project—you might work with a documentation project manager and a test project manager. And, you might or might not manage the people on your project. (See Section 7.3, *Managing a Matrixed Project Team*, on page 128.) The key idea is that every project has to have people who can perform this work, whether they are defined as one person or not.

If you don't have the power to attract, recruit, or eliminate the people you need or don't need on your team, you might be in a job where you are set up to fail. See Section 7.7, *Know When It's Time to Leave*, on page 134.

Tip: Beware of PowerPoint Architects

I've worked on several projects where the architect was like a seagull. He swooped in, dumped a lot of poop in the form of PowerPoint pictures of the architecture, and left as soon as possible. He didn't stick around for the hard part of the project: making the product work in this architecture or evolving the architecture so that the product could work by the time of release.[2]

Not every project requires an architect. If you have no architect, your sponsors should recognize that your team needs time to assess the architecture and see what patterns are emerging.

It's possible to have an architect who acts as a consultant to the project. It is harder when you have a consultant-architect—Murphy's law implies that the architect will be busy on another higher-priority project when you need him or her most.

---

2. As George Stepanek reminded me, seagullishness occurs when the artifact producer does not remain on the project to see the artifact used or converted to product.

But if your architect is overly fond of drawing programs and not fond of writing code and can't really answer the developers' questions about how to make the parts fit into a coherent structure, you don't have a real architect [SH06a]. Eliminate that person from your project, and build time into the project for assessing the architecture as you proceed. Add the lack of architecture as an explicit risk to your project so you can manage it.

Diversity of experience, personality, and role will help the project team identify risks faster, which allows you to manage the risks better. The riskier your project is, the more diverse a team you need.

7.2 Help the Team Jell

Project managers are not the only ones responsible for making the team jell—but their actions or lack of action can prevent a team from jelling.

The best way I know to help teams jell is to have them work together—and not on rope courses or laser tag. When people have a common goal, make commitments to each other about their interdependent tasks, and use an agreed-upon approach to the work, they are part of a team. If you want your team to jell, help them determine some short-term goals that they can accomplish only together. (That's one reason the approach discussed in Section 13.1, *Start People with a Mind-Set Toward Reducing Technical Debt*, on page 255 works.)

But I Thought I Was Building a Team
by Christopher, project manager

I remember the day I was promoted to project manager. I had worked on several projects where we didn't really know each other well—even though the projects lasted between six months and a year. When I became a project manager, I wanted to invest in team-building activities.

I took my team out for drinks a couple of Friday nights. However, not everyone could make it. Some of the guys had families they wanted to go home to.

I tried a paint-ball day. One of the writers flatly refused to go. I think her exact words were, "I don't use guns—even play guns."

I thought a darts tournament might be the ticket. But only three of us were interested, not the whole team.

I was stumped. I asked the team in one of our project meetings what we should do to create more of an atmosphere of teamwork. One of the developers said, "This." I didn't understand and asked him what he meant.

"Working together, solving problems—that's what makes a team for me. I don't care about those other things, although I liked the beers on Friday nights. But I need to see how people work, not how they play. Then I can know more about how to work with them."

OK, I can do that. I specifically made room in our team meetings for group problem solving. I made sure everyone worked together in a variety of ways to help them create and deliver interdependent handoffs. Now we have a team.

It never occurred to me that people wouldn't like the activities, but they really couldn't have cared less. Oh, they liked the fact that I cared enough to want them to team build, but the activities weren't the issue.

Teams Require Adequate Tools to Work Well

You can't just throw tools at a problem and expect it to be fixed. But good tools, with your guidance, can be invaluable in helping a team jell. Remember, the tools themselves aren't the answer, but you will benefit from having both a software configuration management (SCM) system and a defect-tracking system (DTS) in place.

The SCM is vital for helping a team jell. Without one, it's impossible to know the state of the source code. The developers will step all over each other while developing, or they will insist that certain people own particular areas of code that others are not allowed to change. Any one of these will slow down your project. There is great, free SCM software available. (I wrote this book using Subversion.)

A defect-tracking system can be as simple as index cards, if you're using an agile life cycle and you don't have more than a few open defects at any time. But if you have more than five to ten open defects at any time, you need a DTS to make sure you know about the problems, how long they've been open, and the current state of those defects.

Minimum Requirements for Software Configuration Management

Modern SCMs can branch, label, automatically merge multiple authors' changes, and allow for developers to work in their own private work-spaces (sandboxes). There are plenty of other great features in other SCMs. But if your SCM can't do the minimum, dump it and obtain a new one.

Minimum Requirements for a Defect-Tracking System

A useful defect-tracking system needs to provide you with several views into the database of defects: defects for this project and for this product over time, priority and severity, state of defect, age of defect, and the ability to attach other data to the defect report. When you can see defects for the project and the product, you can see how many are similar to each other and how many are different. You might realize that additional documentation, tutorials, or customer training could eliminate large numbers of defects. The priority refers to the developer/tester assessment of when the defect should be fixed. Severity means the impact on the user. The state of the defect can be open, closed, and reopened, to name just a few. Being able to sort on reopened helps you determine whether developers are making progress (see Section 11.2, *See Whether the Developers Are Making Progress or Spinning Their Wheels*, on page 217). The age of the defect might provide some information about how much time people can allocate toward fixing defects. All of this information is management information that you need to steer the project.

If your DTS can't do these things, first review your schema. If you can't make the schema do what you need, dump it and obtain a new one. But chances are good that you can.

Five Stages of a Team

Teams move through the five stages: forming, storming, norming, performing, and adjourning when they have valuable work to accomplish [WJ77]. People need a compelling vision, as in the project charter, to move into norming (see Section 1.6, *Write a Project Charter to Share These Decisions*, on page 11). If enough people on the team don't believe there's any point to this project, they will never move into norming—they just don't care enough.

The *forming* stage occurs at the beginning of the team's existence. *Storming* is when the team starts to work together and tests each other's power in the group. If the team (or you) can facilitate themselves to agreement on group behaviors, they will move into *norming*. In the norming stage, the group can accomplish good work. As the group cooperates more fully, the team will move into *performing*. When the project is complete, the team *adjourns*.

You Participate on at Least Two Teams

As a project manager, you are part of the project team responsible for the project. And, you're also on the project team of other project managers who are trying to accomplish work in your organization. You might not think you're all on the same side, but you are all on one team.

The best way I know to make sure you and your peers are cooperative is to treat your project manager peers (or in the case of functional managers acting as project managers) as if you are all part of one team—even if your management doesn't encourage that.

If the team has moved into performing, bring those people back together for your project. If the team was not in the performing stage, you might be able to nurture the next team past storming into performing.

You can facilitate the team's progress through these stages, but only if you have the time to spend attending to the project's risks, problems, and the interactions of the team. Make sure you're not spending all your time in meetings with people other than on your project team or on the Gantt. If you need a detailed Gantt, ask for a full-time project scheduling person to update the Gantt.

7.3 Make Your Organization Work for You

The most efficient organization for project completion is the project-based organization. That's where the multifunctional team reports to a project manager, who manages the day-to-day work and manages the team's interaction with the rest of the organization.

But few project managers work in project-based organizations. Instead, most project managers work in a functional or matrix organization. In Figure 7.1, on the next page, you can see why the project manager has trouble helping a team jell in a nonproject organization. Each team member has a responsibility to the functional team, as well as to the project team. This reduces the project manager's power to make things happen, as well as slowing work down.

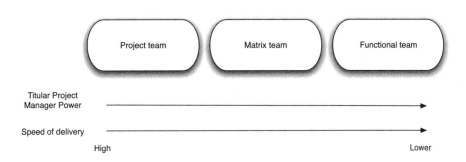

Figure 7.1: COMPARISON OF TYPES OF PROJECT TEAMS

Enlist the functional managers in your work to help make the team jell. You'll work with people to make sure they understand their assignments, not the functional manager. You'll need to help the functional managers understand that the team member's first responsibility is to the project, not the functional manager. And it means that you'll need to discuss the dangers of multitasking with the functional managers. See Section 16.7, *Managing Multiproject Multitasking*, on page 316.

Managing a Functional Team As a Project Manager

Some companies organize their projects so that the developers are a project team reporting to the development manager as the project manager, the testers are a project team reporting to their test manager as project manager, the writers are a project team reporting to the documentation manager as their project manager, and so on. This kind of organizational structure leads to silos and reinforces the need for a phase-gate life cycle.

If you're one of these functional managers also managing your team's part of the project, decide whether you want this organization to continue. Your project will be slower to start, it will misestimate and be off-estimate more, and it will be harder to successfully complete the project. You will have many more defects because the project is handed from one functional team to another and from one project manager to another. The project manager who starts the project (either the requirements manager or the development manager) does not handle the project from beginning to end and might have no responsibility for finishing the project.

You have some choices. You might be able to convince your colleagues that organizing the project as a program will be better for you. Each functional project manager then takes on several features or set of requirements and uses a cross-functional team to finish the project. It's as if the entire project team moves from a functional team to project team, as in Figure 7.1, on the previous page.

If you can't convince your colleagues to change how they work, you're stuck with a difficult (some would say impossible) situation. See whether you can get small groups of developers, testers, and writers (whomever composes your project team) to work on features, even if the organization does not directly support that cross-functional work.

If people seem determined to stay in their silos (both managers and technical staff), see whether one person can be named the overall project manager—someone who has project responsibility from beginning to release. If nothing works, decide whether this is a place you want to remain. See Section 7.7, *Know When It's Time to Leave*, on page 134.

Managing a Matrixed Project Team

When you manage a matrixed project team, each person on the team has their own functional manager in addition to you as the project manager. Your job is to assign tasks and make sure the work of the project is being completed. One of the problems with matrixed teams is that the team members' managers sometimes think it's just fine to multiproject the team members. That means that person is no longer assigned full-time to your project. You will need negotiation and persuasion skills. Consider building a project portfolio (see Section 16.1, *Build the Portfolio of All Projects*, on page 307) and discussing the delays created by multiprojecting to help that manager realize that multiprojecting is not useful.

Discuss with the functional manager who will give the team member feedback and coaching. You (or your technical leads or the other people on the project) will need to give feedback about how the person is doing on your project.

But there may be other discussions, such as career development, that the functional manager needs to provide. Clarify with the functional manager who will discuss which topics with the team member.

Managing a Cross-Functional Project Team

When everyone on the project owes their allegiance to the project, you have more responsibility as the manager. You need to know enough about how everyone performs their jobs to be able to provide effective feedback and coaching to each person on your team.

You might not manage everyone directly. In that case, your subproject managers and technical leads will have to know enough to provide effective feedback and coaching.

7.4 Know How Large a Team You Need

The only thing worse than trying to complete a project with not enough people is trying to manage a project with a too-large team and inadequate management infrastructure. You can manage a team of up to nine people by yourself, although teams larger than six people tend to break into subgroups naturally. If you have a team larger than nine people, you need to have some technical leads or other project managers, depending on the deliverables.

There's a reason for the number nine. Cockburn [Coc01], explains that when the team gets this large the team dynamic changes. Larger teams are not intimate teams (Phillips, and Weinberg[3]) who have interdependent deliverables; they are groups of teams. Especially on multisite teams, you'll need to work even harder to help the team feel as if they are a team [KS99] and not a group.

Technical leads are people who lead the development of a feature or set of features. (If you must develop by architecture, they lead the development of a piece of the architecture.) If you're managing a web-based application, there might be a feature-based team that provides a way to log into a user's account and access the user's profile. The technical lead for that area needs to understand the performance, reliability, database, and usability of the feature set.

If you have a large team—more than nine people—the team has already created its own de facto subgroups. If you assign a technical lead to each subgroup, you've likely managed the issue of a too-large team.

---

3. personal communication

Responsibility and Authority

No manager ever has enough real authority to do what he or she wants to do. There's always someone with a bigger title. (Even if you're a CEO, you report to a board.) Even though titular authority is useful, it's not enough.

If the project is strategically important to the organization, act first (doing whatever the project needs), and ask forgiveness later. You'll know whether the project is strategically important by how many people ask about the status and what levels of people ask. The more people ask at the higher levels, the more strategic the project is.

If the project is not strategically important, don't waste your time trying to accomplish it (RD05). In reality, if the project is important enough to the organization, you have the authority to do just about anything you need to do. (You need the self-esteem to do what you need to do.) But if the project is not important enough to the organization, you can never get enough authority to do what you need to do. Go to the project portfolio, and work on a strategically important project.

Even if the project is strategically important, you might need to use your influencing skills to obtain or have people accomplish what you need. Build relationships to lay the foundation for influence across the organization before you need it. Then when you need help, you can enroll other people to help you push your agenda forward (CB91). I've used sales, service, operations, and marketing people to help me move projects forward.

If you've been working in the organization for a while, you've built influence across the organization. If you're new, you're bright and shiny, and people want you to succeed (most of the time). If you haven't paid attention to your relationships (the organization's politics), do so. Politics is not a dirty word. Politics is the way you can accomplish things in organizations, especially if you don't have the resources to do it all yourself.

As a project manager, you have the responsibility to take authority, rather than wait for someone to give you the authority.

\\\!/
ᴣ℩ƒ   **Joe Asks...**

   Can't I Add More Testers or Writers?

You can add more people to the project anytime you want. And adding more highly capable testers might help you assess risk or offload some of the developers' responsibility for finding defects. Adding more writers might relieve the developers from writing product documentation.

Just don't fool yourself. Adding more people to a project after it has already started will cost the project time.

7.5 Know When to Add More People

You can add people to the project at any time. But you might not be able to add them *successfully* at any time.

Anytime you change the team composition, the team retreats at least to the storming phase, if not the forming phase. And, if you hire additional people, the overall productivity of the team decreases for a few months, unless you've assigned one person as a buddy [Rot04b] for the new hire. (The new hire has a productivity of zero, and everyone helping the new hire has less productivity.) If you assign a buddy, only the buddy suffers from a productivity decrease—and the new hire learns how to work much more quickly.

If you're at the beginning of the project, add as many people as you need, as quickly as possible. Take the productivity hit all at one time.

If you're in the middle of the project, add people carefully. Beware of Brooks' law [Bro95]: adding more people to a late project makes it later.

At the end of the project, avoid adding new people at all. The only time to add people is if your project is hopelessly late and the current staff can't finish it. Add the people you need, and replan.

7.6 Become a Great Project Manager

You've heard the old joke about how to get to Carnegie Hall: practice, practice, practice. It's the same with becoming a great project manager.

But there are requirements for becoming a great project manager: developing your interpersonal skills to work with the team and developing/maintaining enough technical skills to understand and manage your project's risks.

I categorize skills into interpersonal skills (the nontechnical qualities, preferences, and skills); functional (technical) skills; domain expertise; and tools/technology expertise [Rot04b]. See [WJC00] for a different competency profile.

Developing Your Interpersonal Skills

A project manager's interpersonal skills—how you interact with other people—can make or break the project. Here are the interpersonal skills most PMs require. As usual with lists like this, your mileage may vary.

- Listening skills. PMs need to hear what people are saying and ask them questions about state.
- Negotiation skills. PMs need to ask for resources, trade resources, and information.
- Writing skills. PMs need to be able to write down a plan so that everyone understands the plan and the trade-offs. Bullet lists are not enough.
- Oriented toward a goal. PMs need to be able to finish a project and keep people focused on the goal.
- Interested in and respectful of the people who work on the project. The PM doesn't have to be everyone's friend, but the PM has to be able to see when people are struggling, when something isn't working, and when things are working.
- Able to manage ambiguity—to live with the ambiguity and make decisions. Every project I've managed, not just the software projects, has had periods of ambiguity.
- Able to manage the details. Even if the PM isn't a detail person, the PM has to find a way to manage the details.
- Problem-solving skills. Project managers need to recognize which problems need to be solved now, which can be postponed, and how to solve problems. The Rule of Three [Wei85] is a powerful problem-solving tool. (The Rule of Three says, one alternative is a trap, two alternatives are a dilemma, and three alternatives start everyone thinking about real choices.)
- Recognize and seek obstacles that prevent progress. Eliminate them.

- Ability to steer the project—to observe the current state, to note what's different from where you want the project to be, and to be able to guide the project to the new state.

Developing Your Functional Skills

A project manager needs to use several technical skills while managing a project (and learn before starting to manage projects):

- PMs don't need to know the details of *both* the problem to be solved by the project *and* how the problem is solved, but without one or the other—some form of problem-space or solution-space domain expertise—the PM doesn't know enough to make good project decisions. See the sidebar on page 135.

  If you are a nontechnical PM, don't try to cover up your gaps. Be honest about them, hire smart people, and rely on those smart people while you learn about the project's technical issues. If you are honest about your knowledge and show that you're willing to learn, your team will help you succeed.
- Understand different life cycles and which one(s) fit your project.
- Be able to schedule a project.
- Be able to estimate tasks or coach other people in their task estimation.
- Know how to assess risk and manage it.
- Understand how to measure and report on project state.
- Know how to deal with what has been done and what hasn't been done, using either velocity charts or earned value (see Section 11.2, *Earned Value for Software Projects Makes Little Sense*, on page 207). If you have neither measurement, understand what is checked into the SCM and the state of the code.

Developing Domain-Expertise Skills

A project manager for a software project needs to understand how people gather and rank requirements, how to ask whether the design is done, how to evaluate technical risks as well as schedule risks, what it means to have an SCM and how to effectively use it, and what results to expect from testers. The PM needs to be able to select from the varied review activities to help the project team choose the review activities for this project.

This doesn't mean a PM needs to know how to perform these tasks, but the PM needs to know how to organize the activities of the project so that all of these things happen. To understand how to perform these activities, the PM needs problem-space domain expertise and some solution-space domain expertise.

Problem-space domain expertise is the understanding of the problems the project needs to solve. Solution-space domain expertise is understanding how the system implements the solutions to those problems [Rot04b]

The PM needs to rapidly gain an understanding of the domain, specifically the problem space to understand the requirements (and to help with ranking requirements) and the architecture part of the solution space. If you don't know what problem(s) you're trying to solve with the project, how can you know when the project is done? And, if you don't know the architecture, you can't understand the technical risks. You may not understand all the technical risks, but without understanding the architecture, you don't even know what questions to ask.

Note that there's nothing about reading or writing code (or tests) in here. While being a developer or tester might help someone learn the dynamics of software projects, being a good developer or tester does not imply that you will be a good PM. The functional skills are different. Certainly, a PM can be more technical than this, but I don't see how an effective PM can be less technical than this.

Developing Tools and Technology Expertise

If you use yellow stickies, you might never need a project-scheduling tool. But if you're like most project managers I know, you do use a scheduling tool. You need either enough knowledge about the tool to bend it to your will or an assistant who knows.

7.7 Know When It's Time to Leave

Part of being a great project manager is knowing when you're not right for the organization, the team, or the product. If you find that you're in any of these situations, you might not be the problem. Your organization might be the problem, and the situation might be unmanageable.

You always have at least these choices: accepting the current state with your eyes open, moving to another project in the organization, or changing organizations. It's possible you can change the organization [Wei97]. Here are some warning signs for you to consider.

How Technical Does a Project Manager Need to Be?

The project manager does not have to be the technical expert for the project. But the project manager needs to know enough about how the technology under development will solve the customers' problems. And the PM needs to understand the process the team is using to understand the project's risks.

Project managers need to understand enough about the technology so that they can make trade-off decisions (or help product owners make trade-off decisions) about what will actually make it into the release. The more the PM understands the product under development, the better decisions they will make—or guide the project team to better decisions.

Here are the two extreme situations to avoid: the unknowledgeable PM and the PM who would rather be the architect. I've worked with several organizations who thought that PMs in other industries, such as event planning, would make great PMs of software projects. Nope. Not a chance. The PM needs to understand the process of the project. And in addition to the process, understanding enough about the product and the tools can help a PM assess risk and manage it during the project.

In my experience, the PM as architect is just as bad. This PM understands the process and the technology and ignores the work of the PM. If the PM is focused on development instead of managing the project, the project suffers as much (although differently) as if the PM was ignorant of the project.

When You're Not Right for the Organization

You have no choice about team members. Many project managers manage projects where the team members move with them from project to project. And once in a while, you have a team member who's not doing the work you need performed or can't jell with the team. And you can't move that person off your team.

If you can't obtain the people you need for your team, first check and make sure you've explained why you need the people you need. If you can associate costs or benefits with a position, do so. I once asked for a release engineer and was told, "JR, we are not wasting money on a release engineer. These developers know how to check in their own darn code."

\|'/ **Joe Asks...**

Does a PM Need a PMP Certification?

No. A certification shows that you knew how to study enough for an exam and that you have experience working on projects. It doesn't say anything about how successful you were when you worked on those projects.

Why am I so cynical about PMPs? Because the PMBOK describes project management work as if it occurs in a serial life cycle, with the PM large and in charge. (The PMBOK does not require a serial life cycle, but many PMI-only-trained project managers don't know any better.) For many projects—most software projects—it makes no sense to use a serial life cycle. It makes no sense to use command-and-control approaches when a collaborative approach makes more sense, takes less time, and gives a better result.

This doesn't mean there is no value in studying for a PMP certification. The value is in the study and in applying those areas to your project. But a PMP is no guarantee of PM ability. Far from it.

I wasn't worried about checking in—I was worried about the multiple branches and multiple platforms. I asked everyone to log their time for a week whenever they were stuck on problems with the SCM or had to do their own SCM script writing, and so on. In one week, the project team had spent thirty hours on SCM work. I explained this to my manager, who didn't believe it, so I asked the team to log their hours again. The next week, the team had spent thirty-eight hours. My manager agreed to let me hire someone as a contractor, who later became a permanent employee. You might need to explain the need in person-hours lost to the project.

But more often than not being able to hire someone, I see teams where the project manager is saddled with a team member who can't do the work or has problems working as part of a team. If you're in that position, make sure you've first provided effective feedback [RD05]. Assuming you have explained the results you want and you've provided feedback about the work or the person's behavior, it does make sense to move this person off your team.

Joe Asks...

How Many Projects Can a Project Manager Manage?

I'm always amazed when I meet project managers who look as if they haven't slept in days. "I'm managing three projects. I'm not making enough progress on any of them. But my boss thinks I should be able to manage at least three projects. How many should I be able to manage?"

I wish I had the right answer. The best answer is "It depends." If you have an *extraordinary* team who knows how to work together, who can resolve issues among themselves, who can remove obstacles by themselves, who can negotiate for more resources if they need them, and who have enough discipline to monitor their work and steer the project without you, you can manage that project team—because they don't need you—and one other normal one.

If you're multitasking and trying to manage multiple projects, know that you are shortchanging at least one of them, if not all of them. A successful project manager can manage one project at a time. You can make yourself nuts by trying to manage more, but you're unlikely to be successful.

I've tried isolating people on a project team who weren't working well, and I have not been successful. Just keeping those people around makes everyone else edgy—it appears as if the person in trouble is being rewarded for not working on relevant work or for not being part of the team.

You need to be able to move people off your team when they're not working out. If you can't, consider your alternatives. Maybe it's time for you to move to a different project or, more likely, out of the organization.

Meeting attendance is political. If you can't choose which meetings to attend because a Big Cheese is watching who's there and who's not, why are you wasting your time in this organization? Before you assume someone is measuring meeting attendance, ask. You might be making unwarranted assumptions. But if you're not, take your skills and find another job. Your current organization will be out of business soon enough.

Your sponsor hangs you out to dry. You've asked the sponsor to imagine the end of the project where things aren't quite right, and your sponsor says, "I'll have your head." I don't know too many people who work well when they think they're being threatened or feel as if it's all their fault if the project doesn't succeed.

Some project managers think this is an invigorating environment. I don't, but if you do, more power to you. You'll need it. Be aware, though—this is a command-and-control environment, not a collaborative one. And collaboration makes for the most successful projects.

Your sponsor insists that people multitask and won't take "no" for an answer. You've explained the slowdown effects of multitasking. And your sponsor still won't decide which projects are top priority. And, you're on the hook for a successful project delivery.

If the people who are paid the big bucks won't make the project portfolio decisions, ask yourself why you're accepting a no-win position by managing a project that can't succeed. You don't have to do this. You have other choices.

You're supposed to contribute technically to the project. You've got more than three other people on this project. And you're still supposed to write code, test, write documentation, whatever. Somehow, you're supposed to be a technical contributor in your spare time, when you're not managing the project.

Ahem. If you're managing a project of more than three other people and you are their manager as well as project manager, you don't have spare time [RD05]. (It is possible that with just two other people, you can contribute a little technically—as long as you make sure your work is *never* on the critical path.) If your staff is matrixed into your project and they always work only on your project and meet their dates, maybe you can contribute with up to five other people. (If you're working on an agile project, you're the coach or Scrum master, and your team is self-organizing and managing, you have many more hours in the week to produce technical work.)

What I see is project managers not managing the project. They're writing code, but they're not managing the risks, they're not attending to the testing, they're not generating the dashboard, and they're not assessing release criteria. If you work in a meeting-happy place, you'll need to add all the meetings to your list of work.

If you're managing the project, helping people see the goal, removing obstacles, and monitoring their progress, you don't have time to contribute technically [DeM01].

Management imposes silos. Imagine you're the development manager. You start the project, work hard, declare the development done, and march onto the next project. Your peer, the test manager, starts the testing work. He marches into your office two days later and says, "Your developers didn't finish their work. The project is not going to be done in four weeks. I need all of your people to fix the defects." But you had to assign your staff to the Next Big Project. Now what?

Both of you are functional/project managers. Neither of you has responsibility for the entire project—and one of you (most likely the test manager) will be blamed for the late release. But it's not the testers' fault—and it's not the developers' fault. When your management organizes the project into silos and you, the functional managers, allow it to remain that way, it's all of management's fault.

I have some suggestions for actions you can try in Section 7.3, *Managing a Functional Team As a Project Manager*, on page 127. But the real question for you is, Can you make your position work when the organization is oriented against results? Decide whether it's worth your time and energy to change the organization or to change your organization.[4]

All of your projects start with insufficient resources. You're a good person. Your manager says, "Nancy, we want you to start this project. We can't quite give you all the people or computers or space or pens you need right now. In fact, we won't give you the resources you need until halfway through the project. But we have faith in you. Will you do it for the team?"

Oh, it's so tempting to be the heroine and save the company. But you're not doing the team any good when you roll over and accept less than reasonable conditions to start the project. Starting a project with insufficient resources is unacceptable.

If you can't help your management define what's driving the project (see Section 1.2, *Manage Your Drivers, Constraints, and Floats*, on page 3), you aren't right for *this* organization. This organization will continue to take advantage of your good nature and push you into death march projects. Don't fall for it. Either change the project, organizing it against

---

4. Martin Fowler.

the reality of your drivers, constraints, and floats, or leave. Starting a project with insufficient resources is a no-win proposition.

You hear "you're not a team player" all the time. Your job as a project manager is to think your project is the most important work the organization has and to act that way. If you act in such a way to make your project succeed (such as Section 8.4, *Timebox Requirements Work*, on page 148) and you hear, "You're not a team player," then you might not be what this organization needs.

Program managers might need to have a broader perspective than their one project. But even program managers should not roll over and allow the organization to steamroll them. You're the project manager; you're in charge. You have the responsibility to make the project happen successfully; see the sidebar on page 130. Fulfill that responsibility with enthusiasm.

When You're Not Right for the Team

You don't know enough to manage this project. You don't have to have managed a project like this one before. But you do need to understand how the team works and the problems the project is trying to solve. It's not easy to know when you don't know enough to manage the project. But here are some questions for you to ask yourself:

- Do you understand how the team works? If you don't understand the team's workflow and the workflow is working for the team, you might not know enough to manage the process risks for this project.

- Do you understand the problems this project is trying to solve? If you can't understand the problems, you can't help to create useful release criteria. Even more important, you can't assess the release criteria as you proceed.

Your manager inflicts help on the team, and you can't push back. We've all worked with managers who want to inflict help. And sometimes you allow the manager to "help" the team, and you don't push back.

If you can't keep that manager away from your team, you are not removing obstacles from the team. In fact, you're increasing the obstacles the team has to overcome to finish their work. You are not helping the team; you're hurting them.

Stand up for your team and create some distance so that the manager tries to inflict help on you, not on the team. You don't have to take the help; all you have to do is listen, which may be bad enough.

You know too much to manage this project. You have tons of technical experience. And, you've managed projects before. But this project is near and dear to your technical heart. Can you let go of the technical work to *manage* the project?

If you can't remove yourself from architecture or design so that you can concentrate on managing the project, it's time to choose. Either manage this project or become one of the technical staff. But don't try to do both. You'll frustrate the other senior developers by interfering with their technical work, and you won't be removing the obstacles, managing risks, and helping people finish the project.

When You're Not Right for the Product

You don't have the solution-space domain expertise—and neither does anyone else. You don't always need solution-space domain expertise to run a great project. But if you don't have the technical depth in your project team, then none of you understands the technical risks. Decide whether you want to stay with this project.

If you do stay with this project, use an agile life cycle with short iterations. You'll need to prototype and implement by feature to know whether the team is delivering anything useful.

 ### Remember This

- The riskier the project, the more diverse a project team you need.
- Develop all your skills: interpersonal, functional, domain, and nontechnical.
- Know when it's time to leave.

Chapter 8

Steering the Project

You've written the project charter, you've got a plan so people know what *done* means, and you've got some kind of a schedule. The project team is working. You're officially in the middle of the project, where it's your job to steer the project to a successful conclusion.

If you haven't defined your project dashboard (Chapter 11, *Creating and Using a Project Dashboard*, on page 201), do that now. You'll need to take quantitative and qualitative measurements to make sure you understand the project's true state. Once you know the state, you can make decisions about how to steer the project.

Steering the project includes looking for risks and managing those risks. One way to look for risks is to organize the project so you can see the project's rhythm. Anything that disrupts the rhythm is a risk that has occurred. Anything that threatens to disrupt the rhythm is a potential risk. By managing risks as proactively as possible, you can help the project stay on track.

8.1 Steer the Project with Rhythm

Every project has a natural rhythm. Some projects churn, making progress slowly. Others seem to have rocket boosters—every time you turn around, the team is accomplishing more work. All projects have a rhythm, which changes over time. Your job is to see your project's rhythm, and see whether any practices could help your project build and maintain a reasonable rhythm so your project can succeed.

The more serial your life cycle is, the more your project's rhythm will vary by phase [Rot04a]. In the earlier stages, the project might seem to undergo lots of churn, and you'll wonder whether you can ever define the requirements or whether the design will ever stop changing. For projects that "mysteriously" jell, sometime during implementation the rhythm becomes clearer and more focused, because the decisions have been made and you're implementing them; assuming you have adequate staff, the project marches along to its conclusion. For projects that don't jell, you might stay in churn throughout the life cycle, never finding a comfortable rhythm.

In agile life cycles, you might notice churn during iteration planning. But iteration planning doesn't last more than a few hours, so the team finds its drumbeat rhythm once they start an iteration. (If you have an agile life cycle that doesn't find its drumbeat rhythm, chances are good that the team is not following the agile values or using the agile practices.)

I've seen these problems break a project's natural rhythm:

- Not knowing which requirements need to be finished first
- Allowing the requirements-gathering part of the project to take too long
- Allowing GUI changes all over the GUI at any time so that the GUI folks didn't know what they needed from the rest of the project
- Not having a picture of the overall architecture to see where this part fits in
- Not staffing a particular part of the project with people in time for them to succeed

If you see your project struggling to find a steady rhythm, consider the management practices here. Also see Section 16.5, *Start Projects Faster*, on page 311 and Chapter 9, *Maintaining Project Rhythm*, on page 167 for more ideas.

8.2 Conduct Interim Retrospectives

Discovering Why Our Estimates Are All Off
by Stanley, beleaguered project manager

I was stumped. We kept having the problem that we didn't meet our estimates—for anything. We couldn't keep to our timeboxes. It didn't matter how small the estimate was, we didn't meet one. I thought it might be a systemic problem, so I decided to hold a retrospective before the project was done—just to look back at the past few weeks.

At the interim retrospective, several people explained they had been approached by people in marketing and sales to add "just one more thing." I didn't have to say a word. Stella, my technical lead explained, "If we take changes without adding them to our backlog, we will *never* finish what we said we would. We have to make sure Stanley sees those requests."

During the action planning part of the retrospective, the team devised several ways of making sure I received the requests—including walking the person who asked most often for "one more thing" to my office. And, I realized I had to publish the product backlog more frequently; I couldn't just depend on people to go look for it.

Without an interim retrospective, I would never have discovered why our estimates were off. Oh, maybe I would have late in the project. But then the whole project would have been a disaster. This way, I could manage the rest of the project much more proactively.

Retrospectives are a great way to consider what happened on your project and to plan for future projects. Conducting a retrospective at the end of the project is good. And you can use that learning for the next project. But you can conduct retrospectives at any time during the project to learn what to do differently tomorrow.

Agile lifecycle projects need retrospectives at the end of every iteration. Serial, iterative, and incremental lifecycle projects need retrospectives when they meet major milestones. If you have more than one month between major milestones, you can conduct an interim retrospective anyway to see how work is proceeding.

I recommend Derby and Larsen's book [DL06] for a wide variety of ways to conduct interim retrospectives.

8.3 Rank the Requirements

We Have Ultrahigh Requirements!
by Patricia, business analyst, *par excellence*

We have a new product manager, Tommy. He's enthusiastic. He hates to say no to our customers. He promised all of these requirements to the customers in the next release. I couldn't keep up with him—he was partially describing these requirements and then never had time to discuss them with me.

Interim Retrospectives Pay

Pete was a project manager for an eighteen-month stage-gate project. The plan was to gather enough requirements for six weeks to know enough to start prototyping the architecture. But at six weeks, they were nowhere near finishing enough of the requirements to start on prototyping. Pete decided that instead of allowing the requirements phase to continue ("Four more weeks, we just need four more weeks," said the requirements analysts), he would conduct an interim retrospective.

At the retrospective, the team learned all the reasons why they hadn't finished enough of the requirements to be able to start prototyping architecture. And, they learned that if they proceeded the way they had been working, four weeks would not be enough to gather "enough" requirements—they would need at least twelve more weeks. The retrospective at six weeks into the project saved the project from an estimated three-month delay and convinced the project team to choose a different life cycle and commit to it.

The last straw came last week. He decided that we wouldn't have High, Medium, and Low requirements. No, we had Ultrahigh, Critical, High, Medium, and Low requirements.

I explained I was working as fast as I could. I would be happy to work on any of his requirements in any order, as long as they were ordered by number. "Tell me which one is #1. I'll work on that one first, I'll hand it to the developers, and then I'll work on #2."

He enthused, "Great idea! Here, all these are #1!"

"Tommy, maybe I wasn't clear. You have to pick one #1 requirement. Just one."

"But then I'll disappoint some customers."

"I'm sorry that you promised so much to so many people. But we can do only one #1. And one #2. I'm sure that if you think about it, you can choose."

Sure enough, he did. He ordered everything. The next week, he wanted to reorder, but by then we had actually started working on the first set, so he didn't interrupt us. That was a good thing too, because I was ready to kill him. You're not recording this, are you?

If you're lucky, you have all the requirements in one place, and you know which ones to implement first, second, and third. But if you're like most of the project managers I know, you have requirements in a requirements document and in the defect-tracking system. You have them arranged in high, medium, and low priority.

Color me cynical, but here's what I see happening on projects. There are so many high-priority requirements that you might never get to the Medium requirements, and you certainly don't get to the Low requirements. You've got this big bucket of High requirements with no way to differentiate which one to do first.

And for the next project, your requirements givers know that you're in danger of not completing all the High requirements, so they make a higher-than-High category: Critical. Somehow, many of the requirements migrate into the Critical category. You might still have a few High and a few Medium. But now, you can't finish all the Critical requirements in the time. What do you do?

Ranking the requirements, assigning each of them a unique number that starts with 1 helps people see what the team will implement when. Even if you don't implement by feature, you can complete features in the ranked order.

You have several choices for ranking requirements:

Try pairwise comparison. With pairwise comparison, you take each requirement and compare it to each other one, asking "Is this one higher or lower priority than that one?" As you determine which requirement is ranked higher relative to other requirements, that one becomes #1. The next highest-ranked requirement becomes #2.

Pairwise comparison is hard. You'll run into the same problem as you did when trying to decide on a driver for your project (see Section 1.4, *Decide on a Driver for Your Project*, on page 7). You'll need to gently—but firmly—explain that there is only one #1 priority. And there is only one #37.

Do criteria ranking. If you've tried pairwise comparison and aren't making progress, it could be that the group needs to articulate the values and priorities behind their decisions. Articulating the values helps everyone weigh the options explicitly so they can decide.

Generate subjective criteria by brainstorming a list of possible criteria, grouping like items, and assigning a category name. The category name becomes the criteria you will evaluate against. Some criteria I've used in the past are as follows:

- Architectural impact of feature
- Estimated time to implement
- How important this feature is to Very Important Customer
- Availability of specific people to implement or test the feature

Assign relative weights to each criterion. The facilitator asks these questions: Of the items on this list, which is highest? Is there anything else on this list as high as (this one)? Of the items on this list, which is lowest? Is there anything else on this list as low as (that one)?

Once you know the relative ranking, assign weight. The lowest ranking has a weight of 1. Each higher ranking has a weight that's twice the previous one. Assuming each ranking is unique, you'd have weights of 1, 2, 4, and 8. (You can have multiple criteria that are High, Medium, and Low, and weight all the Lows as 1, all the Mediums as 2, and all the Highs as 4.) Then score each alternative against each criteria using a 0–10 scale, where 10 is most favorable. See Figure 8.1, on the facing page.

Develop and maintain a running requirements log: a product backlog. You might find it challenging to rank the requirements when there are a boatload of them—I certainly do. If you can, rank the requirements as you hear about them. Try keeping a spreadsheet or a log of requirements. If you're not using an agile life cycle, keep a quarterly log of what you'll do this quarter and what you think you'll get done in the next three or four successive quarters. See Section 16.6, *Build a Product Backlog*, on page 313, especially the picture of the quarterly backlog.

8.4 Timebox Requirements Work

Requirements Go On and On and On. . .
by Rhonda, CIO

My job is to make sure we finish our projects so the business can receive the value. We had a critical project that was taking too long. It was supposed to be a six-month project. Two months into the project, Sam, the project manager, came to me. "I'm ready to tear my hair out. I can't stop getting requirements. Marketing keeps adding more and more

Criterion	Weight	Alternative # 1		Alternative # 2	
		Score	Weighted Score	Score	Weighted Score
Architectural Impact of Feature	1	10	10	3	3
Estimated Time to Implement	4	3	12	10	40
How Important This is to Very Important Customer	8	1	8	10	80
Availability of Specific People	2	10	20	7	14
		----------	66	--------	137

Figure 8.1: CRITERION EVALUATION

requirements, and they don't finish any of the ones we have, so I don't even know how to get started."

I knew how to fix that. I called the marketing VP and explained his folks had one more week to define requirements. Whatever was fully defined, we would do. If it was only partially defined, we wouldn't do it. That simple.

He tried to give me the runaround, telling me his guys were out of the office. I offered to close the requirements today if his people couldn't use a week. "No, we'll figure it out."

We didn't do everything they wanted—but we did what they needed.

If you must have a requirements phase, timebox it. Otherwise, the requirements elicitation and definition can expand to take the entire project. I once worked with an organization that was trying to reduce its project duration from eighteen months to six months. But the requirements still took four months. They couldn't do anything useful in the two months they had left.

After some digging, I understood what was going on. The marketing department was too busy to meet with the system analysts, so they would postpone the requirements meetings. The analysts would explain that they weren't done with the requirements yet, so they would get more time from the project manager. But then there was no urgency for marketing to finish explaining what they wanted for requirements.

The project manager decided to timebox the initial requirements work to two weeks. Marketing grumbled and at the end of the two weeks sent around several memos explaining why the release was going to be so terrible for the customers. Because the developers had the most important requirements, they could start working on the product. After three weeks, they had a prototype of the original requirements, and marketing had continued to work with the system analysts to define the next set of requirements.

They were able to move to four-week iterations, with marketing taking as long as they needed to define any given requirement. But the project team knew what they were supposed to implement in the next iteration.

Even if you don't move to iterations, timebox the initial requirements gathering and definition. I've done this in several ways:

Timebox initial requirements and continue to gather more requirements. In this option, you can select a reasonably short period of time (no more than 10% of the project's total duration) and ask for the most important requirements. The danger is that you will get the most important requirements for the customer, but not necessarily the requirements that will drive critical architecture decisions.

Timebox all the requirements definition work. This option is personally more dangerous to the project manager. Be ready to hear "you're not a team player" and other such nonsense. You can explain, "I'm doing the best I can to make sure we deliver the product you want. If I let requirements take as long as they took last project, we won't deliver on time. If the release date is not important to you, we don't have to do this, but the last time, you were quite concerned about the release date."

When I've used a timebox for all the requirements work, the project team works with the requirements people to define and refine the requirements. At the end of the timebox, the team implements the requirements that are complete—and only the completed requirements. This approach works well for short projects where you are tied to a serial life cycle.

8.5 Timebox Iterations to Four or Fewer Weeks

We Can't Finish Our Iterations
by Topher, project manager

We've been trying to use four-week timeboxes for about six months now. But we just can't finish everything we estimate we can do in those four weeks.

At the end of the first iteration, we had a few days more of work, so we extended the iteration to five weeks. The next iteration, we had more work, too, so we extended the iteration to six weeks. We got up to eight-week iterations, and we still weren't finishing the work we'd planned for the iterations.

We finally decided to divide by two. That is, make the iterations only two weeks, and see whether our estimates were any good. Turns out, our estimates were good, but because we have support work to do in addition to the development work, we didn't have as much time as we thought to work on development work during an iteration. Our task estimates were fine; our workday estimates were off.

We would never have understood this if we hadn't moved to shorter iterations.

Maybe you've moved to iterations. But the iterations are eight weeks (or more). And now you've got other problems. The testers can't finish the testing in your iterations. Or the developers always estimate too much for what they can do in an iteration. Or, you're using a spiral life cycle that doesn't plan for finishing a feature.

The longer your iterations, the harder it is to maintain a project rhythm. You've probably seen this in a serial lifecycle project, where the whole project is an iteration. If you're having trouble maintaining project rhythm, move to shorter iterations until you can maintain a rhythm.

This might seem counterintuitive to you. "If I'm having trouble with a six-week iteration, how will going to a four-week iteration help?" The answer is more frequent feedback. The smaller the periodicity of iterations, where the project meets a specific milestone (ideally releasable software), the easier it is to see how to start and end an iteration. That's why a Hudson Bay Start (see Section 4.2, *Hudson Bay Start*, on page 52) works. If you can't maintain the project rhythm, either people are not estimating well, they're trying to do too much at one time, they're actually working on several projects, or they don't know what to work on first—or some other reason particular to your project. Shorter timeboxes will make the problems more obvious so you can solve them.

Tip: Use the Divide-by-Two Approach to Reduce Iteration Size

If your iterations aren't succeeding, try the divide-by-two approach. Divide your iterations by two. If they're six-week iterations, make them three weeks. If they are four-week iterations, make them two weeks. If they're two-week iterations, make them one week. Smaller iterations help you gather feedback faster about what people actually do in that timebox.

Once you know what people are doing in the timebox, you'll know whether it's an estimation problem, a multitasking problem, or some other problem. You can then remove that obstacle. But longer iterations mask the problems.

8.6 Use Rolling-Wave Planning and Scheduling

Planning Just a Little Provides Me with More Flexibility
by Donald, project manager

We're stuck with a serial life cycle. We have very strict phase gates and have a management review for each of them. But in between the phase gates, we use timeboxes and iterate on prototypes to know how good our estimates are.

We're in the design phase. And we realize that we can't get the performance we need out of that particular component. It's not going to happen; it violates the laws of physics. It's time to replan what we can do and release a slightly different product.

I'm not worried about the schedule. I plan in detail for only four weeks at a time. I'll have to throw out part of my planning for the next few weeks, but I'll be able to replan without too much trouble. I'm worried about the product, but that's another problem.

At some point during your project, some risk occurs that changes everything from here on out. Software projects unfold in unforeseen ways. One task might complete faster; another task might take longer. If you plan to replan—to iterate the planning—you can improve the overall project schedule. Iterative planning and scheduling can help you on projects with technical risk or schedule risk—when you don't have enough product knowledge or historical data to plan the schedule with certainty or when the project is too long to plan with certainty.

Replanning for serial lifecycle projects. For serial life cycles, first define the phases or major milestones. Make sure you choose milestones that have specific meaning for the team or define what the milestones mean. For example, if you have "requirements freeze," specify what that means for your project. Once you've defined the milestones, attach milestone criteria to each milestone. That way you'll know when you've achieved the milestone. Don't try to plan everything. Just plan the next three to four weeks in enough detail that everyone knows what to do and how they'll get through the next few weeks. (If you know of some specifics you'll have to do in certain parts of the project, such as demos, trade shows, or beta, list those in your milestones, too.)

All you have to do is monitor the project progress, keeping in mind the milestone criteria. Milestone criteria are the necessary achieved tasks to meet the specific milestone. For example, I've worked with teams who used "requirements freeze" in serial lifecycle projects who used criteria such as "requirements for foo feature complete and reviewed." In a serial life cycle, you're unlikely to meet any criteria such as "freeze" or "complete," because you can't know whether earlier phases really are complete until you have working code that represents the requirements or design.

As the project team accomplishes tasks, you can add more tasks to the end of your current detailed plan. If you're on week 3, and you have a four-week rolling-wave plan, you'll be planning week 7 while you're in week 3. It's a little harder to iteratively plan a serial life cycle, because too often you can't assess progress until you're close to a milestone. That's why you need the milestone criteria.

Serial life cycles pose a special problem with rolling-wave planning. Since you're working with phases (requirements, analysis, coding, and so on), it's very seductive to plan as much detail as you can at the beginning. Instead of planning the details, plan just the next few weeks in detail.

As you complete an early phase, start filling in more details for the next phase. Look for technical debt in your project as you proceed—later phases that take longer than you thought can be a sign of technical debt. The more technical debt you have, the longer the later phases will take.

Once you're well into the coding and testing phase, you can plan the final testing and any end-of-the-project activities, such as early releases, betas, and any other major activities before actual release.

You've used rolling-wave planning to build your schedule. And, in a serial life cycle, you'll want to create milestones that say "replan" as you finish a phase. Build the replanning activities into the original project schedule. Use what you know about this project (especially using interim retrospectives) to update the project plan and schedule.

This way the project team realizes the project is under control, but the project team and the project manager can continually assess and manage the schedule risks.

Tip: Build Replanning into the Project Schedule

Unless you're using an agile life cycle, make your replanning activities explicit. And make them often enough that the schedule doesn't fly away from you without you realizing it.

Replanning for iterative, incremental, and agile lifecycle projects. Since all the other life cycles have either iterations or increments (or both), it's much easier to replan those life cycles than to replan a serial life cycle.

Iterative life cycles that don't deliver finished code into the code base each iteration can use the same replanning approach as serial life cycles. You'll have different milestones, such as "prototype 1 explored and results published," but the idea is the same.

Incremental life cycles can use a similar approach as serial life cycles to replanning at the beginning where they tend to have phases. Once the increments start, you'll find it easier to build the rolling-wave schedule, because you're not waiting for a phase to be complete; you're waiting for finished (developed and tested) code to be checked in.

Agile life cyles use the idea of rolling-wave planning as a default, because each iteration is a timebox. You have to plan only enough to start the iteration, monitor progress through the iteration, and make sure the iteration ends with completed work.

> \\// Joe Asks...
> :} ⌣
> ⌢ __Is There Ever a Time to Avoid Iterative Scheduling?__
>
> Iterative scheduling is not for everyone on every project. It is most useful under these conditions:
>
> - When you have an idea of what needs to be done but not a clear idea of how to do it
>
> - When you are pressed for time and want to take advantage of project advances
>
> This leaves out research-type projects or the research phase of a project. To use iterative scheduling on research projects, develop questions you can ask at the end of each timebox. Then you can use iterative scheduling to replan the next timebox. Instead of product deliverables, you'll have answers to questions—or more questions—a different kind of product deliverable.

8.7 Create a Cross-Functional Project Team

Silos Kept Us in the Dark
by Brian, development manager

I'm the development manager for a large transaction processing product. We have a GUI front end, a bunch of middleware, and plenty of databases on the back end.

All the developers worked together to design and develop the product. I managed the project. Then we handed it off to the testers. The test manager, Nancy, took over responsibility to release the product.

Once my guys were done with development, we started on the next project. And then we'd get all these requests from the testers to fix things. Lots of interruptions. And, the customers complained when they started using the product too—they found things neither development nor test had found.

For the next project, Nancy and I sat down and talked. What did we have to do to make sure we finished the project without all these interruptions? We decided we'd integrate the testers into the development team. Nancy took over as project manager. She's better than I am at tracking all those details.

What a surprise! The developers liked working with the testers. And the testers really liked working with the developers. The testers thought of problems during design the developers didn't consider. And some of the developers liked showing off their devious minds, helping the testers develop tests. And, when we launched, so few of the customers complained that we were able to devote all our time to the new project.

We're done with the business of handing off pieces of the product from one person to the next. No more silos for us. We work only in cross-functional teams now.

In Chapter 7, *Creating a Great Project Team*, on page 121, I suggested a number of roles you want filled on your project team. The team membership is cross-functional. Cross-functional teams have several benefits:

- Cross-functional teams finish work faster [Mey93]. Single-function teams finish their individual parts faster, but there's no review or verification that what they've done is any good. The entire work product is not complete. Project teams receive no points for complete requirements; they receive points for implementing a feature *in toto*.

- Cross-functional teams provide a diverse project team. The testers are looking for ways to build in testability. The writers are checking with the developers and testers about how to express how the project works. The analysts are refining the requirements and possibly participating in building acceptance tests.

8.8 Select a Life Cycle Based on Your Project's Risks

The Standard Process Doesn't Work for Us!
by Cynthia, project manager

We're part of a large company—you could call us an institution, and you'd be pretty darn close. We have a project management office (PMO), and they're the ones who define all our project management processes.

A few years ago, they defined the way we would run a "standard" project. A standard project is big—more than 100 people and usually a couple of years long. Of course, none of us project managers had ever successfully run a standard project they way the PMO defined it.

We decided to look at our projects differently. We're smart enough that we can generate the documents and metrics for the PMO, and still manage our projects they way we need to, to achieve success. We have big and small projects, short and long projects, projects with significant technical risk, and some with no technical risk. And, when we have to manage costs, we actually can.

Now, even the PMO says, "Look at your risks and choose a life cycle. Choose practices that make sense for your team and your life cycle." We've been succeeding, partly because we don't do those humongous projects anymore. We start smaller and stay smaller, and we use iterations, timeboxes, and increments as they make sense. And we work with our teams to help them choose practices that work for us, depending on our circumstances.

The biggest thing that helped me was realizing we didn't have manage all projects with a serial life cycle. I had choices! And once I could choose the life cycle, it was easy to choose practices, too.

In Chapter 3, *Using Life Cycles to Design Your Project*, on page 35, you saw the apparent risks and effective risks each life cycle manages. The lifecycle choice is one of the first choices a project manager makes and has a lasting effect on how you organize the project. Think before you decide. If you're not sure, start with an agile life cycle because it gives the project the most flexibility early in the project.

8.9 Keep Reasonable Work Hours

Dinner Every Night on the Company Was Not Reasonable—For Anyone
by Justin, director of development

We had about 150 people working on this next release—of course, it was critically important to the future of the company. We'd just about stopped making forward progress. My boss, the VP, said it was time to have dinner every night at the company.

The plan was this: Every night at 7 p.m., one of the directors would arrange catering for all the people working on the release. We'd get together and have dinner, and people would stay at work and get more done.

It worked for about a week. Then, some people started coming in at 10 or 11 a.m. One guy started coming in at noon. And, people ate dinner and left. I would walk around during the day and see people balancing their checkbooks and calling their spouses or parents. One guy was arranging his kid's play dates for the weekend.

We finally stopped and made everyone just work forty hours a week. All of a sudden, the quality of the code and tests went up! And we started finishing more, too.

It's tempting when you see lots of problems to ask the team to work overtime. But the more overtime people work, the less work they accomplish [DL99]. Here's why.

People can accomplish at most six hours of technical work a day. For short periods of time—up to one or two weeks—some people might be able to accomplish another hour or two a day. But most people cannot manage sustained overtime.

When they do work sustained overtime, they lose the rhythm of their day, spending more time in the coffee room, more time at lunch, more time calling their friends or mothers, more time surfing the Web, more time balancing their checkbooks, and more time paying attention to their human existence. It doesn't take long before the nonwork people are doing complete dwarfs their project accomplishments.

If you find that your project is not proceeding fast enough, think about the tips here to build and maintain the project's rhythm.

8.10 Use Inch-Pebbles

Joe Can't Estimate More Than One Week of Work
by Adrian, development manager

I have a really talented guy, Joe, on my team. Joe does great work—his architecture of that piece last year was phenomenal. Joe can estimate little pieces, but he can't estimate big tasks. Whenever he does estimate large projects or tasks, he's off—underestimating—by an order of magnitude or more.

In this last project, Joe and his team were in charge of a big piece. It was a big lump. Because the tasks were too big, Joe couldn't see all the pieces. He would estimate only the pieces he could see. And we had some tasks that were like icebergs. The only thing you could really understand before getting into the task was the very tip of the task. It wasn't until you were into the task that you could see all of it.

Now that we break every task down into inch-pebbles (sometimes using spikes to do so), Joe is a much better estimator. And I'm not applying some random fudge factor to everyone's estimate.

Projects lose their rhythm when too much time elapses between accomplishments. Team members can't see the end of this task, so they lose their urgency and rhythm. Inch-pebbles help each person maintain their own rhythm and help the project stay on track.

Tip: Help Project Team Members Avoid Student Syndrome

Student Syndrome (see the tip *Help Project Team Members Avoid Student Syndrome*) occurs when people wait until the last possible moment—and sometimes beyond that moment—to start working on a task [Gol97]. Student Syndrome most often occurs when people estimate tasks in weeks, not days or inch-pebbles.

Student Syndrome breaks the project's rhythm by introducing delays into the project. When Tom hasn't finished his work and Jerry depends on that deliverable, Jerry now has a wait state.

Manage Student Syndrome by coaching team members to estimate their tasks in inch-pebbles or by using timeboxed iterations. Either way, everyone has a deliverable every day or so, which helps avoid Student Syndrome. Many people feel a little bit of pressure to deliver their pieces and not keep other people waiting—they don't want to let their peers down. When people can see their progress, they're more likely to keep making progress, allowing everyone to keep reasonable work hours.

8.11 Manage Interruptions

Interruptions Are Obstacles for Us
by Josh, VP, engineering

I've grown this organization from the original seven developers to the few hundred developers, testers, writers, release engineers, and assorted other folks in the past ten years. And the one thing it took me a while to learn was that interruptions were a big problem for us, especially when we were a small organization.

I always knew interruptions were a problem. But it wasn't until one of the project managers, Ted, showed me the list of all the interruptions his team had encountered over the previous week that I realized how much interruptions cost us. I solved the problem by managing the project portfolio, by moving to timeboxed iterations, and by paying much more attention to how we bring people into the organization and onto projects.

We're not perfect yet, but our interruptions no longer overwhelm our projects.

Interruptions destroy a project's rhythm. Any one interruption might be OK, but all of them make a person feel nibbled to death by ducks. People can lose up to 40% of their time because of interruptions [RG05] There are two types of interruptions: other projects and people.

Manage Other Project Interruptions

Your job as project manager is to protect the iteration's work. If you're using a serial life cycle, the iteration is the whole darn project. If you're using timeboxes, the iteration is the timebox duration. In an iterative life cycle, the iteration duration can vary but is related to the work to be finished. In an incremental life cycle, there is no iteration *per se*; the "iteration" is the duration for a given feature.

Postpone all other project interruptions for your project team until your iteration ends. Once it ends, you can postpone the start of the next iteration to deal with the interruption.

Sometimes other people don't realize what their interruptions are costing your project. Keep a one-week log of all the interruptions, and let people know the cost of those interruptions. Be factual, not blaming— your job is to educate and inform.

Manage People Interruptions

You want people on the project to ask questions when they have them. Otherwise, they can't make progress. But every time one person asks another person a question, the second person is interrupted. And in cubicle heaven, everyone around the answer-person is interrupted. What do you do?

You have several choices. My first recommendation is that you encourage pair programming (or pair requirements development or pair testing) so that people work together to learn a part of the system. If pairing doesn't work, make sure people have private spaces they can use where they can talk and not disturb others. If you can't manage private offices, make a project "war room," where you've posted project artifacts such as the dashboard, architecture documents, and the like.

Make sure there are workstations so people have access to the code base and any other electronic documents so people can talk about the same artifact together.

If you've never asked the Furniture Police [DL99] for help before, this might be difficult for you. But the Furniture Police are people too. Review the sidebar on the following page to see what you might do. I've found bribery in the form of brownies and beer[1] works (not always at the same time with the same people).

8.12 Manage Defects Starting at the Beginning of the Project

Defects? We Don't Have No Stinkin' Defects
by Edward, program manager

Let me tell you a story about a time before I got "defect-religion." I was new to software development, even though I had managed other projects, mostly in sales, for a while. The developers were merrily developing away. The testers were complaining they couldn't make the builds work. When I asked the developers, each of them said, "It works on my machine." I thought the testers were just babies.

Our senior manager got sick and had to take extended sick leave. Since I was the only person in our group who had a chance of managing the organization, I started doing the senior management role. The project was supposed to take only another two months, so I brought in a consultant, Janice, to manage the project.

The first thing Janice did was to start listing the defects. She even made the developers use a defect-tracking system. They all came to me and complained. I went to see Janice to ask her about the system. She explained that the developers had ignored all the defects since the beginning of the project. When they did think of them, they think of the one they just fixed, not the ones still left to fix. Janice said, "We will never finish this project if we don't pay attention to the defects. In fact, one of them just said this to me: 'Defects? We don't have no stinkin' defects!'" Then Janice told me that she thought we had several hundred open defects. She told me, "These defects are preventing us from moving forward with testing. And they will prevent our customers from using the system. To be honest, I think the defects are preventing several developers from developing their code, too."

---

1. Be aware of your organization's policy on alcohol at work. Few organizations have any policies on sugar.

Prepare for Influence

As long as you're willing to give up the illusion of command-and-control, learning to influence is easy. It might require a change of mind-set on your part. Here are some tips to consider:

- Remember that you don't own the whole problem by yourself. Sometimes as a project manager, you think you must have all the ideas and answers. You don't. On a project, the release date, the feature set, or the level of defects is everyone's problem. Don't take a problem as only yours. You have the responsibility to make sure the team solves the problem, not to dictate how.

- Think of the value you bring to the organization. Once you know your value, you can start thinking about what that value means to other people (CB91). That value helps you ask people to help you and know what you can give them in return.

- Discover the other person's or team's WIIFM (which stands for *what's in it for me?*). Some people are motivated by doing interesting things, some by public or private recognition. Many people want to do a great job and know that what they are doing contributes to the overall project success. Most often, a team on a multisite project has a particular motivation. Learn what that is.

- Suggest that you and the person (or team) own the problem jointly. That way, you can be friendly and open to the other person's ideas and concerns. If you tell other people what to do, they can develop a bazillion reasons why your answer is wrong. If they develop the answer themselves, they are much more likely to implement it.

- Listen to the team. Your team will tell you what they need to be most effective. If you're asking people to work in a different way, they might need a different workspace or more equipment or something else.

- During a discussion, allow others time to think. Make sure you're not pushing your ideas without giving others a chance to really consider and question those ideas. Some people might need more time to provide valuable input.

Prepare for Influence (cont.)

- Don't be overly tied to your ideas. Once you've agreed to work collaboratively, which is what you do when you work through influence, others might be able to improve on your solutions. Be sure you don't get in their way. Sometimes, we all find it difficult to let go of ideas that have served us well in the past. Remember that you can use your ideas as a starting place for a particular problem.

 **Joe Asks...**

How Do I Manage Interruptions When We Have Operations and Development?

It doesn't matter what life cycle you use. If you're trying to develop a product and operations work keeps popping up, your estimates are wrong. (It's the same problem with support and development.) The operations interruptions will kill your project.

Here are some ideas:

- Take some people out of development and assign them to operations full-time for a week or two at a time. Rotate people through the operations work.
- Assume that everyone can work only two or three days per week on development and the rest of the time will be on the ad hoc tasks. Each person has the responsibility to not multitask on the same day.
- Add more people to the team, people who like the fire fighting associated with the ad hoc tasks. Their first responsibility is to the ad hoc tasks, with a secondary responsibility to the project.
- Start a group of people whose job is operations.
- If you're using iterations and estimating using relative sizing and duration, estimate each operation's piece and add it to the product backlog.

Whatever option you choose, you need to account for the operations work and the development work.

> Janice and I talked some more. She convinced me there was a problem. She was right—the defects we had accumulated over the project prevented us from meeting our original two-month deadline. It took us another four months to release. But we did, and our customers were happy. I don't wish away defects anymore.

Many project teams take a laissez-faire approach to defects during the project and start to seriously manage defects only at the end of the project. And if you're using a serial or iterative life cycle, you might not have any coding defects to review at the beginning of the project.

But if you don't start managing defects at the beginning of the project, they will manage you. The project will increase its technical debt (see Appendix B, on page 335), and you won't even know until the end. You'll have too many defects to fix at the end, and you won't be able to fix them all.

You have several choices. If you can, move to an agile life cycle, where the developers and testers are developing and testing simultaneously. The team will report fewer defects overall, you will know about the defects faster, and you have the immediate choice of how to deal with them.

If you can't move to an agile life cycle, move to an incremental life cycle, and make sure the developers use continuous integration (Section 9.1, *Adopt or Adapt Continuous Integration for Your Project*, on page 167) as they proceed. Make sure the testers can test in a variety of ways to evaluate the features as the developers finish them.

If you're stuck using a serial life cycle or an iterative life cycle, start a culture of looking for defects from the beginning of the project. That means reviewing documents and tracking problems to make sure they are fixed.

When you organize defects in the defect-tracking system, consider how you want to categorize the defects. You can assign each defect a severity and priority. And, you don't want to play the promotion/demotion game (see Section 15.4, *Avoiding the Promoting/Demoting Defects Game*, on page 299) for defects late in the project. Severity is about the technical ramifications of the problem. If severity is high, the system can't run or delivers incorrect results. Priority is about the business impact of the problem. If the priority is high, the customer will be adversely affected by the problem.

Defect #	Short Description	Priority	Severity	Exposure	When to Fix?
17	Name is address; address is name	High	Low	High (our customers will be confused!)	This iteration

Figure 8.2: DEFECT TABLE FOR EVALUATION

Some project teams use a table similar to the risk analysis table when trying to evaluate defects. The defect in Figure 8.2, is an example of a problem that's not a huge technical problem (Low on the severity scale) but so confusing that it's High on the priority scale.

The "When to fix?" field in this table might be in the table or the defect-tracking system. I've seen teams use dates, releases, and iterations successfully in this field.

Remember This

- You, as the project manager, take the lead on considering which management practices to adopt or adapt.
- Evaluate your project's issues, and decide on the practices to adopt/adapt based on your issues.
- Look for management practices that will establish and maintain your project's rhythm.

Chapter 9

Maintaining Project Rhythm

In addition to steering the project with management practices, you can also make great gains when you invite the team to change their technical practices. This chapter contains a collection of practices that might benefit your project. You and your team will have to judge whether you can adopt or adapt these practices to work in your context. Don't mandate these practices. If you think they can help, introduce them to your team, and invite your team to try them.

9.1 Adopt or Adapt Continuous Integration for Your Project

Continuous integration occurs when a developer writes some code for a short while—no more than a couple of hours—compiles it, tests it, has it reviewed, builds, runs the smoke test, and verifies the changes haven't broken the system, and checks it into the code base.[1]

Continuous integration buys the developers immediate feedback on their work. They tend to start thinking in smaller pieces (which allows them to proceed faster) and to recognize the integration risks earlier in the project. Continuous integration helps developers produce a little bit every day, helping the project team members find their natural rhythm.

Staged integration occurs when a developer waits to check code in until he has finished an entire piece of code. Some developers integrate once a week. Unfortunately for some projects, developers integrate only once a month or two. Staging the integration breaks a project's rhythm. People who are designing and coding new pieces are interrupted by build problems. They are forced to remember lots of little details from the

---

1. See http://www.martinfowler.com/articles/continuousIntegration.html.

Frequent Builds Are for Developers and Project Managers

If you introduce the idea of daily builds, your testers might complain, "We can't use the builds that fast. We can use only one build a week." Frequent builds, such as every hour or even just every day, are not for the testers. Frequent builds are feedback for the developers and a piece of project status for the project manager.

If the testers can run their tests to take advantage of a daily build, that's wonderful. But even if they can't, the developers will obtain valuable feedback by trying to maintain the rhythm of a daily working build.

---

beginning of the project until they start integrating. And when they forget, integration slows the project down because the team finds defects and has to remember all the details of code they might have written months ago. That's a form of multitasking that's particularly insidious. People are working on the same project—possibly even related tasks—but because they are no longer working at the same level of abstraction (design is a higher level of abstraction than debugging) and because they are no longer working on the same feature, they have to change context. All the context switching costs occur here (see Section 16.7, *Explain the Cost of Multitasking Technical Work*, on page 317), including losing the next great idea for the feature under design and the potential for injection of defects into the design.

When you can't integrate your changes into the code base, you can use a variant of continuous integration. Say you're managing a project team that's extending the design of an already-existing product. Your team is working on a piece of the product that is the base of the entire product. If your stuff doesn't work, nothing works. You don't want to check into the code base and break the entire product for the three months it's going to take you to add and replace functionality in the product. What do you do?

You do the next best thing. You make a branch off the main code base and have your developers do all their work on the branch. Every time they check in some code, they also update their branch by syncing with the main line. Your developers are always working off the latest and greatest code base, and they're integrating with it. When they're done with their work, they merge everything back into the main line.

This is an adaptation of continuous integration. Use this when you have to rewrite an already-existing piece of code and don't want to break the system while the changes are under development. This also works if you are managing a project that provides common services to a group of products, such as a library or a platform.

9.2 Create Automated Smoke Tests for the Build

Whether or not you use continuous integration, create some automated smoke tests for the build. Smoke tests merely verify the build is not broken. Don't let me dissuade you from adding as many regression tests as you like, but the idea behind a smoke test is to know whether the build is useful to anyone.

Automated smoke tests help the project team know whether anyone has broken the build. If you know as soon as a build is complete, you can do something about it. If you have to rely on another developer or tester to know whether the build is broken, you can't act as quickly as you might like to fix the build.

Don't Let the Smoke Out!
by Meredith, senior tester

As a tester, my job is to find problems. And, I'm really good at it. I have a motto, "Don't let the smoke out."

I was on a new project at my company. The developers had never worked with a professional tester before. They were astounded when I walked up to one of them with a list of fifteen defects, and said, "You wanna talk about these, or do you want me to submit them to the defect-tracking system?"

I explained that each of these defects could have been found by an automated smoke test. None of them required my specialized training and experience. I didn't want to waste my time on defects that were easy to find. I wanted to find the nasty defects—the intermittent problems, scaling problems, and reliability problems. I wanted to sink my teeth into the code and shake the damn thing until the defects fell out onto my feet.

The developer paled and caught his breath. "Uh, yeah, I want you to do that too. What do you need from me?"

I explained about my motto, "Your job is to keep the smoke in. My job is to make this puppy bleed all over the floor. Got it?" He agreed. I think I heard him tell the other guys I was a bit bloodthirsty. But, heck, that's OK with me.

I checked in my tests to start the automated smoke test framework. Little by little, the developers added to the smoke tests. Whenever I found a problem that the smoke test could have found, I marched up to the developer who'd put that defect in and gave him the "Don't let the smoke out" talk. Pretty soon, every time people saw me headed over toward the developer cubes, someone would yell out "Who let the smoke out?"

We work really well together now. These developers are really good at their jobs. And they help me be good at my job. And the product kicks ass. (Can I say that?)

Keeping the build working helps establish and maintain project rhythm. Knowing as soon as a build is broken helps you bring the project back to its former rhythm—or understand what is preventing the project team from maintaining rhythm.

In fact, if you're managing a project that is supposed to release on multiple computers, databases, or firmware, make sure your team always compiles and builds for all platforms every day. If you don't, you'll have a rush at the end of the project to fix problems you've found only then. It's easier to deal with incompatibilities early in the project so developers can keep them in mind as they continue to develop.

9.3 Implement by Feature, Not by Architecture

Implementing and Testing Feature by Feature
by Harvey, Vijay, Dao, Randy, Ken, and Mabel, the alarms feature team

I'm Harvey, the lead for the team. Vijay, Dao, Randy, and Ken are the other developers. Mabel is our tester. We all have specialties, in the GUI, the platform, the hardware integration, and so on. Mabel knows it all. (Laughter in the background.)

At first, we tried to write architecture and design specs to tell each other what we were doing. We would each implement our piece of the architecture and put it all together at the end. Nothing worked the way we expected it to work. That's because even though we had specs, we changed things a bit as we developed our components.

Mabel had heard about implementing by feature and talked to me. I asked everyone whether they were willing to create a feature-based team—well, really a set-of-features-based team. We would do all the alarms, one at a time, from the front to the back. Mabel would test.

It wasn't easy to start, but once we got going, it was amazing how fast we added features. We didn't have to add lots of code and try to integrate it; we just added what we needed for each alarm and tested that. Mabel kept track that we didn't screw things up at the system level—we kept track at each alarm's level.

We were done so fast that we got other feature sets to do. Now, some of the other groups are trying to do what we did. The whole project is much faster. And, our customer gets to see what we're doing as we do it, so we get feedback.

Many project teams are organized as architectural teams: such as platform, middleware, GUI for a web-based product. But implementing by architecture means that you don't know whether the features will actually work once you integrate the whole darn product. It's difficult to do continuous integration when implementing by architecture because you can't build and run tests—no features are actually complete at the beginning of development; they tend to be finished at the end. In addition, you can't count anything as done.

All you've done is create "waste" [MP06]; you haven't created anything of value. Once something is done, you can count value. But until something is done, you can't count it.

Implementing by architecture can break your project's rhythm, because you have lots of partially implemented features. You don't see complete features until the end of development—too late for feedback to the developers. When you implement by feature, the development team implements just what they need for a given feature all the way through the architecture. If you have a web application, you organize a small feature-based cross-functional team of enough platform people to do the platform work, enough middleware people to do the middleware work, and enough GUI people to do the GUI work just for this *one* feature. If you have people with different interests and technical skills, such as GUI or firmware skills, those people use their skills feature by feature. (You may have to help them organize the project to use their time well.)

Project teams who believe in Big Requirements Up Front and Big Design Up Front have trouble moving to implementing by feature. In those cases, explain what a feature would look like (how small it is), and help them see how little they can do (Section 5.3, *How Little Can You Do?*, on page 78) and still have a feature with enough architectural integrity that it will work even when they implement the next feature. Remind these teams that they are familiar with debugging by feature and testing by feature.

> ## Architecture Reflects Organization
>
> You may have noticed that the product's architecture reflects the organization of the teams that created the product. The bigger the product (in size and complexity), the more obvious this is. This is Conway's law (Bro95): any piece of software reflects the organizational structure that produced it.
>
> The more architecture-oriented your project team is, the more components the product will have. That prevents people from finishing work together, slowing the project. Not only will they be less likely to work together to complete features, they will lose the opportunity to refactor the system into a larger cohesive piece as they proceed. The organization prevents them from doing so.
>
> If you're seeing very small pieces of code with just one or two people working on that piece or a whole mess of code that seems to be coupled to other pieces or doesn't appear to be cohesive, look at the organization. Both of these extremes will break the rhythm of the project—in fact, the project may not have a rhythm at all. And surprisingly enough, by fixing the organizational structure, you can fix the project.

Some people will still object, saying they need to know how the whole architecture works before they can think about one small feature. In that case, it's helpful to have a draft architecture (see Section 3.5, *Managing Architectural Risk*, on page 45) but not commit to the architecture until the team has implemented several features.

Implement the Highest-Value Features First

When implementing by feature, implement the most valuable features first. Leave the riskiest features until later. If you're lucky, you won't have to do them. If you do, the developers and testers know much more about the entire system, so they will be able to maintain their rhythm.

Some teams are afraid to implement by feature because they don't know which features to do first. Some people on your team will want to implement the riskiest features first. Some will want the most valuable features first. If you're in this position and no one will rank the requirements, it's hard to know which features are the most valuable.

Without the customer or customer-surrogate input, you, with help from the team, take the responsibility to develop and publish a product backlog (see Section 16.6, *Build a Product Backlog*, on page 313). You'll decide which features you'll implement in which order.

But if you do work with people who are willing to make the decision about the value of features, implement by value—even if that puts the architecture at risk.

The more valuable the features are and the more finished you can make those features, the more flexibility you've bought yourself and the team for this project. You might be able to release early (if the riskier features can't fit into this architecture), which is valuable for many of your customers. Postponing riskier and less valuable features maintains your project rhythm and reduces risk for this release.

Debugging by Feature

Some groups insist on implementing by architecture. And when it's testing time, the testers test by feature. In that case, your group will end up debugging by feature, even if they didn't build the product that way.

You'll need a cross-architecture group (or access to everyone) to debug by feature. If you haven't already created cross-architecture teams, your project's rhythm is disrupted. However, you can't fix the problems without the cross-architecture teams.

If you find yourself debugging by feature at the end of the project, consider implementing by feature from the start. You'll have less project disruption and a more even rhythm.

Testing by Feature

Testers test the system by feature, sometimes because that's how the requirements are written and sometimes because that's how the testers have access to the system. When testers report problems, they rarely report against small architectural components in isolation. Instead, they report a problem during a test case, "When I tried to open a bank account, I could see the data go through the middleware to the DB, but I didn't see the return acknowledgment." The tester has reported a problem with the middleware but not precisely where.

\\// Joe Asks. . .

How Can I Implement by Feature When My Product Has a Hardware Piece?

If your product has a hardware component, you might not be able to fully implement by feature from the beginning of the project. But here's what you can do.

Plan to iterate on prototypes as the hardware team finalizes their design. You might be able to implement pieces of features, with stubs taking the place of actual hardware implementation. But be aware that any code you develop is really a prototype, not final code. If the hardware folks can supply you a simulator or emulator, your code will be much closer to final code.

The hardware folks will have ambitions for their work that they may not be able to fulfill. Until the hardware is in physical form, you won't know whether they are able to implement those features in hardware or whether the response is fast enough for the design you thought the software could take. Plan to iterate on prototypes.

You can make those prototypes as good as you can make them—if you don't care about the cost of software development. And for many hardware/software combination projects, you don't care about the cost of software development. But if you do care about software development costs, make sure you don't spend any more time on the software prototypes than necessary.

Once the hardware is in initial physical form, you have a firmer idea of what can be done in hardware and what needs to be done in software. You can start implementing by feature. Implement as little of the hardware/software interface as needed for each feature—you'll have less to debug, and it will be clearer where the defects lie.

Developers are accustomed to taking these reports (whether they are debugging or testing reports) and backtracking to determine how the feature interacts with the architecture to understand the problem. Implementing by feature helps the developer see these potential problems as the developer designs and writes the code, not wait until the end of development to see them.

9.4 Get Multiple Sets of Eyes on Work Products

Invite your team members to review each other's work. It doesn't matter what approach you use for review—pair programming, buddy review, peer review, walk-throughs, or formal code inspections—every part of your project will benefit from being reviewed. Offer your project team a variety of possibilities. These possibilities are in a particular order: least ceremony to most ceremony. In my experience, these are also most effective and sustainable to least effective and sustainable.

Pair programming. Before you assume "No one here will do that," offer pairing as an alternative. (And remind people that they've already done pair debugging.) I've asked for volunteers who could choose to pair. I suggested they check out a variety of resources, such as [WK02], [SH06b], and http://www.pairprogramming.com before they start.

Without fail, some people want to try pairing. They learn how and become much more productive than either of them alone.

There's a huge benefit to pair programming, aside from the fewer defects and faster code development. The benefit is having two people who are completely familiar and comfortable with one piece of code. And, assuming people switch off to work with different people as pairs, they will all become familiar with the parts of the system the team is working on. And, there's no delay in feedback to either author.

It doesn't matter what life cycle you use. You can always use pairing as a technique to get multiple eyes on the code.

Buddy review. Buddy review does not have the same learning benefits as pair programming does. Yes, each person will learn about that area of the product, but not in the same depth as the author. There's a small amount of delayed feedback to the author—the duration of time it takes to complete the review.

Peer review. Peer review is the same idea as buddy review (give your code to someone else), but most people tend to review a whole file or several files (an entire module) at a time. Reviewing large chunks of code is much harder—it's harder to make the time to review, and it's harder to keep all the ideas in your head.

Peer review does not have the same learning benefits as buddy review does. In my experience, too often this is a review for style, not content. The feedback delay to the author can be as long as a week.

Walk-through. In a walk-through, a number of people gather in one room. The author proceeds to explain the work product, walking through the document. There is little, if any group learning. There is often substantial feedback delay to the author—the time it takes to organize the meeting.

Formal inspection. Formal inspections, if done right, can help the group learn the work product under discussion. But I have yet to see formal inspections as a sustainable practice in organizations. Even those who start with inspections have difficulty maintaining the momentum of inspections.

Maintaining inspections is difficult because the inspection of someone else's code disrupts every person's rhythm individually and the project's rhythm. To perform a Fagan-style inspection, people must context-switch out of their tasks, read the work product in detail, and be ready to comment on what they see. My rule of thumb is that it takes several hours to a day to prepare for a two-hour inspection meeting.

9.5 Plan to Refactor

Refactoring is the simplification of code, whether that code is production code or test code. Refactoring is not redesign; it's just simplification. The refactored code doesn't change its contract; it's simplified.

My Code Goes Away
by Hal, junior developer

I'm only on my second project since school. On my first project, my manager listened to my estimates for coding, and said, "OK, since you're new here, why don't we add some time at the end for you to integrate what you've learned into the code?" I thought he was nuts, but that was OK. I worked hard, met my deadlines, and then had to change things as I got feedback on how the whole system really worked. I needed all of that extra time and a little more. What really surprised me was this: I didn't

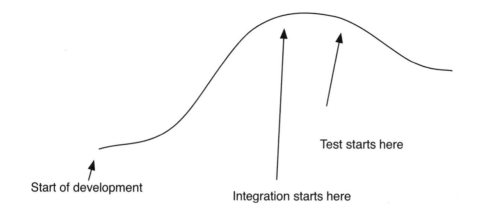

Figure 9.1: TYPICAL CODE GROWTH IN A SERIAL LIFE CYCLE

write more code to fix problems; I simplified things and removed code. My code went away.

For this project, I'm using continuous integration, and I'm refactoring as I go. Simplifying and cleaning up as I go—not changing the design—is really helping me see what I'm doing and how quickly I'm proceeding. And, my code is still going away.

If you've ever tried to count lines of code as a project proceeds, you'll see an S curve of code growth in a serial lifecycle project or any project where integration and test occurs at the end of the project (see Figure 9.1). Note the reduction in code size starting after integration and test; that's refactoring. (Yes, it may also be some redesign, but in my experience, it's primarily refactoring.) If you don't plan for refactoring at the end or if you can't pay down your technical debt from the serial life cycle, the code size stays high. That reduction at the end does not occur.

In an agile lifecycle project, you tend to see something more like Figure 9.2, on the following page. The code grows much more slowly because the developers are building only what they need now for this particular feature. And because they refactor as they proceed, the don't have that push at the end to fix a huge number of defects. (For many defects, removing code is the answer.)

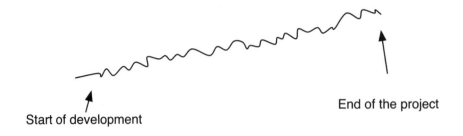

Figure 9.2: TYPICAL CODE GROWTH IN AN AGILE LIFE CYCLE

You can plan to refactor as you go. You can plan to do it at the end. But if you want to release a product with as few defects as possible, you will need to refactor. If you plan to refactor as you go, the refactoring cost is very small. If you plan to refactor at the end, the cost is very high—and too often, you'll think you don't have time to do so. Or, your management directs you not to refactor. The high cost arises from the delayed feedback to the developers and the difficulty in knowing what to refactor and how, because the developers are no longer thinking about this piece of code.

9.6 Utilize Use Cases, User Stories, Personas, and Scenarios to Define Requirements

One good approach to reducing unnecessary code growth is to think about who is using the system and how to develop what the user needs.

Too many projects attempt to define requirements by defining functional and nonfunctional requirements. But these requirements don't explain how a person will use the system or under which scenarios this functionality has to perform. Use a requirements approach that provides the project team with the context to understand the requirements.

Who Wants That Checking Account?
by Clarissa, senior manager

My project team was stuck. They had partly implemented a whole bunch of features, but nothing was working. I called a meeting to determine what to do.

At the meeting, I asked which users were top on their lists for finishing the work. They looked at me with blank faces. "Look people, we are a bank. We want to capture the eighteen-year-old off to college for the first time, the suburban mom with other assets, the seventy-year-old grandmother, and the fifteen-year-old who has been mowing lawns. We have different accounts for each of these people. We want to capture their business if they walk in. Have we thought about what we need to do for each type of customer?"

They had been so focused on the internals of the system that they had forgotten about the people who would use the system or be served by the system. We rank-ordered the people we wanted to capture, which helped them finish defining the requirements and finish pieces of the system.

It's always the people, isn't it?

The developers, testers, and writers all understand how to develop, test, and write about the system when they understand the context of the requirements. If they don't understand, they can ask better questions about the requirements than if the requirements are stated only in functional and nonfunctional requirements.

9.7 Separate GUI Design from Requirements

Requirements are the problems you want the system to solve. GUI design is how the GUI guides the customer to use the system to solve those problems. It's amazing how many projects fall into the paralysis of GUI design in the guise of requirements. If your project takes forever to get out of requirements, see whether the problem is partly the GUI design.

The GUI Is Design, Not Requirements
by Karen, program manager

I started at a new company, trying to rescue a project stuck in "requirements hell." The requirements document was already 300 pages, and it wasn't even close to done.

When I started reading it, I realized why. All the GUI design was in the requirements document. Instead of designing the GUI in the design part of the project, the business analysts and GUI designers were trying to define the GUI requirements in the requirements document. They were using high-powered graphic design tools and developing the GUI in the requirements document.

When I asked why, they looked at me, and said, "These are the GUI requirements." I suggested that they were actually looking at the GUI design and that the design needed to be integrated with the problems the application was trying to solve. The GUI design does not belong in the requirements document.

They finally agreed to try it my way, and we were able to stop the requirements hell. And, since I reorganized to implement by feature, we were able to integrate the GUI design into each feature. We periodically reviewed the entire GUI for consistency, but that's not about requirements; that's design.

It's tempting to start designing a GUI at the beginning of the project and call it requirements. But if you do, your project will never find its rhythm. It will stay mired in requirements until it's too late to do anything the customers want—although you will have a gorgeous GUI.

9.8 Use Low-Fidelity Prototyping as Long as Possible

Low-fidelity prototyping allows people to comment more fully on the problems to solve. Higher-fidelity prototyping narrows feedback.[2] At the beginning of the project, you want bigger-picture feedback, not narrow feedback. Paper prototypes are like sticky-note scheduling: they keep the team involved, and people are more willing to consider options on paper than they are in electronic versions.[3]

Paper Prototypes Save the Day
by Karen, program manager

After we got out of "requirements hell," I realized the UI designers were behind. I investigated and discovered they weren't using paper prototypes—they were using beautiful images of the new logo and all the graphical content. They hadn't started designing the workflow first; they had started designing the graphics first.

I explained how paper prototypes help people see and comment on the workflow. There's plenty of time to get the logo and other graphics just right—but the workflow can change the architecture. If you get the workflow right, there are many fewer changes to the GUI at the end of the project.

The UI designers were suspicious but agreed to try paper prototypes. Then they moved to wireframes. Finally, they integrated wonderful

---

2. See http://headrush.typepad.com/creating_passionate_users/2006/12/dont_make_the_d.html.
3. See http://www.uie.com/articles/prototyping_tips.

graphics with their graphics tools. They had many fewer workflow changes at the end of the project, because everyone understood how the system was supposed to work. They still had tweaks to the actual graphics, but those changes didn't change the underlying product. We actually released on time.

Low-fidelity prototyping isn't just for the GUI. I once worked with a project team who was debating several architectures to deal with some tricky timing issues. We used a large conference room and arranged ourselves into the several queues we were considering, with pieces of paper representing the data we were transforming and moving. The project manager started the simulation, calling out the sequence of events—when and where we had to transform or move data. We discovered some timing and resource contention issues we had not anticipated. After the people simulation, we also developed electronic prototypes. But we had much more knowledge about where the risks were.

 ## Remember This

- You can invite your team members to consider some of these practices, but you can't make them perform any of them.
- If you have to use all your influence for only one practice, consider continuous integration.
- The practices you adopt/adapt will help maintain your project's rhythm, allowing your projects to start and finish faster.

Chapter 10

Managing Meetings

As a project manager, you could spend your whole day in meetings. There is nothing inherently wrong with that as long as you are careful to attend or call only those meetings that are of real value. Unfortunately, you won't always be able to be the person who can determine what's valuable. In this chapter, you'll learn to tell the difference between good and bad meetings and learn how to spend more of your time in productive meetings and less in those that seem to serve no useful purpose.

Too many project managers waste time in meetings. Your time, and your project team's time, is too valuable to waste in meetings. Don't just run from meeting to meeting; decide whether any given meeting is worth your time. You'll need to decide which meetings to call, which to attend, which to delegate, and—most important—which to ignore.

Tip: Seek and Destroy Time-Wasting Meetings

As you organize your project, look for time-wasting meetings. If you find one, cancel it. It's the simplest and most effective way to focus the team on the project [DeM01].

10.1 Cancel These Meetings

Your job as the project manager is to protect your team from outside influences and interruptions while helping them make progress toward a reasonable deadline. You can help your team by protecting them from meetings they don't need to attend. Cancel meetings that are of no value to anyone, and excuse team members from meetings in which they will neither give nor receive any value. You might encounter some resistance

\\// Joe Asks...

Is This Meeting Worth It?

Look around the room at the next meeting you attend and calculate the cost of that meeting. Suppose you have a dozen people attending, half of whom make around $80,000 a year. Well, $80,000 a year is roughly $40 an hour. Those six people are costing $240 for the hour they are in the meeting. That's not counting the time it will take them to get back to work after the meeting and the time it took them to get to the meeting.

Add the cost of the rest of the people at the meeting—don't forget to add the cost of your own time. Did the meeting provide at least that value to the company? We aren't even accounting for the lost value of the work the attendees might have provided had they not been in the meeting (lost opportunity cost).

from some team members who think you are judging them as not being important enough to attend the meeting. Stress instead that you think they are too important to attend the meeting.

While you are reducing the time at nonproductive meetings for your team members, don't forget to look for meetings that you can be excused from as well. After all, if you are in the back of yet another meeting in which you aren't really listening and you have nothing to contribute, you aren't doing the work you were hired to do.

Avoid Meetings That Don't Require You to Solve Problems

Lots of organizations have a bazillion "status-y" kinds of meeting every week. If you don't have to participate in making a decision or solving a problem at a specific meeting, you don't have to attend that meeting. Really. I wouldn't lie to you.

Some of you are thinking, "Huh, JR. Not in my company. You don't show up at a meeting, you're no longer working on something important." It's possible that in your organization, project managers are promoted based on the face they show the organization, including the meetings. In that case, decide whether you want to change the culture, continue to waste time at meetings, or leave. See Section 7.7, *Know When It's Time to Leave*, on page 134.

But more often, the meeting started for a good reason (a few years ago), and that reason is over. The only thing left is the meeting. You can be courageous and explain that you need to be with the project, so you'd love to see the minutes of the meeting, but you don't need to be here.

Try it once. See whether it works. If it does, you can continue to pick and choose meetings to attend. If not, wait a while and try it again. Your job as a project manager is to assess and guide your project to a successful conclusion, not to sit in meetings that prevent you from doing your job.

Never Conduct Public Serial Status Meetings

Never hold a serial status meeting. Never.

A serial status meeting occurs when the project manager sits there and listens to each person explain what he or she did last week and what he or she will do next week. It's boring for everyone except the person talking and the project manager. Serial status meetings waste team members' time. They encourage people to "multitask" at them: reading email, IMing someone else, surfing the Web...all work that is not advancing the state of the project. The team members are not paying attention to anything anyone else is saying, and they are not paying attention to the meeting. Serial status meetings aren't meetings; they're ceremonies [DL99].

If you're holding project team meetings that don't solve problems, you're holding project team meetings that delay the project. Stop now, and reconfigure your meetings.

"But, JR, my team members really like knowing what other people are doing." In my experience, on small projects, people already know what everyone else is doing. And in bigger projects, no one cares about the small status; they do care whether other people are going to meet their deliverables.

If you're convinced your team members like the status meetings, first conduct one meeting with no status component. Then use ROTI [RD05] or ask people—anonymously—to tell which kind of meeting they prefer. If they still like the status meetings, go ahead and keep them. Remain aware of how long your status meetings take, and make sure they still retain value for your team over time.

Avoid These Meetings

Here are the meetings to avoid:

The meeting that no longer has a reason to exist. Some meetings have existed since time immemorial. The original meeting owner has left his or her original job, and the original purpose is long gone. The only thing left is the meeting. Don't go to those meetings. Usually, people won't even realize you're not there.

Meetings with no action items. One of your colleagues calls meetings at the drop of a hat. Everyone sits around the table and discusses issues. You might even decide something. But there are no action items. You don't have to go to those meetings. How could anyone know whether you didn't attend?

Your manager's serial status meetings. OK, this one takes a little nerve on your part. Your manager is still holding serial status meetings. And since all of you are managing independent projects, you *really* don't care what Jim-Bob is doing.

Skip the meetings, and send your status in email instead. It's worth giving your manager feedback about the value of the meeting for you.

Any meeting where you're prevented from bringing your laptop. Ellen explained about a particular meeting at her company: "These meetings are sooo boring. I'm not supposed to bring my laptop or my PDA. I'm supposed to sit there, pay attention, and not look bored out of my skull."

Have a one-on-one meeting with the person who runs that meeting, and explain that you need your laptop to solve problems. Provide feedback to that person, explaining that you're most effective at helping when you have all the tools of the trade. If that person says she needs to hear status from everyone, explain the alternative ways to obtain status (see Section 10.5, *Determining Project Status*, on page 188).

10.2 Conduct These Types of Meetings

Whatever kind of project manager you are, you can expect to hold these kinds of meetings for or with your project team:

- Project kickoff meetings.
- Release planning meetings.
- Status meetings which report status to management.

- Project team meetings.
- Iteration review meetings.
- Project retrospectives. See Section 15.4, *Plan for a Retrospective*, on page 300.

10.3 Project Kickoff Meetings

The project kickoff meeting is your first project team meeting. With just a little care, you can set a positive tone for the whole project.

If you haven't yet written the project charter, you can use the project kickoff meeting to write the charter with the team. You have the answers to what's driving the project (see Section 1.4, *Decide on a Driver for Your Project*, on page 7), and you can use the kickoff to write the charter as a team (see Section 1.6, *Write a Project Charter to Share These Decisions*, on page 11).

If you have written the charter, hold a walk-through of the charter. This helps people see how to start reviewing work products, as in Section 9.4, *Get Multiple Sets of Eyes on Work Products*, on page 175.

10.4 Release Planning Meetings

If you're running an agile project, you'll hold a release planning meeting instead of a project kickoff meeting. The release plan shows everyone (the team, sponsors, and customer) how you expect the project to evolve. You'll plan which features you *expect* to deliver in an iteration. Since you'll rerank the product backlog between iterations (see Section 16.6, *Manage the Product Backlog*, on page 315), the details will change. At the beginning of the project, this is your best first guess.

First, the project team estimates the relative size using planning poker (see Section 5.1, *Planning Poker*, on page 72). The team estimates its velocity and predicts how many iterations they might need and what they think will be in an iteration. Especially if the team is new to working in iterations, delivering potentially releasable software, their initial estimate of what they can accomplish in an iteration may be off. That's OK—you'll be measuring velocity as you proceed through an iteration. You'll know whether you need to do another release plan at the end of an iteration or wait until you've finished a few iterations to replan.

Once the team has estimated the relative size, the customer/product owner ranks the features. The team organizes those features into iterations. The team and customer might take a few iterations to plan for which features in which iteration. You might have to help the team and customer focus on just the first couple of iterations, and you should also plan to replan.

At the end of a release planning meeting, you should have these work products: some definition of *done*; a potential release date; and a backlog of sized features, possibly organized by iteration [Coh06].

10.5 Status Meetings

Status meetings come in two flavors: those between you and the members of the project team in a one-on-one meeting and those between you and management. You probably noticed in the earlier list that I did not include team status meetings. That's because public status meetings that are not daily standup meetings are serial status meetings and a waste of time (see the tip *Seek and Destroy Time-Wasting Meetings*, on page 183).

Determining Project Status

Here are the techniques I recommend you consider for obtaining project status from team members:

- Daily standup meetings (see Section 10.5, *Daily Standup Meetings*)
- Weekly one-on-one meetings between you and each project team member (see Section 10.5, *One-on-One meetings*, on page 190)
- Weekly email status reports (cf. Section 10.5, *Obtain Weekly Email Status Reports from Team Members*, on page 192)

Daily Standup Meetings

If you're using an agile life cycle, you most likely use a daily standup to see project status. In fact, any project team can use a daily standup, as long as the team members have created small enough tasks to do so. If you're not using inch-pebbles (see Section 8.10, *Use Inch-Pebbles*, on page 158) or other techniques to decompose any task into its one- or two-day components, standup meetings make no sense. Your best bet is to use one-on-ones to help the project team members decompose their tasks. The longer the task, the more likely you'll run into the 90% Done schedule game (see Section 6.14, *90% Done*, on page 115).

Here's how a daily standup meeting works. Everyone on the project team gathers in one area at a specific time for up to fifteen minutes. Everyone stands up. (If you hold the standup in a meeting room, people will sit down, and the meeting will take an hour.) Each person, when it's their turn, answers these questions:

- What did I finish yesterday?
- What am I planning to do today?
- What are my obstacles?

You can see that it doesn't take much time to hold these meetings. Since there's only one day's worth of accomplishment, it's not a problem to conduct these meetings in fifteen minutes or less. If you're having trouble keeping to the fifteen-minute time slot, see Section 10.9, *Troubleshooting Meetings*, on page 195.[1]

Some of you are saying, "OK, that sounds great in theory. But I have twenty-four people on my project. How the heck do I do this with twenty-four people?" If you have team leads or subproject managers on even larger teams, they do this with their people and report obstacles to you.

"Ah, but all twenty-four people report directly to me." I'm sorry to disappoint you, but you are not capable of directly managing twenty-four people. Your team has separated into smaller groups on their own (which is fine). Ask yourself these questions: What do I gain by having all those people report to me directly? Can I organize differently to make obtaining status and helping the team move through their work better? Too often, when project managers do not have technical leads, they become the bottleneck on the project—they are responsible for too many decisions.

I recommend you have no more than six people report to you on a project. (See the discussion in Section 7.4, *Know How Large a Team You Need*, on page 129.) Once about eight people are on a project, they tend to self-organize into smaller teams, whether those teams are functional or cross-functional. Let the team self-organize, and you can reap the benefits of easier communications.

"But how will I connect with everyone?" Unless you're on a project with short (one-to-two week) iterations, it's worth conducting one-on-one

---

1. Also see Jason Yip's article at http://www.martinfowler.com/articles/itsNotJustStandingUp. html.

meetings with everyone weekly or biweekly. Otherwise, the team leads will be talking with each person daily, providing feedback and small course corrections.

One-on-One meetings

If you're managing a serial or iterative life cycle, or even early in an incremental life cycle, you'll need weekly one-on-one meetings with everyone on the project. In other words, the longer you try to forecast the project, the more you need weekly one-on-ones to verify the project state. (If you're heading a large project or programs, each project lead has these meetings, and you meet with the leads individually.) For agile life cycles, the *project manager* does not need to meet with people; the manager does. If you are also the functional manager, see [RD05] for the other parts of the one-on-one meeting.

When you're a project manager for a matrixed team, be careful about the issues you discuss in one-on-one meetings. Use your one-on-one meetings for project status, not career development. Expect to provide feedback and coaching about how this person is working on the project. Just be careful that your one-on-one doesn't duplicate the functional manager's one-on-one. Talk to the functional manager in advance. Set goals and boundaries for each of you. Periodically meet with the functional manager to make sure you're still coordinated.

Here's the format of the one-on-one meeting when you're not the people manager also:

- Greeting. Make sure you say "hello" when a person walks into your office. Use the greeting to context switch *into* the one-on-one. Turn off your cell phone, and turn away from your computer.

- Discuss status and progress. Review the person's inch-pebbles here. If you're coaching the person about how to develop inch-pebbles, this is the time to coach. The more serial the life cycle, the more you want to see indications of visible progress. It's too easy for people to become stuck and not realize it.

- Discuss their obstacles. You might have to help people realize they have obstacles. I once worked with a project team who had become so accustomed to the idea that setting up an environment took several hours, they didn't realize that was an obstacle.

- Review all action items—yours and theirs. If you had some action from a previous one-on-one meeting, report on your progress. Take notes during your one-on-ones so you have a record of your action items and issues that arose.

The purpose of the one-on-one is for you to see visible status and for people to be able to tell you that they need help. If you do only public status, people will tend to keep pushing on their own to finish the task—even if they are stuck. The project is headed toward the Schedule Chicken game (see Section 6.13, *Schedule Chicken*, on page 114). Private, one-on-one status meetings help you see when people are stuck. And the best way to see whether people are stuck is to *see* their work progress.

Seeing Visible Progress

Ask people to explain the status of their work, including what they'll do next week and how they'll track status. Request that people think of their tasks as to-do lists with inch-pebble-level work. Explain that you won't put their inch-pebbles into the project schedule. All the inch-pebbles make the schedule too complex, and your job is not to baby-sit each person's work. Explain that your job is to understand when people are making progress and when they are not. Inch-pebbles are a technique for people to monitor their own state and let you know.

Ask people to monitor when they are stuck and to tell you whether they need help in some way. Asking for help is fine. Floundering is not. If someone is working on a big work product, ask them to consider what they want to show you: marked-up interim designs, performance measurements of algorithms, number of scripts they threw away, or something that shows you progress. Since the team members determine their tasks, their deliverables, and when they need help, you're not micromanaging them.

Every so often, you'll run across a team member such as Dave, who thinks his work requires privacy to complete. When that happens, tell Dave that you don't know how to manage the project adequately with his need for privacy. Ask what he is willing to show you or give you so you can see his progress. That doesn't always work, so ask him when his deliverables will be complete.

If Dave gives you a date of more than two weeks, explain that that's too long. In many projects, you might be able to afford for one person to be off by one week, but I've never worked on a project where any one person could slip a deliverable by more than two weeks without affecting the entire project. If you're willing to give Dave the benefit of the doubt, ask whether he can develop deliverables that are fewer than two weeks in duration. Maybe you can wait to see the status at the end of those two weeks. (If a team member can successfully deliver work every two weeks, I'm still nervous, but I can manage my nervousness.) Once Dave misses a deadline, negotiate a different way to track tasks and status. You need to know that people are making progress.

When you explain why you need information and the level at which you need the information, most team members will be willing to work with you. You'll obtain visible progress about the project state.

Obtain Weekly Email Status Reports from Team Members

If you're using an agile life cycle, you don't need weekly status reports from the team. You already have all the information you need in the standup meeting. And since you can use the standup meeting to generate the project dashboard, you don't need any more information.

For the other life cycles, I ask for all the same information in an email status report as in a standup meeting. In addition, I request the next few weeks worth of inch-pebbles. Yes, this is asking people to perform rolling-wave planning. And, you will find that it works. Forcing people to decompose big tasks into smaller deliverable pieces and to look ahead just a few weeks will help them (and therefore you) understand whether the project is headed toward success—or disaster.

Here's my status report template.

Email Status Report Template

Accomplishments. Bullets or a brief paragraph (two to three sentences) of accomplishments for the past week.

Future Milestones:

Task Description   Planned Date   Expected Date   Actual Date

On projects where outside events keep changing what project team members do, add another column on the right: How Many Times This Estimate Has Changed.

Obstacles. Team members add their obstacles to completing work. Expect to take action items from this list.

Report Status Weekly to Your Team

On serial, iterative, and incremental projects, send out an email every week explaining the state of the project. Collate everyone's status report to you, except for their obstacles. That way you provide transparency into the project and don't need serial status meetings. Explain where the project dashboard (see Chapter 11, *Creating and Using a Project Dashboard*, on page 201) is and what the numbers mean. Make sure you keep people focused on the end goal and aware of interim milestones.

On agile projects, status is much more obvious to everyone on the project. Since there's a standup meeting every day where everyone explains what they've completed, obstacles they've run into, and what they're going to do, you don't need to send a weekly email to the team. If you have to prepare a report to management on project state, email that to the project team also.

10.6 Reporting Status to Management

One of the best ways to keep your sponsors involved in your project is to send them a periodic status report. Even if you have micromanaging managers, maybe supplying them with data on a regular basis will prevent them from trying to micromanage you.

If you're managing with timeboxed iterations, you need to send a status report only at the end of the iteration to management, if you can't convince them to attend your end-of-iteration demo. Because everyone can see the product at the end of an iteration, a status report is not as necessary as with other life cycles. For the other life cycles, consider sending the status report weekly or biweekly. If your management is unaccustomed to timeboxed iterations, consider sending an interim status report for three- or four-week timeboxes.

Start with a summary of the project dashboard, such as the weather report. Include a few bullets of accomplishments, especially if you've met a particular interim milestone. Refer them to the dashboard, and invite them to ask you questions if they have any.

If you work for a senior manager who loves all the detailed data, make sure you send all the supporting data from your project dashboard. You might need to indulge this manager with a periodic meeting to discuss the data. Don't think you can avoid this manager's need for data. You can't. Your best bet is to gather the data and plan on discussing it with the manager.

10.7 Project Team Meetings

Keep your project team meetings problem-solving meetings. If you have an agenda item for discussion, make sure that the item serves to solve or prevent a possible problem.

Here's an agenda template that serves the purpose of helping people stay focused on problem solving, not status.

Project Team Meeting Agenda

Title line: Agenda for (project) team meeting, date, time, location.

Expected attendees: Name them all.

Major milestone review: For any life cycle other than agile, listing the major milestones and when you expect to meet them can help people see the context even while they're working on their piece. If you choose to ask about EQF (see Section 11.2, *Track Your Original Estimate with EQF*, on page 209), this is the place to do so. Add the duration you expect to spend on this item.

Problem of the week: If you have particular problems you need the team to solve, this is the place to list them. Add the duration you expect to spend on each item.

Any obstacles? Ask for equipment needs, any other obstacles that may have arisen since your one-on-ones. Include the duration for this item.

New business? Ask whether there are other topics people want to discuss. Include the duration for this item.

Review old action items: Use a simple list of action items: date due, person responsible, and what the action is. Include the duration for this item.

Next Meeting: Specify the date, time, location.

Pending items/parking lot: Include a list of items you and the team doesn't want to forget but don't need to address yet, organized by date you need to start paying attention to each item.

This agenda has only those items that the entire team needs to discuss. If you have a problem that you think is for the entire team but you discover can be solved by a couple of people, thank them for dealing with this later, and move on to the next topic.

You can always end the meeting early. It's possible you don't have an hour's worth of meeting issues. That's great. Start the meeting on time and end early. People will thank you—they will feel as if they have an extra half hour in their day.

Don't forget to send everyone a list of all the action items after the meeting. As people finish their items, they reply to that email explaining what they did and when.

10.8 Iteration Review Meetings

At the end of an iteration, the team shows the working product to the product owner. Yes, that's a demo. The idea behind agile is that you inspect and adapt [Sch04] as you proceed. That's why you need to demo the product to your product owner.

In addition, the team discusses the velocity charts and anything else the team creates as part of their project dashboard. Finally, the team holds an interim retrospective to learn from what happened during this iteration.

If you use agile approaches, you can shortcut all the meetings and manage with just the release planning, daily standups, iteration reviews, and retrospectives.

10.9 Troubleshooting Meetings

Here are some problems your meetings might encounter and how to troubleshoot them:

Your daily standup takes more than fifteen minutes. Make sure people are standing up. Once people sit down, the meeting takes longer.

Make sure people report on *finished* work. If people report on work in progress, they're not decomposing the requirements into small enough features, or they're not breaking their tasks down into inch-pebbles.

No one arrives on time for your meetings. If this is just a problem for your project, renegotiate the time of the meeting. Maybe you've interrupted people's flow by having the meeting at this time. I once held all project team meetings over lunch (because the team requested a lunch meeting). I called the meeting for 12:15 and explained I was starting at 12:15 whether they were there or not—and we would be done by 1:00 p.m. That worked for the project team.

Usually, this is not a project problem, but an organization's problem. I start the meeting when I say I'm going to, and if there's no one there, I get to make all the decisions, including the people who were assigned problems we needed to solve. (Yes, this is a bit high-handed.)

Make sure you're doing your part by sending out meeting agendas at least twenty-four hours in advance of the meeting and sending minutes with action items within twenty-four hours of conducting the meeting.

Make sure you're not wasting people's time at the meeting. If you're including serial status information at your meetings and you're not holding one-on-ones, you are wasting people's time. You can ask people whether their return on time invested [RD05] is enough to keep the meeting going. Maybe you're trying to meet too often, or you're not solving project problems.

Make sure your team members are not boycotting your meetings because they are a waste of time. See the tip *Seek and Destroy Time-Wasting Meetings*, on page 183.

No one completes their action items for the next meeting. Make sure you've sent the minutes from the last meeting within twenty-four hours of that meeting. If you have a section with action items, make sure each item has a name and a date associated with it.

For the next meeting, send the agenda at least twenty-four hours in advance. That will remind people they have open action items.

People who are not part of the project want to attend your team meetings. The reason for articulating the attendees for a project team meeting is to help people realize who will be making decisions about the project's issues. When other people want to attend your meetings, first discover why, and then create a role for that person.

If you have a senior manager who wants to "help" your team accomplish more work faster, show the manager the project dashboard. Make sure that manager understands your velocity and how people are assigned to the project. If your team is multiproject multitasking, the manager can help by developing the project portfolio and managing the priorities.

If that manager still wants to "help" by "motivating" the team, help the manager understand that for knowledge workers, motivation is intrinsic, not extrinsic [Koh93]. If the manager still wants to say something, give that manager a timeboxed few minutes to say something in the meeting. Then allow the project team to solve the problem of speeding up the project—without the manager in the room.

None of these actions is easy, and they will require all of your negotiation, influence, and perhaps appeasing skills. But remember, your job is to protect the team from outside interference. Do what you need to in order to protect the team.

If you still have a manager (or other people) who wants to observe your meetings, create an Observer role for those people. Arrange chairs behind the chairs around the conference room table, and direct the Observers to sit there. Remind the Observers that they may observe and write down their observations, but they are not to interfere. I make this offer, "If you can't stand it and need to say something, write me a note. Here are index cards—you can pass me a card with your question or comment." If Observers can't remain quiet, you are well within your rights as meeting owner/facilitator to ask that person to leave.

You might want to invite other people to your meetings to obtain their input on decisions or gather data that will help your team to make good decisions. If that's the case, clarify the other person's role and how you will use input from that person *in advance* of the meeting.

10.10 Manage Conference Calls with Remote Teams

You might not be able to conduct in-person meetings with your team. If you need to hold teleconferences, this section has tips that might help your calls.

Conference Call Hell Is Now Heaven
by Wendy, project manager of a worldwide project

I'd had it. I had been running these conference calls for a month, and I couldn't have a conversation because Jack was eating lunch, Pierre was eating dinner, not all the people were on the call when they needed to be, and more. It was a disaster. I finally laid down the law.

First, I got my managers to buy reasonable speaker phones and headsets. Can you believe one guy was supposed to use one of the half-duplex speaker phones? Unbelievable.

Then, I worked on my facilitation skills and made stronger agendas. Then, I explained how we were going to treat each other on the call. Every site would have a facilitator, and people would switch that position every week. I asked one of our admins to take notes so we could review action items every few minutes.

I started to enforce the rules of "only one voice at a time" and "no aural eating." Everyone had a good time teasing me about that. But it's working. Our calls run much more smoothly now.

Here are some helpful hints for running conference calls. Some of these hints may be difficult for you to institutionalize. Persevere. Gently.

General Facilitation Guidelines

When you facilitate a conference call of more than two people, try these guidelines:

- Make introductions; ask all sides to announce their name and their role.
- All participants should agree that facilitation is necessary.
- Use the "one conversation at a time" rule. If one person is speaking, let that person finish. If you have a pauser on the line, ask whether that person is done before speaking.
- Say who you are when you speak.
- Say the name of the person if you are addressing someone in particular.
- No eating (especially no eating something noisy or in noisy packaging). If you can meet only during someone's dinner or lunch time, request that person mute their side of the call while they are eating.
- If you are interpreting to another language, lay down the ground rules (interpret after each complete thought), and don't be afraid to enforce them.

Logistics

Aside from facilitation, make sure everyone on the call has checked these logistics.

- Make sure you have a mute button that doesn't play music and really mutes you. I was once on a call when someone said, "That Johanna, she's a tough cookie, isn't she?" I agreed. The other person was quite embarrassed.
- Use a good speakerphone with full duplex sound.
- If you're initiating the call, make sure everyone at your site is in the room before calling the other groups.

Plan the Call in Advance

Your conference calls might need just a little extra planning. Decide what to do in these circumstances.

- What happens if not everyone calls in, and you don't know where they are? One of my clients has a rule: if not everyone is there after fifteen minutes, reschedule.
- What happens if you can't reach the other teams or someone needs to call you? Give the other teams a cell phone number to reach you in addition to the conference call number.
- People need to know what you want to discuss. Send out an agenda in advance that everyone can see—this is even more critical than in a face-to-face meeting. During the meeting, if you have to modify the agenda, make sure everyone understands where you are in the current agenda.
- Make sure everyone knows the topics under discussion. Aside from choosing the topics in advance, you'll need to keep topics focused. You'll need to plan in advance to organize the attendees to make sure you have the right people to discuss those topics.
- Publish a meeting objective, and make sure the meeting objective is clear.
- Vary the order of participants (who speaks first, and so on), especially for regularly scheduled calls.
- If there is no good reason to meet, cancel the meeting (beware the meeting that won't die).
- Have an end time. Stick to it.
- Use collaboration software when it makes sense to do so.

Meeting Facilitation

It's harder to facilitate meetings across physical locations and time zones. Consider these suggestions for facilitating:

- If someone joins the call late, have someone else, not the facilitator, summarize what has happened so far and say who is on the call. The facilitator can stay on track and only the two people (the late person and the person explaining what's happened) are distracted.
- Use mirroring (repeating what the person said).

- Use focused conversations [RBS00], a technique that helps people separate the objective data, reflective data, their interpretations, and their decisions.
- Monitor all discussions so you know when the discussion is too detailed. Know when to cut off specific questions.
- Ask for people who do not agree (in other words, "Does anyone not agree or not understand?"). Do not assume silence means agreement.
- Be sensitive to when other people have lost the conversation.
- Organize the agenda by topic. When that topic is complete, confirm completion.
- Be aware that it is much harder to understand a non-native speaker over the phone.
- Check that people have not been cut off in the middle of the conference call. I like to also have everyone's cell phone number so if that person isn't talking, I have another way to reach them.
- Summarize partway through and at the end.
- List action items at the end of call.
- Announce when the meeting is over.

Your Work After the Teleconference

You still have some work after the conference call.

- Always send a summary of any decisions made along with action items to all participants as follow-up afterward.
- Make sure you know when the call has really ended. Check to see whether the speakerphone is still on.

 Remember This

- You can decide whether a meeting is useful and worth your time—or any of your project team members' time.
- Avoid serial status meetings like the plague.
- Monitor your meetings for how well they meet the needs of everyone involved.

Chapter 11

Creating and Using a Project Dashboard

Most of the questions you answer come down to some variant of this question: "Where are we?"

This could come from senior management trying to figure out whether you're going to hit a deadline or from the project team asking about their status. It soon feels like they're in the backseat of your car on a long trip asking, "Are we there yet?"

The key to understanding a project is to make regular measurements—both quantitative and qualitative—and display the measurements publicly. When project managers display these measurements as part of the project status, teams are able to adjust their work and proceed more successfully.

This collection of measurements comprises your *project dashboard*. Taken together, the project measurements display your velocity, distance, consumption, and location—much as a car dashboard does.

Creating a project dashboard provides feedback to the team and reports status to other interested people. Use a Big Visible Chart or Information Radiator [Coc04] so that everyone can see the project's progress.

11.1 Measurements Can Be Dangerous

Measurement involves three big problems: the project team spending too much time on measurement to the detriment of the work, gaming the system, and measuring the people instead of the project.

It's easy to spot and fix people spending too much time measuring. Are your project staff members generating paperwork and measurements rather than performing the work? The measurements in this chapter are all obtainable by you, the project manager. Most of the project staff shouldn't have to help you obtain project measurements. You might need help from someone who manages the SCM or the DTS. (If you need to measure performance or reliability, you might need developers or testers to help you measure that.) If you need help from more than a couple of people, work on your project infrastructure support. The goal of the dashboard is to use the data to assess the project state, not to spend time creating the dashboard.

It is often harder to spot people gaming the system, but the cause is often that only a single factor is being measured. You're likely to see schedule games (see Chapter 6, *Recognizing and Avoiding Schedule Games*, on page 87) and other behavior that doesn't help the project progress. There's a famous Dilbert strip where the boss says he'll pay each developer some amount of money to fix defects. Wally, one of the characters says, "I'm going to write me a minivan." Wally is planning to write a whole lot of defects and then fix them. If you measure only one thing, you encourage people to optimize for that one thing. Make sure you have multiple measurements for assessing project progress.

When you choose measurements, make sure you measure the project and the product, not the people [Aus96]. If you measure anything that can be traced directly back to one person or another, you are measuring people, not the project or the product. Measuring people begs them to game the system, preventing you from understanding the project's state and possibly preventing the project from completing. Never measure people.

It's easy to measure some facets of a project, such as the project start date, the current date, and the desired release date and say, "We're X percent of the way along," because the project team has used that percentage of time. (See Section 11.2, *Earned Value for Software Projects Makes Little Sense*, on page 207.) If all you measure is the schedule, you're guaranteed not to meet the desired deadline.

In fact, measuring any single dimension can't give you a full enough picture of the status of your project. If you're driving a car and look at the mileage for this tank of gas but don't look at your miles per gallon and the miles left to drive, you still don't know whether you have enough gas to get you to your destination.

To obtain a true picture of the your project's state, choose at least four out of six dimensions of the project drivers, constraints, and floats from Section 1.2, *Manage Your Drivers, Constraints, and Floats*, on page 3 to measure and display on your project dashboard. Those four dimensions capture the areas you are most likely to be able to modify during the project. And if you don't measure them, you can't see what to change to make your project succeed.

Tip: Use Multidimensional Measurements to Assess Project Progress

> There are any number of references that say, "You get what you measure." And, as you saw in Section 11.1, *Measurements Can Be Dangerous*, on page 201, it's possible people will want to game the measurement. Since you will get exactly what you measure, make sure you measure enough information about the project to provide an honest assessment of project progress.

Rob, a VP of engineering called me, confounded. "JR, those freaking testers! They can't do anything right." Rob's project had 1,500 developers and about 350 testers. I had met a few testers before, so I said, "That's funny, the people I met seemed to know what they were doing." "No way," Rob quipped, "the developers meet every single milestone. The testers don't meet any. I need you right away to do an assessment."

Well, developers meeting every milestone is a suspicious statement. I know a lot of developers. And even the best don't always meet their schedules. I started the assessment with an open mind. Maybe all 1,500 developers really are incredible.

But here's what I discovered. The developers have to report only dates to the project managers. That's it. And the project managers measure only dates from the developers and defects from the testers. There's no measurement of anything else on the project. When I talked to developers about their work, it all became clear. Danny grimaced and explained, "I have to start the feature when the Gantt says to; otherwise, I get marked down on my performance evaluation. I put stubs in, so I 'finish' it on time. When the testers report a problem, I fix the problem."

> ### ⅍ Joe Asks...
> #### Can I Ever Start Measuring Over?
>
> You can. I don't recommend it, because generally the system (the process and the people) that's creating problems—such as starting the project a month late—doesn't recognize the system is doing this. Without a chart to show why you've been behind since the beginning, you won't be able to change the system of how projects start.
>
> Instead of remeasuring, draw a line on the chart with something like "Original Start Date" and "Actual Start Date." Then show the triggering event that led to the "Actual Start Date." (See Figure 11.7, on page 214.)

Rob's organization has broken projects (and products)—projects that don't deliver what Rob needs. As long as he persists in single-dimension measurement for a group of people (dates for developers and defects for testers), they will have broken projects. The only cure for Rob is to have the project managers measure all around the project so that they can tell more accurately where the project is.

11.2 Measure Progress Toward Project Completion

By using several measurements from the drivers, constraints, and floats, you can measure the team's progress toward project completion. Project completion is a function of how accurate your original estimate was and how much progress you've made. But measuring only the schedule progress is not good enough. The only accurate way to measure progress for a software project is to measure how many features the project team has completed, how good those features are, and how many features are left to implement.

Use Velocity Charts to Track Schedule Progress

If you're implementing by feature, a velocity chart (such as Figure 11.1, on the facing page) is a great progress indicator to how much progress

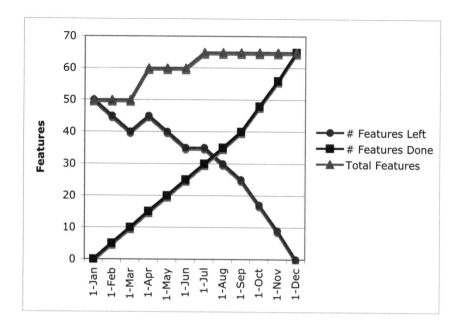

Figure 11.1: VELOCITY CHART FOR A PROJECT

the team has made on the project.[1] And it can give you an indication about how much work is left.

Here's how you make a velocity chart. Add up the number of features—that's your total features. As you finish a feature, add 1 to the number of features done, and decrease the number of features left. If you have to add more features during the project, add those extra features to the total features. Even if your features aren't normalized to be the close to the same size, this chart will help.

If you use inch-pebbles and you're not implementing by feature, tracking inch-pebbles (Section 8.10, *Use Inch-Pebbles*, on page 158) can help you know where you are. But that won't be as accurate as implementing by feature. Whatever you do, don't just ask people whether they've met their milestones without looking to see how good the stuff is that they are producing.

---

1. See http://www.xprogramming.com/xpmag/jatRtsMetric.htm.

Tip: Velocity Charts Are the Single-Best Chart

If you can make only one chart, choose a velocity chart. Velocity charts use three measurements (requirements, completed work, and date), all on one chart. They don't provide a picture of defects or cost, two more measures you might like to see. But they provide an overall picture of progress on one chart.

Because you're measuring several trends on one chart: total requirements and *completed* work, including all the testing and documentation and whatever else your project requires over time, it's the single-best chart. If you're working without implementing by feature, the chart shows no completed work, which is exactly the state your project is in. Velocity charts are your friend.

Use an Iteration Contents Chart to Track Overall Progress

In addition to a velocity chart that tracks implemented features over time, you might want a finer-grained look at what's going on in each iteration. (Even if you're not using timeboxed iterations, generate this chart over a fixed time period. That will help you see when requirements changes and defects arrive in the project.)

In Figure 11.2, on the facing page, you can see how the release's contents change over time. In this project, the team started with a velocity of six features per iteration. By they time they got to the ninth iteration, they were down to two features, plus two changes and four defects. At that point, the project manager realized things could only get worse and stopped changing the iteration's backlog during the iteration. That allowed the team to make much more progress in the last three iterations.

Until the project manager generated this chart, no one had any idea about the cost of the changes during an iteration and the introduction of defects those changes caused.

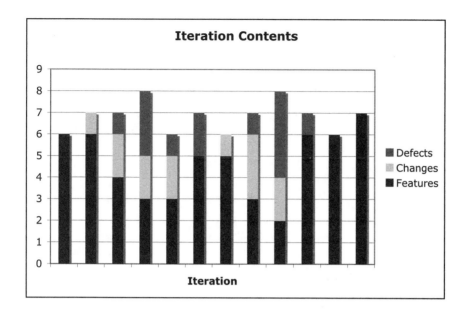

Figure 11.2: Iteration Contents Chart for a Project

Earned Value for Software Projects Makes Little Sense

Earned value is a measure of the value of work performed to date.[2] But because software is ephemeral and ever-changing, it's close to impossible to calculate the true earned value. If you can't clearly define it, you can't really measure it. Resist the attempts from your organization to have you report on earned value. For a tangible product, it's easy to calculate earned value. If you're building a table, you can calculate the cost of the materials and time to see whether the legs and the top have value even before you put the table together. But earned value is different for software.

Here's an example. Say you have five requirements to complete in ten weeks. Imagine that you and the project team believe it will take the entire team two weeks per requirement. And, imagine you have five people on the team. Your estimate is ten effort-weeks per requirement, a total of fifty effort-weeks. Imagine the team has finished the first three requirements, including testing them, as in Figure 11.3, on page 209.

---

2. © 2007 R. Max Wideman, http://www.maxwideman.com; reproduced with permission.

> ## ⌣ Joe Asks...
> ### How Can We Have No Completed Work?
>
> You've been working hard for months on your project. No one has been slacking off. But when you try to use a velocity chart, it shows you no (or virtually no) completed work. How is that possible? It's possible—and even likely—if you're using a serial life cycle or implementing by architecture in any life cycle, without planning how to finish features.
>
> When a project team uses a serial life cycle or implements by architecture, they have lots of partially completed work. Partially completed work is called *waste* in the lean community. It's waste because it's not done. Because velocity charts show you completed work, you can tell whether the team is producing waste or a completed product.
>
> The more you use incremental, or even better, agile techniques, the more your velocity chart will show what you've done. Being able to show the project team what is done helps maintain the project rhythm and helps people accomplish more.

The customer sees what the team has done so far. "Looks great, but I really need it to do foo over here and blatz over there."

The "foo" and "blatz" features will cost another two team-weeks each. Your original calculation was that you had 60% of the work done in 60% of the time. You were on track. You are now not even close to on track. But you have feedback from the customer earlier than the end of the project, and you can give the customer what the customer wants.

How much value do you have? I don't know how to answer that question, because it doesn't account for the fact that the customer didn't realize what he or she wanted wasn't enough for the time allocated for the project. The initial measurements were wrong. Your project has some value. Maybe the work to date has even more value than you thought because the customer realized early that the requirements weren't quite right. But you are no longer 60% done; you're at some other percentage.

Some organizations like to use "Percent Complete." I don't agree with that either. All too often this refers to only the development piece, but

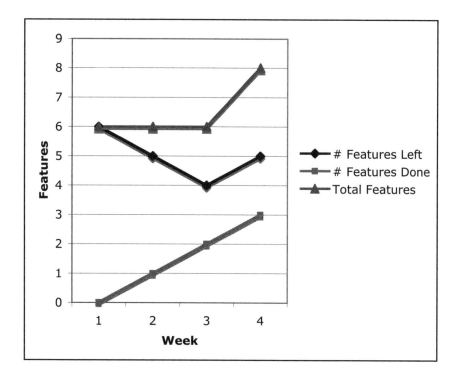

Figure 11.3: A SIX-WEEK VELOCITY CHART

not the testing part. Pieces of the product that haven't been tested aren't complete. Using "Percent Complete" begs people to start with schedule games such as the one covered in Section 6.14, *90% Done*, on page 115.

If you want to know your progress, use a velocity chart showing running tested features. A velocity chart shows the team's actual progress against the planned progress. And it shows that change happens to a project and how much change is occurring.

So, just say no to earned value. Use velocity charts instead.

Track Your Original Estimate with EQF

Tom DeMarco in [DeM00] described a measure called *estimation quality factor* (EQF). EQF helps you understand how good the initial estimate was. At periodic intervals during the project, the project team answers

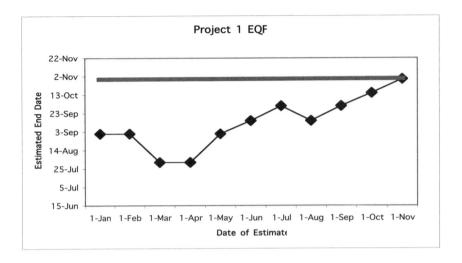

Figure 11.4: ESTIMATION QUALITY FACTOR

this question: "When do you think we'll be done?" Each data point is the consensus agreement on when the project team believes the project will be finished. At the end of the project, draw a line backward from the release date to the beginning of the project. For an example, see Figure 11.4. The area between the line you drew and the when-will-we-be-finished line is how far off your estimation was. This is a great technique for people to use as feedback on their individual estimates. But even if you don't use it for feedback, it's a great technique for the project manager to see what's happening.

Maybe you're concerned: there's a penalty in EQF for discovering new requirements later. That's true. EQF is not a perfect measure. But if you're not going to use an agile life cycle, late requirements (or late-learned requirements) do bring a penalty. I'd rather see why the project is suffering from a delay than not know why.

If you're using an agile life cycle, your velocity charts will provide you a quantitative answer, rather than a qualitative answer. But if you're not using an agile life cycle, EQF is a great qualitative measure of how close your estimate is.

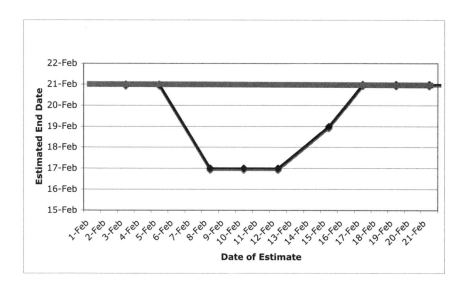

Figure 11.5: TOMMY'S ESTIMATION QUALITY FACTOR

Figure 11.4, on the facing page is a chart of an EQF for a project that was originally supposed to be nine months long. For the first couple of months, when the project manager asked when people thought they'd finish, they said September 1. And for a couple of months, they were optimistic, thinking that they might finish early. But during the fifth month, team members realized they didn't know enough about some of the requirements. What they discovered changed the architecture and pushed out the date. For the next few months, they still weren't sure of the date. They realized in the last three months of the project that, because of the changing architecture, they were encountering many defects they hadn't anticipated. Evaluating EQF, a qualitative metric, was helpful to the project manager and the project team as a check against the progress charts.

EQF isn't just for software projects. A person can use this technique when performing any project work. I used it when writing this book. You can use it with developers (or testers or writers or whomever) to coach them about their estimation.

Tommy was working on a feature that he thought would take him three weeks to complete. He made sure he had several deliverables each week, his inch-pebbles. As he completed an inch-pebble, he updated his EQF for the feature. See Figure 11.5, on the previous page. He thought he was lucky with delivering the pieces early. He didn't change his EQF until about halfway through the feature, even though he had managed to complete most of his deliverables early for the first part of the feature.

As Tommy proceeded, he didn't quite make the progress he thought he would. He was still on track for his original estimate but was not going to meet the earlier date.

Schedule estimates are just guesses, so anything you can do to show and then explain why your schedule varies from the initial plan will be helpful to anyone who wants to know "Where are we?"

More Measurements Tell the Rest of the Story

Project completion measurements might be all your managers want to see, but if you're a project manager or a technical lead on a project team, I'm sure you'd like some early warning signs that the schedule might not be accurate. To keep my finger on the pulse of a project, I monitor several measurements:

- Schedule estimates and actuals, aside from EQF. If you use velocity charts, you get this as part of velocity.
- When people (with the appropriate capabilities) are assigned to the project vs. when they are needed.
- Requirements changes throughout the project. If you use velocity charts, you get this as part of velocity.
- Fault feedback ratio throughout the project if you're not using an agile life cycle. See Section 11.2, *See Whether the Developers Are Making Progress or Spinning Their Wheels*, on page 217.
- Cost to fix a defect throughout the project, especially if you're not using an agile life cycle.
- Defect find/close/remaining open rates throughout the project.

Note that these are assessment measurements, not measurements that are trying to find the problems in the project. These measurements will expose problems but might not be sufficient by themselves to see the real problems. The power from the measurement comes from looking at all of these measurements together.

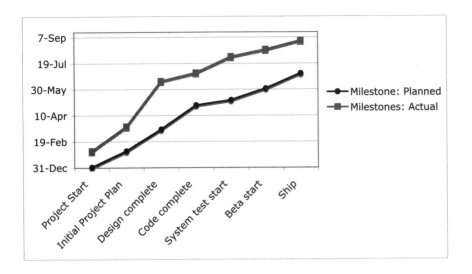

Figure 11.6: SCHEDULE ESTIMATES VS. ACTUALS

Measure the Schedule When That's All You've Got

Maybe you're in an organization wedded to a serial life cycle. Or, you've just joined the project, and things are not going well, according to your boss. First measure the schedule to see what's happening.

That's right. Note that I'm not telling you to measure only the schedule, I'm advising that this is the first measurement to which you should commit. But don't just use Gantt charts. You have many tools available. For example, look at when the project team expected to meet a particular milestone and when they actually met that milestone, as in Figure 11.6. If the project team starts the project late (no matter what the first milestone is), that project is not going to meet the desired end date.

Time lost is never going to be regained.

Figure 11.6 shows what happened with one project. This project is a modified waterfall life cycle (the next phase can start without the previous phase being complete), but there are no iterations. Notice that the project started a full month late. When the project manager posted this chart, he also said this to senior management: "Don't expect us to pull in the schedule by a month. We started late; we can't make up the

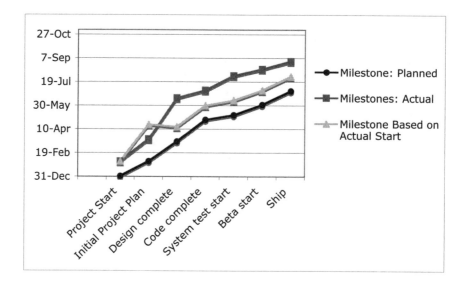

Figure 11.7: SCHEDULE ESTIMATES VS. ACTUALS WITH REAL START DATE

time." To the project team he said, "I'd like you to work as intensely as you can, without working overtime and getting tired. We don't have time for you to make mistakes. Do the best job as quickly as you can, and we'll keep tracking where we are."

As a pragmatic project manager, you might even want to show the project team how well they are progressing, assuming they started on time rather than always being a month late. To see how it might look, see Figure 11.7.

Chart When Qualified People Actually Work on the Project

It's altogether too common for projects to start starved of resources. Most often the resources the project is missing is the people. And, people are the one resource a software project requires to proceed. But not just any people—people who are capable of performing the work required on *this* project.

Planning to start a project with a small team and adding people later is OK—if you plan for it. That's a project where the plan says, "We need this many people right now. We'll need more later." That's not the same as starting a project starved of the people you need. I've started projects

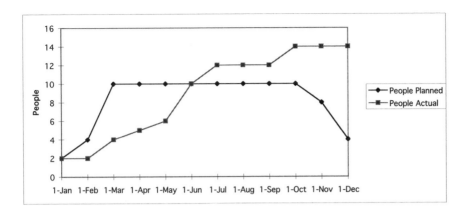

Figure 11.8: PEOPLE SCHEDULED FOR THE PROJECT AND ACTUALLY ASSIGNED TO THE PROJECT

where I had people prototyping and when I had technical leaders on the project. I've started projects where I asked the developers to fix defects when I was missing technical leaders. I've started projects using short iterations when I had developers but no testers. In each case, we had a plan to integrate the rest of the project team when it was time for them to join the project.

But starting a project starved of people is asking for trouble. (Starting a project without enough computers or desks or other resource might be acceptable if the people can manage the problem of the scarce resource.) You need to know how many people you have and whether those people can get the work done.

If you're in this position, use timeboxed iterations, and measure iteration velocity. You can show the data to the team and keep explaining the data to the people who haven't freed the necessary resources yet. If this happens to you repeatedly, read Section 7.7, *Know When It's Time to Leave*, on page 134, and decide whether this job is worth it.

Figure 11.8 is a staffing history from a real project. The people needed in the second month were still working on their previous project (that project had slipped). Instead of waiting to start the project, senior management told the PM to start, and he did. By the third month, the project was staffed with only four people, instead of the ten required.

Given this information, the project manager and team could have changed how they worked. But they were being told that the other people would start "any day now"—and the PM and team believed it.

By the six-month mark, the project was fully staffed. But the velocity was very far behind. To catch up, the PM asked for and received more people—testers. (This was a serial lifecycle project.) The testers found lots of defects, so the PM asked for more developers. The developers created more defects, and the testers found more defects, until finally they got to a reasonably stable point.

This chart measures the trend of the people assigned to the project, not the total number. If you add up the total numbers, the actual person-months used by the project was about 1/3 more. And since people cost is not always a constraining driver for a project, that might have been fine. The real problem is that the project team delivered only about 2/3 of the desired feature set, and the system was not particularly stable.

If you're faced with a situation of not enough people on your project, make sure you don't fall into the same trap as this PM did—thinking you don't have to redesign your project. Because this project had so many people still assigned to it at the end, the next project was ready to be starved of people. But the PM had learned from this project and asked the two developers available for the next project to implement by feature in one-week iterations. When you're faced with insufficient numbers of people to complete the project *as you designed it*, change the project design. For me, that almost always means moving to agile development, because it gives me the maximum flexibility with the people I have.

Determine the Rate of Change on Your Project

If you're using a serial life cycle, you might not be able to produce velocity charts that mean anything because you're stuck in the dynamic of having too much partially completed work but not enough actually finished (see the *Joe Asks...* on page 208). Although I still recommend velocity charts, you might need to split the chart into its component pieces. In that case, you can use a requirements change chart, such as in Figure 11.9, on the next page.

I was the project manager in a situation like this. I had arrived in the middle of a serial lifecycle project. I couldn't measure velocity; we had too much partially finished work. But I could start measuring

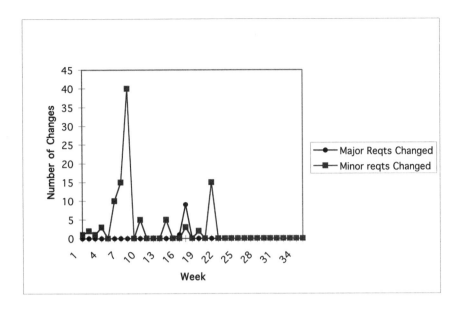

Figure 11.9: REQUIREMENTS CHANGE CHART

requirements changes. In this project, I had a simple criterion for deciding whether the requirements change was major or minor, based on the principle that interface changes between modules tend to create defects. A minor change affected one module, and a major change required changes to more than one module.

In Figure 11.9, there are lots of small changes—something most of us expect on projects. But we also encountered some major requirements changes late in the project (week 22). When I saw these requirements changes, I was able to explain to senior management that either the project would be later than we expected or the number of defects would rise. But with these changes, it was clear that the original date and the original feature set with the small number of expected defects was not possible.

See Whether the Developers Are Making Progress or Spinning Their Wheels

Once the project team is writing code, you can measure the fault feedback ratio (FFR). The FFR is the ratio of the number of rejected fixes

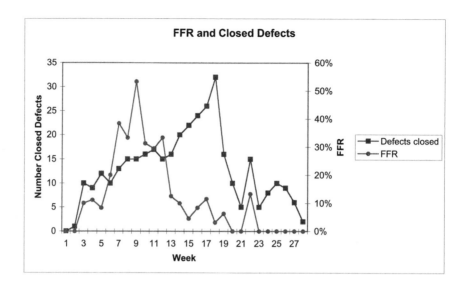

Figure 11.10: FAULT FEEDBACK RATIO

(fixes that don't actually fix the problem) to the total number of fixes. In my experience, an FFR of 10% or more says that the developers are having trouble making progress.

Because successful agile projects tend to use test-driven development and pairing and unit test development for every line of code, the FFR tends to be quite low. But projects that don't use continuous integration and continuous code review tend to build up defects and substantial technical debt (see Appendix B, on page 335). That's when it's useful to measure FFR (as in Figure 11.10), taking a look at how many defects the developers can actually close, compared to the number of rejected fixes.

In Figure 11.10, when the developers reduce the FFR, the overall number of successfully closed defects increases. And, when the FFR remains high, you can be sure that the developers will fix fewer defects until they fix the defects that are preventing them from making progress.

Measure the FFR on a weekly basis, and use it as data to initiate a discussion with the developers and testers. If you see a week where the FFR is high, first check to see how many total problems were fixed that week. If only four problems were fixed and one was rejected, the developers and testers are probably OK. But if you see twenty defects fixed and five of them were rejected (25%), it's more likely that somebody, or a few somebodies, are having trouble. In Figure 11.10, on the facing page, notice that the FFR starts to get high around week 6 and stays at more than 10% until week 13. Once the project team hit the second week of high FFR, the project manager instituted peer review on all fixes. That helped, but there was a delay between the start of peer review and the reduction of FFR back to numbers where the fixes didn't interfere with progress.

To identify trouble areas, first ask the developers whether they are running into trouble with their fixes. I generally phrase the question this way: "When you fix something here, does a problem pop up over there?" I'll ask other questions, all leading to asking the developers whether they need any resources to fix this problem. If I hear that the developers want to redesign a module, we discuss the issues for that redesign.

My next question is for the testers: "Are you able to define all the conditions that create this problem?" I start with those questions to see whether the developers are fixing one piece of the problem at a time or whether the testers understand the system sufficiently to test thoroughly enough.

FFR is a late measure that allows you, as the PM, to ask questions to help the project team solve the problem. Although you can use FFR on any work product, people don't tend to reopen defects in design docs or requirements docs. Since you can't measure FFR until there is code, the earlier you start measuring FFR, the more feedback you can get in a serial life cycle.

Measure How Much It Costs You to Find and Fix Problems

If you're using any life cycle other than one with no more than four-week iterations, a key measure is the cost for the project team to find and fix problems. You've probably seen "industry-standard numbers" that look something like this:.

Phase	Requirements	Design	Code	Test	Post-Release
Cost	1	10	100	1000	10,000

Phase	Requirements	Design	Code	Test	Post-Release
Project 1 cost	Not measured	Not measured	.5 Person-days	1 Person-day	18 Person-days
Project 2 cost	.25 Person-days	.25 Person-days	.5 Person-days	.5 Person-days	8 Person-days

Figure 11.11: ACTUAL COST TO FIX A DEFECT FROM TWO PROJECTS

The idea here is that it costs you 1 unit to fix a problem in the requirements phase; 10 units to fix a problem in design; 100 units in code; 1,000 units in test; and 10,000 units in post-release. We usually think of units as dollars or some other form of currency.

I've measured cost to fix a defect,[3,4] and the numbers I find are different. Figure 11.11 shows costs from a couple of projects. Project 1 did not search out defects as they occurred and remove them. The Project 1 team only halfheartedly looked for problems during code. Most of the problems were detected in test. Project 2 took a very proactive approach and actively looked for defects from the start of the project.

Remember, it's not just the cost per defect; it's the cost per defect times the total number of defects. If you're not looking at the overall cost, you can't know where to spend your time. Based on cost to fix a defect from previous projects, you might decide to be proactive and use inspections of key project documents, test-driven development, or pair-programming from the start of the project. Or, you might choose to act just for more challenging defects. Or you might decide to monitor cost to fix a defect and take a more reactive response, such as peer review of fixes or inspection of all code.

If you haven't performed any proactive defect-finding activities, the cost to *find* a defect is fairly small. But the cost to *fix* can be high, and the overall cost to fix all the defects is very large, because you're guaranteed to have more defects if the project team does not have a proactive culture of finding and fixing defects. If you have been proactive by

---

3. See http://www.jrothman.com/Papers/Costtofixdefect.html.
4. See http://www.stickyminds.com/s.asp?F=S3223_COL_2.

using techniques such as test-driven development, pair programming, inspections, or peer reviews, the cost to find a defect can be higher— because you've already looked for defects. The cost to fix a defect tends to be much lower when a project team finds defects early. And the overall number of defects is lower, lowering your total cost to fix defects for a particular release.

I monitor cost to find and fix so I can see whether the developers or testers are surprised by what's in the code base. I have a couple of rules of thumb, assuming the developers have not been proactively looking for defects:

- The longer it takes developers to *fix* a problem, the more likely it is that the developers are afraid of touching parts of the system. It might even be the case that the developers don't understand parts of the system.
- The longer it takes the testers to *find* problems, the less they know about the product or the less they know about multiple techniques to test the product.

The higher your total cost to fix a defect, the more defect risk management you'll need to do: when to stop accepting fixes for a release and what to fix.

Understand Whether the Developers and the Testers Are Making Progress with Defects

Almost every project measures defect trends. I've seen some intricate defect trend charts, but my favorite chart shows just three things: number of new defects found per week, number of closed defects per week, and number of remaining open defects per week, as shown in Figure 11.12, on the following page. I specifically do not chart defects by priority because the project team and senior management become too willing to play the promotion/demotion game (see Section 15.4, *Avoiding the Promoting/Demoting Defects Game*, on page 299). Besides, the developers have to read through all the defects, even if they are supposedly a lower priority. I just count all the defects.

I count the number of remaining open defects so I can see when the close rate passes the find rate, enough so that the number of remaining open defects starts to decrease. I look for the knee of that remaining open defects curve, knowing that as the slope of the remaining number of open defects goes negative, the risk of release lessens.

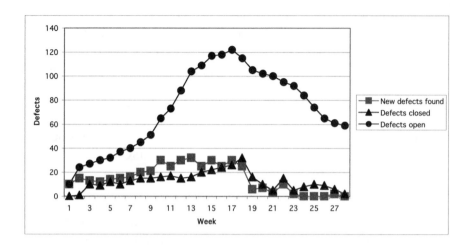

Figure 11.12: DEFECT TRENDS OVER THE COURSE OF A PROJECT

Display the Testing Progress

Once testing has started, you can chart the progress of the testing. I recommend you integrate testing into development, no matter what life cycle you choose. See Chapter 13, *Integrating Testing into the Project*, on page 255 for suggestions.

In Figure 11.13, on the next page, you can see how the number of planned tests continues to increase over time. That's because the requirements kept changing. And, you can see that the number of tests the team was able to run steadily increased, as did the number of tests passing. But there's a significant gap between the number of tests passing from the number of test run.

This graph is from a real project; it was for a new release with new functionality. The team started with 900 tests already available as automated regression tests. But only 600 of them passed by the time the testers started. Those regressions occurred because the team would not use continuous integration and used staged integration at the beginning. When they saw the chart and realized how much work they had created for themselves, they started to move toward continuous integration.

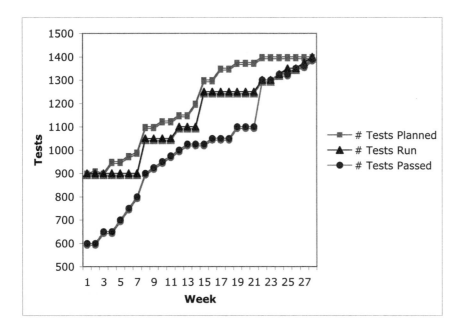

Figure 11.13: TESTING PROGRESS

The test progress chart is useful as a measure of test progress. But it's also an indication of (possibly unanticipated) requirements changes and an indication of how well the developers are integrating as they proceed.

If you're using an agile life cycle, where the testing for a specific feature occurs within the iteration that the feature is developed, you might not need a chart like this. But if your project team has trouble keeping the testing in an iteration, a chart like this might help, especially if you graph it by iteration. When you use iterations and add new features for an iteration, expect the number of "Tests Planned" to jump in a straight line at the beginning of an iteration.

Display Qualitative Data

It would be easy if all the project data could be displayed on trend charts. But you need a different kind of chart, especially when you're trying to explain the status of something.

Feature or Area or Module	Last Test Date	State	Next Planned Test
Feature Set 1	Mar 3, Build 145	Pass	Build 150
Performance scenario 3	Mar 1, Build 140	Fail. Waiting on Jeff and Andy to fix.	Build 150
Feature 14	Mar 2, Build 142	Passed all regression tests	Build 147 for customer acceptance
Overall Status	**As of Mar 3, 10:08 am**	**Partway done with this iteration's development, seems to be on track**	**Projected last build for this iteration: Build 165**

Figure 11.14: TEST DASHBOARD

I've used progress charts like the one in Figure 11.14, when trying to explain the progress of algorithm development, performance scenarios, and testing,[5] especially for longer iterations or serial life cycles.

Chart the Practices Agreed to by the Team

In Chapter 9, *Maintaining Project Rhythm*, on page 167, I suggested a number of technical practices the team could adopt or adapt. When the team agrees to use practices, you might find it helpful to let the team chart their practices. Don't chart the practice adherence yourself. Your project team members are adults. Treat them as adults. If they don't perform the practices, you need to understand why. That's the management part of project management.

---

5. See http://www.stickyminds.com/s.asp?F=S7655_COL_2.

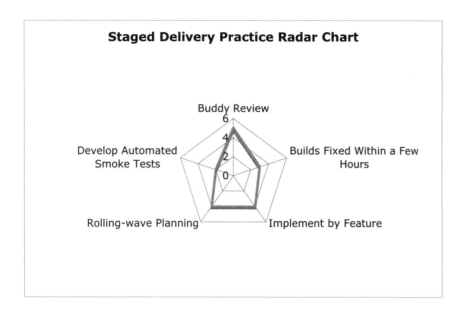

Figure 11.15: STAGED-DELIVERY PRACTICES CHART

Most likely, there is something preventing them from performing the practices. Your job is to remove that obstacle. Have them chart their practice adherence during a retrospective (see Section 8.2, *Conduct Interim Retrospectives*, on page 144).

Figure 11.15, is what a practice chart might look like for a staged-delivery project. This team chose five practices they wanted to use to help them succeed on their project: buddy review, builds fixed within a few hours, implement by feature, rolling-wave planning, and develop automated smoke tests. They're doing well on buddy review, implement by feature, and rolling-wave planning. They're not succeeding as well with automated smoke tests and fixing builds within a few hours. When you look at this chart as a PM, your job is not to flog people to do better. Your job is to discover what's preventing them from succeeding.

Here's what Tina did when she looked at this chart. She called a project team meeting where solving this was on the agenda. She gave everyone sticky notes and a pen. "Something is preventing you from developing automated smoke tests and fixing the builds.

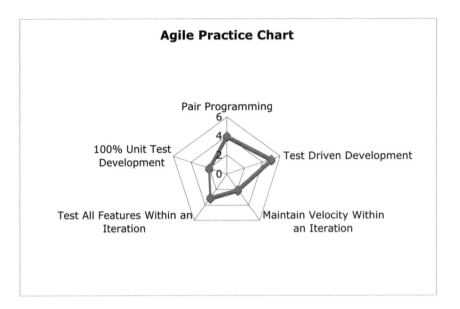

Agile Practice Chart

Figure 11.16: AGILE PRACTICES CHART

Write down what you need in order to develop automated smoke tests and to fix the build within a few hours. One idea per sticky. When you have your stickies, post them on the flip chart that says *automated smoke tests* or *fix build.*"

Once everyone was done (about seven or eight minutes later), Tina read the stickies aloud. She asked the team to affinity-group them by looking for related ideas and grouping the organized ideas [RD05]. It was clear the problems were related (for this team). And, surprisingly enough, the problem was with the source control system for the automated smoke tests. Tina made that a new requirement for the project (not a goal) and assigned her two most talented people to the task. Within a couple of weeks, they had reorganized the smoke tests and the build so that people could independently check in their changes and additions without stepping on each other's toes.

Tina would never have known what the problems were unless she'd asked the team for their obstacles.

Figure 11.16, on the facing page, is what a practice chart might look like for an agile project.[6,7] This chart has some data that might seem strange to you. How can people rank themselves high on test-driven development but low on 100% unit test development? When Charlie asked that question at the team retrospective, Mario explained, "Well, I use test-driven development to start. And then I get excited and forget to always write a test first. I ranked myself high on test-driven but lower on 100% unit test development. I figure I'm at about 98%. That's good, but there have been a few times when if I had really done all the tests first, I would have found some problems earlier."

Team practice charts open the door for conversations about the practices the team has chosen, what's working, and what's not working. Your job is to understand how to interpret the charts, help the team learn what's causing the problems, and remove those problems.

Measurements for Agile Projects

If you're using an agile life cycle, with iterations of no more than four weeks and with all the people assigned to the project and not reassigned during an iteration, and if you complete the iteration's work within the iteration, including finding and fixing all the defects introduced in that iteration, you might need only velocity charts, testing progress charts, and the iteration contents chart. Ask the team whether they want to track their practices.

11.3 Develop a Project Dashboard for Sponsors

Your sponsors (or whomever you report project status to) might have their own preferences for status. With any luck, it will include your project dashboard. But if your sponsors don't want to see everything, collect the dashboard as feedback for the project team. Your sponsors want to know when you'll be done. And the way to help them understand that is to show them your risks and the project's progress toward meeting release criteria.

Display the Risk List

You started developing the risk list when you wrote the project plan (see Section 2.3, *Develop a Project Risk List*, on page 25). The risk list will change as you progress through the project.

---

6. See http://www.xprogramming.com/xpmag/BigVisibleCharts.htm.
7. See http://xp123.com/xplor/xp0012b/index.shtml.

Numbered Risk	Explain the Risk	Probability of Occurrence	Severity If It Occurs	Exposure	Trigger Date	Mitigation Plan
1	Lucinda and her staff won't be available for prototype review when we need them	High	High	High,High	May 1	1. Explain schedule to Lucinda 2. Keep her apprised of progress. 3. Warn her 1 week in advance.
2	'Supply chain' thing will change entire db design if it occurs before Sept 1	High	Medium	Medium, HIgh	Sept 1	Continue to talk to Lucinda about the disruption these changes could make. Give her a date for when we can take changes.

Figure 11.17: INITIAL RISK LIST

The risk list is the list of things that could prevent the project team from meeting the project's drivers, constraints, and floats. Although I have met some sponsors who want to take an ostrich-like approach to risks, more sponsors realize that ignorance is not helpful.

One of my project management classes decided they wanted to see a constellation of risks, as in Figure 11.18, on the facing page. They found it useful to see how many risks were in the upper part of the chart and how many were in the lower chart so they could see a big picture of the risks. I know of at least one senior manager who prefers to see the constellation risk list first, before diving into the data below.

Display Progress Toward Meeting Release Criteria

Progress toward release criteria can help your sponsors see your progress, as in Figure 11.19, on the next page. If they haven't wanted you to use increments or iterations, they will not be able to see much progress toward release criteria until the end of the project. If you want to move toward more iterative or incremental (or both!) development, start tracking progress toward meeting release criteria. (Yes, this is a form of guerilla process improvement.)

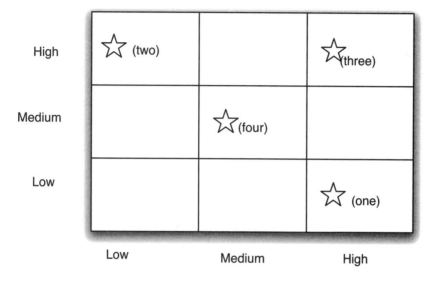

Severity of Occurrence

Probability of Occurrence

Figure 11.18: CONSTELLATION RISK LIST

Criterion	Status	Status	Status	Status	...
Reliability Criterion #1: run for 13 hours	Build 121, fail	Build 123, pass, but defects x, y, z discovered	Build 125 pass	Build 127 pass	
All online help reviewed	Build 121, Module A reviewed	Build 123, Modules B, C reviewed	Build 125, Module D reviewed	Build 127, All except Module G reviewed	

Figure 11.19: RELEASE CRITERIA

11.4 Use a Project Weather Report

Sometimes, your sponsors or management (or even clients) want to know how things are going daily. That's micromanagement. But, people tend to micromanage when they don't have data or when they have data they can't understand. If the data in your project dashboard is at too low a level for these folks, they will keep asking you for information. Remember, senior managers think in high-level bullets, and not too many of those bullets. I've used a weather report[8] for reporting status to those folks who want details but not at the level of the project dashboard.

Most often, I've seen these managers micromanaging during the final testing, so I've seen weather reports more often based on data from the testers. However, if your managers are trying to micromanage your project, generate a "balanced scorecard" (looking at the whole project) weather report in addition to the project dashboard.

Project weather reports assess the state of the project to compare where it is to where it should be. I've seen project managers use the traffic-light model—red, yellow, and green—to denote the project's state. The traffic-light model shows today's state and is easy to understand. But for many projects, there are more nuances than a three-state traffic-light model can supply.

Also, I've met a number of sponsors who want to know when the light will turn green. *Never* is a politically incorrect—although accurate—response. I've also met many project managers who either chose or felt forced to choose to game the traffic light. They only had yellow and green projects until the last week of the project, when the project suddenly became red.

Projects tend to continue in the direction the team is heading—unless the team or project manager takes specific action to change direction. The weather-report model assumes that unless the project manager and the team take some action, the weather will not get better. It's more difficult (but not impossible) to game the weather report, because there are more states.

---

8. See http://www.stickyminds.com/s.asp?F=S10522_COL_2.

Most senior managers want to see a weekly project status. Most of those managers don't want to wade through your project dashboard—they want your quick assessment of project state. And, that assessment needs to help you and your audience see where the project is and where it's headed.

A weather report gives you a quick perspective about the project—where the project is vs. where it should be—the project "weather." If the weather declines over time and nothing is done to resolve the issues, one could predict that the project will continue to get worse (forecast future project weather).

Define Weather Report Icons with Care

Since the traffic-light model of project status doesn't have enough states, make sure you define what each weather report icon means for your organization. You can tailor the definitions to your organization's needs. Here's a set of definitions that works for one of my clients:

Sunny
The project schedule is on target.

Partly Cloudy
There is minor project schedule concern, but the schedule can be met.

Overcast
There is schedule concern; the schedule can be met with extra efforts.

Cloudy
The current schedule or feature set is highly risky.

Rainy
The schedule or feature set cannot be met under current project conditions.

Severe
We cannot meet the project schedule or the desired feature set.

Why do I recommend you use Rainy and Severe? Rainy means "Hey, senior management, let's talk. We can't do what you want, but we still have room to maneuver. We can drop some features, possibly add more people (see Section 7.5, *Know When to Add More People*, on page 131), extend the schedule, or somehow replan this project." Severe means "We blew our opportunity to replan this puppy. We will keep working until you pull the plug."

A Tale of Traffic Lights and Weather Reports

Ben was a project manager on a six-month project that had more than its share of problems. Of the twenty people on the project, one had suddenly gotten married. One pregnant developer had to be on partial bed rest. One tester broke his leg skiing. And of course, the customer for this project was a Very Important Customer, who wanted several more features.

Ben described the project state as yellow for the last three months. They had another six weeks left in the project. Ben explained to the Very Important Customer and to his management that the project was at risk for a couple of the new features. Yes, the project team was working hard. They were doing everything in their power to finish on time, but they weren't sure they could make it. Every status meeting, Ben's manager and Very Important Customer slapped him on the back, assuring Ben they had faith in him.

Ben decided to try using a weather report at the next status meeting. He described the project as Cloudy. "Cloudy? Do you mean you can't do this for me?" boomed the Very Important Customer. Ben's manager suggested a quick break and took Ben aside, "Ben, what do you mean? The status has been yellow all along. You always manage to make something happen with the yellow projects."

Ben explained that although other projects had been yellow before, they hadn't been this close to not being done. "And we need some good luck."

The Very Important Customer asked what else Ben needed and offered the use of his lab and testers as early as next Monday if that would help. Ben explained that it would because they could start testing the already-completed features and continue to test in parallel with development. They made the date, missing only one of the extra features the Very Important Customer desired.

In this case, traffic lights lulled the sponsors into believing Ben was just being pessimistic, instead of realizing what the issues were. Here, the weather report assisted the sponsors into a discussion of what the issues were and how to solve them. By changing the status representation, weather reports can do the same for you.

Say you're on a project that has few risks and is proceeding on schedule. You'd give that project a full sun.

But imagine your risk list is increasing daily, and you're not sure if two features will be completed on time. Although the schedule hasn't yet slipped, you are sure it will. Say it's early in the project, and your test team cannot run—never mind run successfully—the number of tests they thought they could. You'd probably give the project a Partly Cloudy designation. After several weeks of Partly Cloudy, you might move to Cloudy if the developers and testers are still not making enough progress.

And if the project risk list is increasing, the developers are spinning their wheels, and you're finding more and more defects, you might select Rain.

The weather-report model uses assessment of the project data to predict project progress, as if the project had a season. The prediction arises from our experience with the weather; seasonal weather doesn't change much day by day. Even if there are days with rain, snow, or abnormally high or low temperatures, the weather generally continues on as expected for the season. A project progresses in the same way. You might encounter a problem you can fix on a project, but if you encounter problem after problem, you're not going to stay with your original assessment. As weather icons change (or remain the same), readers will be more aware of the project's status and might want to understand the dashboard data in more depth.

Build Credible Weather Reports

Weather reports can lose credibility if they change dramatically from week to week, unless something dramatic has changed for the project. Problems that could change a weather report in one week include losing a significant percentage of people to other work, a vendor missing a deadline, or realizing late in the project that the architecture won't support the planned feature set.

Another way to hurt credibility is to use less-than-professional weather icons, especially if your managers care about how things look. In the same way your project dashboard needs to be clear to your readers, the weather report icons need to add to your credibility, not diminish it.

If you're already gathering a variety of project data—schedule data, velocity charts, defect trends, test coverage, people assignments, and risk lists—then the weather report is your best assessment of the over-all picture. If you're not collecting that data, resist the temptation to use a gut feeling for the weather report. Instead, use progress toward release criteria for the weather report.

Publish Weather Reports Weekly

The goal of the weather report is to help people understand the project assessment and avoid surprises. Projects with more than two months left should have a weekly weather report. At some point—if the project state is still changing rapidly—or near major milestones, the weather report might need to increase to a couple of times a week.

Weather reports are one more tool in your project status arsenal. Choose a project dashboard as your first measurement and status reporting technique, but use whichever approaches will fit your organization and context.

 Remember This

- Use velocity charts and iteration content charts as your first choice.
- Data is a tool for your use, not an end in itself. Remember, the charts should serve you.
- If you can't acquire data you think you need, you have a bigger problem than the data. Fix that problem first.

Chapter 12

Managing Multisite Projects

Your project is bigger than seven or eight people all sitting together. In fact, you're managing several teams in several locations. Those locations could be as varied as down the hall, on different floors, in different buildings within a few miles of each other, or in multiple countries with multiple time zones and multiple cultures. Welcome to the world of geographically distributed projects: multisite projects.

Once your project has more than one site, the communication alone makes the project much more complex. And the more global your project is, the harder it is. Not only are the time zones different, but the culture for each team is different.

You might not have a global project. You might be lucky enough to have two teams separated by just one floor. Don't fool yourself—you have a geographically dispersed project. Any project where the people are separated by more than 30 meters (about 32 yards) is a geographically dispersed project [SR98].

You might not have the same cultural problems as teams across multiple physical sites or time zones, but you do not have a collocated team. (If part of your team is an elevator ride or stairs away from the rest of the team, you have a geographically dispersed team [TCKO00].) Anytime that the distance or time zone discourages or prevents people from communicating, you are separated. You'll need to manage the team, cultural differences and all, as a multisite project.

12.1 What Does a Question Cost You?

Cockburn suggests the costs for even walking down the hall are very high.[1] You might never have thought about it this way, but you might be literally paying a price for having teams split among several locations. Let's assume a developer (fully loaded) earns $500/day. That's $1.04/minute. How much does it cost that developer to get a question answered? (The costs are similar for other team members, but teams tend to have more developers, so the example is developer-centric.)

In a collocated team, the cost is reasonably low. When a developer has a question, they either work with the person who can answer the question or sit down the hall from the person who can answer the question. If the developer is working with the person who can answer, there's no lag time for the answer. The cost of a question is $0. Imagine the developer needs a question answered from someone down the hall. Getting up, walking over to the other person, asking the question, and getting the answer takes three minutes. That's a cost of two minutes for one developer to walk and ask the questions, plus one minute for the other developer to answer, a cost of $3.12. If the team has ten questions a day, that's a total of thirty minutes a day lost to the project and a cost of $31.20. (I'm not factoring in the additional time lost because of interruptions on either developer's part. See Section 16.7, *Explain the Cost of Multitasking Technical Work*, on page 317 for more on that cost.)

But as soon as the people have moved to another floor, two things happen. The cost of asking the question escalates. First, the walking time is longer. Because the walking time is longer, developers wait much longer to ask questions. Or they muddle through with their assumptions, not checking with anyone. Even if we don't account for the cost of the questions that are not asked, the questions that do tend to get asked are more complex. The questions need to justify the effort of walking to the other floor to find the answer, so the questions take longer to answer. As a result, the time to answer a question is closer to three minutes. Instead of a developer dealing with a two-minute interruption, the new developers have an eleven-minute interruption. And the person with the answer has a three-minute interruption. The cost is fourteen minutes, a total of $14.56 per question. Let's assume that developers ask only five questions a day. The total time lost from the project is 70 minutes, at a cost of $72.80/day.

---

1. See http://alistair.cockburn.us/index.php/Harnessing_convection_currents_of_information_060.

Over the course of a week, that's 350 minutes, almost six hours—darn close to a person-day of work. The monetary value of that time is $364. Every week. Without even trying, this project is losing a person-day every week. The actual time loss estimates here are conservative. There's a good chance that your project is losing even more time and money.

Maybe you're saying, "Oh, we just IM everyone. We don't need to *see* people." Sure, some of the questions can be answered with IM. But not all. And not the ones that take a long time to answer.

If you're a project manager, do whatever you need to do to move the entire team together.

12.2 Identify Your Project's Cultural Differences

The cultural differences might not be obvious if all the sites are in one country, but they exist. I once managed a project where we had a Boston team and a Los Angeles team. We were all part of the same company, but the practices each team used was different. Both teams did nightly builds, but in Boston, everyone checked in their code every day (continuous integration). In Los Angeles, they checked in their code when it was ready for other people to use (staged integration). The difference became most obvious when one of the Los Angeles developers was frustrated with one of the Boston developers. "How could you release code into the code base that you know doesn't work?" The reply was, "How can you make us wait to see what you're thinking?"

Same company. Same products. Different expectations of behavior. That's one of the many ways cultural differences appear.

Expect cultural differences in what people believe they can discuss, in what's rewarded, and in how people treat each other. The example of continuous vs. staged integration is an example of what's rewarded by the functional managers and how people treat each other. In Los Angeles it was unacceptable to promote "unfinished" code into the common code base. In Boston, it was unacceptable to hang onto your code for more than a day before checking it in. Cultural differences appear even within the same social culture. Different teams in different locations develop different customs—their own culture.

When you manage a multisite project, be prepared for all kinds of culture clashes. Remember, the entire project doesn't have to use all the same life cycle, approaches, and practices, but the entire project team must use complementary life cycles, approaches, and practices.

12.3 Build Trust Among the Teams

The most important management technique for multisite projects is to help the teams learn to trust each other.

Teams who have common commitments and interdependent deliverables learn to trust each other as they complete their deliverables and follow through on their commitments. Your job is to help each team develop their commitments and define their deliverables. You can manage the schedule and delivery of interdependent pieces in three ways: make sure each site has complete deliverables to the project, make sure your teams can cooperate with each other, and help people meet each other in person.

Make Sure Each Site Has Complete Deliverables to the Project

When you organize the project, assume each site will complete some unique set of features. Yes, the deliverables are interdependent—they all need to exist in the final product—but each team has responsibility for a functioning deliverable. If you have some developers in one place and testers in another place trying to create working software, you are likely to be disappointed. The necessary communications take too long or don't exist at all. Single-function teams in different sites have this problem.

In addition to not creating single-function teams, don't create team "bits" of developers (or testers or writers or whomever) in multiple places. If you have two developers in Chicago and two developers in Paris, you've got team "bits." It is too hard for people to collaborate on interim deliverables when they're spread over multiple sites. That guarantees blaming each other when things don't work. It is even worse when you have developers in one location, testers in a second location, and writers in a third location.

Make sure that each site has a complete team, which can deliver a complete deliverable to the project—fully running and tested features.

If you don't have enough people in one place to make a team, think of ways for each person to stay in close contact with the rest of the team.

Joe Asks...

Developers in One Site, Testers in Another?

Your management has decided your testers will be separated from your developers. What do you do to succeed?

Organize groups of people across the sites who are responsible for features. "You three developers from Milwaukee and you two testers from Bangalore—you folks are responsible for this widget." You'll need to help the teams build trust and understand how to work together. It's hard.

If you have any choice, reject this option. Opt for cross-functional teams in each location.

Staying in Close Logical Proximity
by Guy, software developer, Switzerland

I'm the only developer in a sales office. I'm working on a project because I have specific skills that the team needs. But I'm the only one here. We have people in Paris and London, too.

To combat my "solo-ness" and make me more of a part of the team, we have an open Skype connection to each other all the time. We each have a camera, so everyone can see what we're doing. It took me a while to get used to be on camera all the time. It's not perfect, but it's better than nothing.

We stay in close logical contact, if not physical contact. That certainly helps me deliver my parts. It would be close to impossible without our contact.

Make Sure Your Teams Can Cooperate with Each Other

As the project manager of a multisite team, your job is to make sure the system doesn't keep people from cooperating. As soon as the teams are in competition with each other—especially if they're concerned about keeping their jobs—you'll be lucky to get any product out the door.

Help People Meet Each Other in Person

If it's financially feasible, bring everyone on the project together at one site for a few days of working together. In addition to working together, include some social activities, such as meals, so people from one site

Interdependent Teams Cannot Be in Competition with Each Other

I once worked with an organization who was trying to reduce the cost of development. They decided the best way to reduce cost was to use lower-cost developers in another part of the world. They had four development teams across Europe and Asia. The European managers were told that if they missed their deadlines, all the work would move to Asia.

The European managers weren't stupid. First, they cherry-picked the features, making sure they took the features they knew they could complete in a short time. The Asian manager realized this after the second time they met to divide up the features, and he was able to obtain some of the not-impossible features.

The European managers started encouraging their architects to design by whiteboard (only) and email small fuzzy pictures of the whiteboard to the Asian developers. The European architects fulfilled the corporate dictum, "Send copies of your architecture to every site," but they ignored the intent of the dictum. Even increasing the size of the picture still left the Asian team confused by the architecture design.

The VP was concerned by the project's slow pace. After talking to the managers, I explained to the VP what one of the managers had said, "I won't help the Asian project team if you insist at putting my developers at risk. I'll make sure we do what we need to do, and that's it. You want cheaper development? Stop pitting us against each other."

This problem was obvious to an outsider. But it was hard to see from the inside, primarily because no one trusted anyone else. Putting teams in competition to keep their jobs is a no-win situation. It destroys trust, encourages people to think of themselves first (and only), and reduces the project's output. Sometimes, the output is not just zero; sometimes people destroy already-achieved features because they were "fixing" something.

Make sure your multisite teams have a common goal—that of the project or program. Never pit team against team.

have a chance to learn about the humanity of the people from other sites. This is different from mandatory fun, as in Section 7.2, *Help the Team Jell*, on page 123. This time together will help the team communicate better when they return to their home sites.

If you can't bring the entire teams together, bring the project managers and technical leads together. The more people, the better. But even a couple of people from each site who meet each other and learn about each other are more likely to trust each other after a few days of working together than people who don't take the time to meet. And, once everyone has met each other, continue to allow periodic travel to and from different sites to maintain that relationship.

You'll need to visit each site periodically as a project manager of a multisite team. You might not need to visit each site every week, or even every month. But make sure you spend some time at each site. I like to conduct project/program team meetings from each site, just so people can see me as I run the meeting. It helps them "see" me when I'm back at my home office.

Once you've started building trust, you can help a multisite project succeed. But if you haven't started the project thinking about how to build trust, you're going to need a lot of luck (and a few miracles) to make your project successful.

People need to meet so they have a context for how people talk in IM or in email. Imagine you see this question in email: "Anything new with you this week?" Try an experiment. Put a different emphasis on each word. With the emphasis on *anything*, people might hear sarcasm or frustration. With the emphasis on *new*, people might hear frustration or impatience. With the emphasis on *you*, people might hear you personally or the project team or your part of the world. The farther away people are, the more likely they are to misunderstand you; they can't hear the context of your conversation.

12.4 Use Complementary Practices on a Team-by-Team Basis

Complementary practices include the project's life cycle and any development, testing, or other management practices the team uses. It does not work for one team to use a waterfall life cycle, delivering everything at the end, and to have another team use an iterative life cycle, looking for periodic feedback.

> ### ᕯ Joe Asks. . .
>
> #### Do I Have the Authority to Ask Each Team to Work in a Specific Way?
>
> You might not think you have the authority to make sure the team is using complementary life cycles and practices. You do. You have to—you're the project manager. If you don't think you can ask people to work in a specific way, ask for results. "I don't care how you accomplish this, but we need that feature developed, integrated, and tested so the Manchester folks can use it in two weeks."

Use Complementary Life Cycles

First make sure each subproject team is using complementary life cycles. Don't use a serial life cycle for a multisite team. It's too hard to obtain feedback early about the project, and the early milestones are too easy to game. Serial life cycles for multisite projects encourage schedule games such as the one discussed in Section 6.13, *Schedule Chicken*, on page 114.

I've been successful when each team used a staged-delivery life cycle across the project. I've also been successful with some teams using early iterations to prototype and obtain feedback and then moving into some form of incremental development. For one project, we timeboxed an eight-week iteration called "Prototype Exploration." Each project team prototyped some of their major features. We then spent two weeks evaluating the prototypes and the architecture that emerged from their prototypes. We moved into three-week timeboxes to implement and test each feature, continually integrating at the end of each timebox. This is a combination of an iterative life cycle (the prototype exploration part), followed by an agile life cycle (the timeboxes part).

A colleague is managing a project where the U.K. team is using two-week XP iterations, the Israeli team is using four-week Scrum iterations, and the California team is using a staged-delivery life cycle. They have to carefully manage who implements what when (which they do using the concepts in Section 16.6, *Build a Product Backlog*, on page 313), and it's working for them.

I don't know how to make multisite projects meet the desired release date with all the features using a serial life cycle, unless you don't care about defects. If you care about time to release, the feature set, and the level of defects, don't use a serial life cycle. At least use iterations, if not some combination of iterations and increments. Especially for a multisite project, the developers and testers need feedback as early as possible.

Define the Milestones and Handoffs for Each Team

Each project's life cycle doesn't have to be identical, but the outputs of each group must match the expectations of the other groups. This matching of expectations reflects complementary practices among the project groups.

As you organize the schedule, make sure everyone agrees on the meaning of important terms and milestones.

Define Each Term's Meaning

Project terms vary from team to team as much as practices do. Many teams have their own interpretations of terms such as *fix, verify, feature freeze,* and *code complete.* You don't have to be part of a multilanguage team to have trouble with terms.

I once managed a second-line support group for a multisite global team, in which there was some confusion about the term *fixed.* The job of the Boston-based group was to fix the defects that the first-line support group could not fix and that were time-critical for our customers. We had a recurring problem with two of our European first-line support groups. The Europeans repeatedly promised imminent fixes to very high-profile customers, because they thought the defects were fixed. However, the defect fixes were not complete. The Boston group was using the notation "Fix" for defects that had been investigated, the cause known, and a fix was in test. "Verified" was the notation for finished fixes—fixes that had been tested and verified as actually fixing the problem and not breaking anything else. It never occurred to our European counterparts that "Fix" was not truly fixed. Just as it never occurred to the Boston group that "Fix" was a final state, instead of "Verified."

Other terms some teams have found confusing are any project milestones containing the words *freeze* or *complete*, such as feature freeze, code freeze, and code complete. (This is another good reason not to use a serial life cycle.) I once worked on a project where the U.S. developers thought *code complete* was the first time they froze the code to create a build. The Russian developers thought *code complete* was the last freeze to create the final build to generate the production master. The technical leads kept arguing during schedule development, until they realized they weren't using the same terms.

Define What the Milestones Mean

Not only does the project team have to agree on what the project's terms and milestones are, you'll need to make sure everyone agrees on what the milestones mean. Many years ago, I was a program manager, trying to bring together project components from Boston, Los Angeles, and Japan. The technical leads and I were working on the schedule. Everything was smooth until we tried to agree on the first milestone: feature freeze. To the Boston team, feature freeze meant that the low-level design was complete. However, to the Los Angeles team, feature freeze meant that they had a good idea of the high-level design. The Los Angeles group couldn't understand why Boston would want complete module interface designs—Los Angeles wanted maximum flexibility to add features to the product as late as possible. The Boston and Japan teams wanted to define the features early, and freeze the interfaces as early as possible, to allow for the customization of the product for Japan.

I brought the technical leads together to talk about what each group needed and when. Initially, the Japanese technical lead was reticent to express his views, concerned that he was pushing his perspective on the entire team. We revisited the project requirements: release the English and Japanese versions of the product within the same calendar month, and create a public API for the English language market. We didn't have time to retrofit features in for the Japanese market.

Instead of pushing for a resolution, I asked each team lead to talk about their problems and what solve their problems. The Boston team needed to freeze the API in time for the Japan team to develop their customizations and for the writers to document the product. The Los Angeles team needed to create enough product infrastructure that they wouldn't have to change the API for the next release. The Japanese team needed to modify the GUI and the data structures for the Japanese market.

The later Boston and Japan defined the features, the harder it was for the Boston and Japanese developers. The earlier the Los Angeles team defined the features, the harder their job was. Once we realized that we were all on the same project but we had different goals, we were able to better articulate what we wanted at which time.

As a project team, we were able to develop our major milestones together by focusing on interim results (what did each group absolutely need by when?). It took us about a week to come to a consensus about what each milestone meant, especially "freeze" milestones, and how we knew we'd met those milestones. Not everyone liked the whole schedule, but we could all live with it.

I call this technique of defining milestones by the results you want *discuss and publish*. Some teams chose to define interim milestones in addition to the milestones defined in the overall project plan. When the teams agree on what each project milestone means, you can develop a joint project schedule and understand what you have to do to achieve those milestones.

Define How the Team Will Know the Team They Met a Milestone

When managing multisite projects, don't mandate how each team should work to achieve their deliverables. Clarify the results you want. Already-established teams generally have some built-in practices, including work product review, configuration management, product build, product test, and others. For example, although I strongly believe in nightly builds and smoke tests, I don't demand each project team perform nightly builds. Instead, I focus on defining the results I want and managing the risk of achieving those results. I ask for Big Visible Charts, posted on an intranet site that every team can access.

Say you're managing a project with three sites: Manchester (England), New York, and San Francisco. You've got your hands full with the time zone problems, but you and the team leads have agreed on a standard time to have conference calls. You're using four-week timeboxes to complete features. And you've worked with the New York team before. You're a little concerned that they don't know how to finish the testing within the timebox. You need an approach that will help you and each team know that they're finishing the work within the timebox.

Since you want to manage by looking for results, not what people have done, you can ask the team leads to explain their testing status on specific days of the week, so you—and that particular team—can know whether their testing is maintaining the same pace as development. You can also ask the team to publicly post their test status with a testing dashboard. See Section 11.2, *Display Qualitative Data*, on page 223 for one approach to show progress.

When the team is responsible for some Big Visible Chart, the team is more likely monitor it and their progress.

Tip: Manage for Results

For any team, manage for results, not for approaches or practices. This is especially critical for multisite teams, where you can't manage by walking around and listening [RD05].

Use retrospectives to help people assess their practices and decide what to continue or change. But don't mandate a particular way of working. Be clear on the results you want.

Discuss How the Team Will Review Work Products

After you agree on the milestones, attack the subject of technical reviews. All projects benefit from reviews. If people aren't collocated, you might have to suggest a variety of approaches to reviews. (I have never seen pair programming work across physical locations. Sure, it can work once in a while, but I haven't seen it as a sustainable practice where some people are in one location and other people are in a separate location.)

And especially on multisite projects, technical reviews provide an additional communications framework and a context in which to discuss the project issues. Some people are uncomfortable talking about the projectwide issues. Those people might be less reluctant to discuss the technical side of the project, and requirements and architecture reviews provide a framework for them to air issues. Given your life cycles, consider how to schedule requirements and architecture reviews for the project. Don't forget about other documents if you have them, such as design or functional specs, and especially code.

This is why an agile life cycle is so helpful for multisite teams. The life cycle enforces the idea that reviews are necessary, as well as makes sure all development (including testing and documentation) is completed during timebox.

Understand the Effects of Time Zones on Team Progress

In the early days of multisite teams, many senior managers thought, "I have teams working across the globe. They can make progress on my project twenty-four hours a day."

Don't drink the Kool-Aid. It is possible to make some progress with teams all over the world, assuming your project is not responsible for considerable innovation and the cost of development doesn't matter.

The more innovation required, the more accessible the project team members need to be. If Dan (in San Mateo) has a great idea at 11 a.m. and wants to share that idea with Vijay (in Bangalore), it's 12:30 a.m. the next day. Dan and Vijay they need to find time to discuss it together. Dan is not going to call Vijay then. He's going to wait. That costs the project time and money; see Section 12.1, *What Does a Question Cost You?*, on page 236.

The more critical time to release is, the worse the effect of time zones on your project. If you are stuck with teams all over the world, move to short iterations with each team responsible for their deliverables, so they have as few questions as possible.

The more time zones in your project and the more cultural differences in your project, the harder it is to make multisite development work.

On multisite projects, people across sites rarely have the ability to even informally pair. If you create a review mechanism anyone can use, you're more likely to have a solid product than if you don't.

If you initiate technical reviews at the beginning of the project, the individual project groups are more likely to continue with technical reviews for their pieces of the project. I do this by having charter, plan, and schedule reviews at the beginning of the project. Even if you don't want to have the project teams review all of your work, hold a programwide review of release criteria. Ask them how they will turn the program's release criteria into their release criteria for their part of the project.

When you encourage your project team to review your work, you are creating an environment that encourages other people to ask for review.

That environment is great for any project and is especially useful for multisite teams. The more work product review, the more people are likely to understand how their piece fits into the whole and how the whole product is supposed to work.

You might find that your multisite project requires more formal requirements and architecture reviews than other projects; the formalism helps reduce the risk of communications problems. Some people might not comment except in a formal review mechanism—some people might not realize you want them to comment unless you have a formal review mechanism. Even if people are willing to comment on requirements and architecture, if you don't make time in the project, the people from various teams will not be able to comment. After all, on an multisite project, you're not going to run into each other in the cafeteria.

You can use formal requirements and architectural reviews to ensure that everyone on the project understands the project objectives. The formal reviews should include at least one technical representative from each project team. These participants agree that the requirements are correct and can be implemented by the team.

For iterative and agile life cycles, I request that the requirements and architecture discussion be limited to *this* iteration's requirements and architecture. For incremental life cycles, I request that the discussion be limited to this deliverable or set of deliverables across the project (this staged delivery piece) and that the team will review the next piece before implementing the next piece. Ask the teams to focus on reviewing the interfaces, not the internals of the feature.

Review and inspection of documents across the world (or even just thirty miles away) is not easy. I have encountered problems with email-only reviews and inspections of requirements and architecture documents in these areas:

- The people who first read the work product "direct" the discussion. Some people are too shy to bring up their issues electronically. Those shy people don't participate, reducing the value of the review.
- Some people don't read the product once other people start commenting. They assume someone else will take care of the issues.
- It is difficult to get people to agree on a consistent commenting style. If you can arrange an early entire project-team meeting in one location, this is one problem the team could address.

What's different about these problems in multisite projects? The more sites and the more time zones apart the participants are, the more the cultural differences show. And, the harder those difference are to resolve. Also, people tend to use written documents, including email, as a CYA (which stands for *cover your tush*) technique, instead of a helpful review. If you want to resolve issues without threatening anyone, talk to the other person. Again, time zone issues make this difficult.

The cultural differences (specifically what people feel free to discuss and therefore the focus of the discussion) cannot be bridged without some audio contact. I prefer face-to-face discussions, but when that's not practical, videoconferences might work. For a team with a successful history, conference calls might be adequate. In my experience, the way people use and understand language to write specs and their comments tends to prevent effective email reviews. This is especially true when most of the project teams are native English speakers and a minority are not native English speakers. I prefer to get the technical people together in person to review requirements and architecture documents. I find that the travel cost is significantly less than the potential risk of product failure.

If you're working on a very short project and are willing to take the risk of inadequately meeting the needs of some potential customers, consider some of the Internet-based tools for meetings, coupled with an excellent audio connection. Make sure the moderator is a skilled meeting facilitator, especially when it comes to conference calls. (See Section 10.10, *Manage Conference Calls with Remote Teams*, on page 197.)

12.5 Look for Potential Multisite Project and Multicultural Problems

Multisite projects might well have their share of technical problems. Multisite projects tend to be larger and require program as well as project management. In my experience, any strictly technical or product problem solving is secondary to managing the people interaction issues. When managing multicultural projects, look for problems in these areas:

- The teams in each site might define their milestones and handoffs differently. That leads to the teams misunderstanding their commitments and handoffs to other groups. Sometimes the different definitions are because of a lack of understanding of the actual words. Sometimes, people differ on their meaning of commitment—is a commitment a best-effort agreement, or will the team do whatever it takes to meet the commitment? Whatever the cause, different meanings for milestones can be overcome with complementary product development practices, especially in project planning, project scheduling, and technical review.

- Expect to see uneven project communications and reporting of project state, especially at the beginning of the project. Not being able to see what other people are doing can lead to lack of trust in other teams. If you don't know what other people are doing, you might not think you can trust them. Especially when geography and culture separate teams, this lack of trust can be a huge obstacle to project success.

- Especially with teams whose native languages are different, you might not know what other people are saying. Language differences and everyone's relative ability to use one common language can create many problems in a project. What language are you using as the default language? What kinds of ambiguities do you have in that language? How fluent are all the project participants in the project's language? Is everyone willing to talk to everyone else, or are there cultural mores that make some people uncomfortable talking to certain teams or team members? Make sure that the language you use for written and spoken communications is adequate for everyone.

- There can also be communications problems with regard to holidays, vacations, and overtime. Be specific about what vacations mean, the impact of everyone's national holidays on the project's schedule, and general expectations about overtime—these will all affect how the project participants work with each other and report on project state.

- Make sure everyone knows what the "end of the day" or some other time for a deliverable is. For example, 5 p.m. in Boston is 2 p.m. in California and some other time in Taiwan or India, depending on the time of year.

- Uneven ability to use common tools, such as the configuration management system, defect-tracking system, and the project's intranet. The tools encourage sharing designs, source code, tests, and other project information. When some members of the project team can't use the project resources, they might resent the people who can use those resources. In addition, they might stop trying to share their work with the rest of the project team.

Interim retrospectives (see Section 8.2, *Conduct Interim Retrospectives*, on page 144) can help identify—and solve—these problems and others that are particular to your project. If you can't bring everyone together, use retrospectives at each site, and gather the site project managers to solve the cross-site problems together.

12.6   Avoid These Mistakes When Outsourcing

I wanted to call this section "How to Outsource Successfully." But I can't. I can't claim to have experienced true success on outsourced projects. I have managed outsourced projects where we met the date but did not save money. I've managed outsourced projects where we saved the money but did not deliver what the customers really wanted. And I've rescued too many outsourced projects where the defects overwhelmed the project team, the schedule was wishful thinking, and the project cost 200–500% more than the hoped-for budget.

If you have to use an outsourced team as part of your project, keep these tips[2] in mind:

- Train the outsourcing staff. The outsourcing staff needs to know how the product works, both from the internals and from the perspective of knowing the problems the customer wants to solve.
- Qualify the vendor. Does the vendor have domain knowledge? Is it financially viable? Are there contractual safeguards in place to keep control over the intellectual property you give it?
- Assign one of your best project managers as your internal project manager. Sure, the outsourcer has a project manager. That person will need to talk to people in your office to make sure their team understands deliverables and handoffs around the organization.
- Develop a trusting relationship with a manager or the project manager at the outsourcer to help you understand the reality of what's happening in the project.
- Plan for your in-house staff to shift their work hours, as well as the outsourcing staff, so that people can make time to talk to each other. If you don't shift enough people to work earlier or later in the day, then someone across the world who has a problem won't have someone to talk to. Too often, when an engineer at least eight time zones away needs information, no one is in the office, and no

---

2.   http://www.computerworld.com/managementtopics/outsourcing/story/0,10801,84847,00.html.

one can be reached. Instead of round-the-clock work, the work is stopped until the engineer can determine the answer.

This is a lot to ask of people. You're asking people to change their work hours to accommodate people who might be taking away their jobs or who have taken away the jobs of people who used to be down the hall. Don't expect your staff to agree to this and stick around—unless the economy is so bad they can't find another job.

- Document the requirements. If your native technical staff can't read your mind about what you want in the product, how can geographically distant, non-native English speakers understand your requirements?

- Develop an appropriate change process. Especially if you have development occurring in multiple sites around the world, you need a clear change process to make sure only the changes you want are allowed.

- Select outsource projects with nonvolatile requirements. If your requirements change frequently and you need to check out the evolving product with the user, development across the world makes that much harder.

- Plan for each project to take longer and cost more, especially at the beginning of an outsourcing relationship. My rule of thumb is to increase the estimated time by 30% for the first project. Then monitor the project to see whether you need to increase that estimate.

- Insist that the outsourcing company keep the same team for your project's duration. Otherwise, the time you spent training their people on your product is wasted, and you'll have to start the training process again.

- Make sure you have the tools, information systems, and processes in place to support the outsourced teams. They'll need access to the source code, defect-tracking system, database or other platform applications, builds, and so on—the same project tools that the internal teams need.

- Verify that the people who said they'd be working on the project are the ones actually working on the project. U.S. firms have been using the bait-and-switch approach to contracting for years. Senior staff sell the project and then proceed to the next potential sucker—er, client—while new college grads and other underexperienced staff work on your project.

Well, guess what? The non-U.S. outsourcing firms have learned the same technique. If you don't verify who is working on your project, your project could be the learning ground for their staff to build their resumes.

Remember This

- Any team that's not collocated on the same floor within about thirty feet is a multisite team.
- Managing multisite teams takes longer and more facilitation skills than collocated teams.
- If you can't build trust with remote teams, your project cannot succeed.

Chapter 13

Integrating Testing into the Project

Testing is more than system testing or unit testing. There's a whole range of testing you need to consider for your project. You might need unit testing with stubs if you have product with firmware or hardware or a number of other systems to integrate. You might need several-features-together testing before final system testing. Because each project is unique, you'll need to think about the testing required. Use your project's risks to decide what kinds of testing you need.

I'm suggesting that you, the project manager, initiate the planning for testing. If you don't plan to integrate testing into the development, it won't happen. You'll end up with testing as a separate set of project tasks and tasks that will start later, take longer, and turn whatever life cycle you have into a serial life cycle, extending the project and delaying feedback to the developers. Concurrent development and testing will help you integrate testing from the beginning of your project.

13.1 Start People with a Mind-Set Toward Reducing Technical Debt

It's the first day on a new project, and your team is assembled and ready to go. You have everything in place—everything except the requirements. You can start the project team fixing defects from a previous release. It doesn't even matter whether the product they are working on is a predecessor of the one on which they will be working.

The key is to help the developers and testers start the project thinking about the consequences of taking shortcuts in their practices.

If you're working on a follow-on release, the team's work will pay down technical debt (see Appendix B, on page 335). If you're working on a new product, you can assign some of the team to prototyping activities and some of the team to use their defect-fixing activities as a way to learn what temptations to avoid in this project.

If you decide to pay down technical debt first, explain your goal to the project team. "We took a lot of shortcuts on the last project, and it bit us in the tush. As you fix things, see which practices we want to make sure to use on this project so we aren't bit again." You can even hold a short retrospective [DL06] before the team starts the new work in order to incorporate what they've learned from fixing problems.

13.2 Reduce Risks with Small Tests

Your project isn't easy. You've got serious technical or schedule risk. The wider variety of testing you use on your project, the more you can reduce risks. If you need to choose just one type of test to begin with, make it unit tests. The best way to implement unit tests is with test-driven development (TDD), but if you can't get your team to write their tests before they write the production code, at least get them to write the tests soon after writing the code.

The reason to choose TDD over any other kind of testing is simple: TDD is actually more about design than it is about testing.

TDD has been around since the 1970s [Bro95]. It's more accepted and practiced on projects now, because it's one of the core practices of XP. But you don't need to be practicing XP to use TDD. Any life cycle can benefit from using TDD. See Section 13.3, *TDD Is the Easiest Way to Integrate Testing into Your Project*, on the facing page for more details.

Developers Write Code *and* Defects

Developers write code. (They also architect, design, and elicit requirements.) But some of them forget they also write defects. If a developer is having a bad code day, it's possible for a developer to write many more defects than lines of working code [HT03].

If your developers wait until the end of the project to find their defects, they're ignoring the earliest and cheapest feedback available to them: unit testing their code. Unit tests, developed either just before writing the code (test-driven development) or just after writing a few lines of code, are the cheapest way to find and fix defects. It's also a great prevention technique for preventing more of the same defects (and waiting until the end of development is expensive; see Section 11.2, *Measure How Much It Costs You to Find and Fix Problems*, on page 219).

Even with the great compilers we have today, it's possible for developers to make coding mistakes. Unit testing will find coding mistakes, and not just those caught by design environments or compilers.

Maybe your developers are saying, "Hey, we're using a real high-level language, so we're not able to have memory leaks or any of those foolish mistakes. We don't need to unit test." The higher level the language, the more the developer can make logic mistakes. The worse the logic mistake, the harder it is to find it on the system testing part of the testing continuum. It's much easier to find those mistakes with unit testing.

There's an even better reason to develop unit tests, especially when a developer uses test-driven development. Those unit tests help the developer design the system, not just discover defects. The act of writing a little test before writing the code helps the developer see what to do in the code more clearly.

Unit tests find defects and help a developer design the system more cheaply than any other debugging mechanism.

13.3 TDD Is the Easiest Way to Integrate Testing into Your Project

You think integrating testing with development is a good way to go. And you're not sure whether your testers can manage to keep up with the developers. But you know that if you don't somehow integrate testing with development, your project is not going to be successful. There is a solution.

TDD will help you (the project manager and the project team) integrate testing into the project. In fact, if you can't depend on having dedicated testers and dedicating testing machines, test-driven development will dramatically reduce the testing risks on your project.

TDD follows this flow:

1. The developer (or pair of developers if pair programming) creates a test for a new feature that has not yet been written. That test should fail, because the code to implement the feature doesn't exist yet.
2. Then the developer/pair adds the simplest code that can make the test pass.
3. The developer/pair reruns the test. If the code does pass the test, the developer refactors to simplify the code. If the code doesn't pass the test, the developer fixes the code. During the fixing, the developer refactors the code, revising it to make it simpler, faster, more maintainable—preventing technical debt.
4. As the developer/pair continues, the developer/pair runs all the tests to make sure they have not introduced any regressions. The developer/pair follows this loop until all the features are implemented.

Test-driven development is developing from the inside out. Does that mean you can't design up front? No, but it doesn't make sense to do highly detailed design (also known as *big design up front* [BDUF]), because the developers will be able to take advantage of symmetry in the code (which they will see when they refactor) and the evolving, emerging design. In my experience, emergent design is simpler than what you think the design will be at the beginning.

Projects with any life cycle can use test-driven development. If you're using a serial life cycle, you can ask the developers to use test-driven development to reduce the risk of finding too many defects at the end. Of course, if you're using an agile life cycle with two-week or less iterations, you'll need to use test-driven development to meet the goal of releasable software at the end of an iteration.

If you want to reduce risk in your project, start with TDD on the highest-risk areas. If you want to increase the value of your eventual product, start with TDD on the highest value areas. Talk to your developers and testers about whether to start with the highest risk areas or the highest value areas. See Section 9.3, *Implement the Highest-Value Features First*, on page 172.

If you're exploring prototypes at the beginning of a project, it's possible you might not need TDD. But I don't recommend it, especially if your developers don't throw away their prototypes. In my experience,

Joe Asks...

How Can I get My Developers to Use TDD?

TDD looks like a project-saver to me. How do I get my developers to use it?

First, make sure you're not measuring developers just on meeting their dates. When anyone tries a new practice, it will take them a little longer to accomplish work because they're trying something out of their normal routine. The time you lose in the coding phase in a serial life cycle, you'll more than gain in the testing part of the life cycle. But make sure the developers have the schedule flexibility to try a new practice.

Second, offer articles, blog entries for reading, and training. Do not expect people to adopt a new practice without any training. And if you're worried about the cost of training, measure your cost to fix a defect. (Review the last project, during the final testing phase and post-release. My rule of thumb is that the cost of training is generally lower than one post-release defect and much less than ten to twenty prerelease defects.)

Then, ask for volunteers. Do not make TDD a mandatory practice. Say something like this: "I am worried about the risk of finding too many defects at the end of the project, when we have fewer choices about what to do. I hear that TDD can help us with this. Anyone want to try it for a couple of weeks and see what happens?"

You might not get any volunteers at first. If not, be prepared to measure velocity (see Figure 11.1, on page 205) and defects (see Figure 11.12, on page 222). Remember, you can't count anything as done in the velocity chart until it's complete, meeting milestone criteria. Show the project team the charts on the Big Visible Chart you've set up.

At the end of the project, especially if the defect counts are too high, you can institute TDD as part of your practices before checking fixes into the code base. Once the developers have tried it once, they are much more likely to do it again on the next project.*

---

*. For more information about TDD, see http://www.testdriven.com and http://behaviour-driven.org.

developing the tests first helps drive algorithm and structure design in the code. The more data the developers have about the code, the better their decisions will be—and the lower the project risks will be.

Unit Testing Is Not a Panacea

Even though unit testing is the fastest and cheapest way to find defects, unit tests are not all created equal. The key is that developers must unit test all their code to reap the benefits of unit testing. You can use a code coverage tool to measure this. Often even talented, well-meaning developers are not providing the range of tests needed to truly exercise their code. When developers don't see unit testing as being part of their job, the unit tests they write are worse than none at all. You have the false sense that the code is being tested when it isn't.

Bryan was a developer who didn't believe in unit testing. But the project team decided everyone had to write tests. Bryan wrote tests. If he needed four tests for a given piece of code, he wrote four tests. He wrote four of the same tests. He didn't write the four tests to exercise the code; he wrote one test four times, varying data values. (For some code, varying data values would be helpful; in this case it was not.)

Bryan had another trick when it came to fixing defects. He would write a unit test for pieces of the code, except for the part he had fixed.

Eventually the project manager booted him off the project. Don't think that just because your developers say they're unit testing, they actually are.

Don't audit your developers or punish them for not unit testing. Make it worth their while to unit test. Introduce them to TDD. Explain why you want unit tests. Track the cost to fix a defect and explain how many of those found defects could have been caught in unit testing. In Bryan's case, the project manager could have asked people to peer review code and unit tests. Bryan would have received feedback from a peer much earlier. Use your influence so developers want to unit test.

13.4 Use a Wide Variety of Testing Techniques

Testing illuminates the risks in your project and reduces technical debt (see Appendix B, on page 335). The more encompassing the testing (the more at the system level), the more it illuminates overall product risks. The more focused the testing is on a certain piece (the more

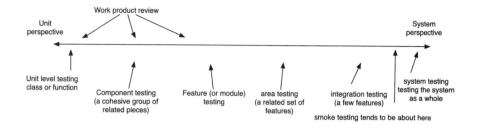

Figure 13.1: A CONTINUUM OF TESTING

transparent—white box—the testing is), the more it reduces technical debt.

I encounter too many project teams where the only testing is system-level testing from manual black-box testers. Our systems are too complex for manual black-box testing to be your only testing technique.

When I talk about integrating testing into the project, I mean all kinds of testing, not just what the testers do. In Figure 13.1, you can see there are many types of testing.

Unit level testing, a developer job, is testing that the few lines of code the developer will write, or just wrote, works. In my experience, it's difficult for developers to maintain 100% unit test coverage unless they write the tests first.

Component testing occurs when the developer organizes a few units together to see whether they work as advertised. Again, component testing is easier to do (and know that your team has done) if they use test-first development.

Feature testing is when you test a feature in totality. If you're not implementing by feature (why not?), this could also be module testing. I prefer that developers perform feature testing first so they can verify that the feature does what it's supposed to do (positive path). Then I ask the testers to test to see that the feature doesn't do anything else (negative path).

Area testing, to see how a number of features intersect with each other, tends to be a tester job, not a developer job.

> ## Joe Asks...
> ### Why Should I Care About Unit Test Coverage?
>
> You might think 100% unit test coverage (basis path coverage, covering each decision) seems like a lot to ask, especially for developers who haven't used TDD before. But 100% unit test coverage provides benefits to the developers and the rest of the project:
>
> - If you need to refactor a scary piece of code, you already know your tests will tell you whether you've made a mistake.
>
> - Unit tests promote better interfaces, because the developer has to use her own interface to test the code. *
>
> - The cost to find and fix a defect becomes quite small.
>
> - Finally, 100% unit test coverage allows the original developer to move on to other assignments, because it's clear how the code works from the tests.
>
> Even with 100% coverage, the code might have logic mistakes. You won't know what the code is missing. But you'll know more about the code than if you don't have any tests or just a small number of unit tests.
>
> ---
> *. See http://haacked.com/archive/2004/12/06/1704.aspx.

Integration testing tends to happen in multiple steps. If the developers are using continuous integration, you'll get positive-path integration testing for free. You might not learn whether there are subtle side effects until the testers get their mitts on the code.

Developers write smoke tests, which are tests that verify that the system can do something after a build.

Testers develop and run system-level tests.

Work product review (buddy review, peer review, inspection) can occur at a variety of levels. People who are technical peers can review each other's work, whether those people are developers or testers.

Testing is about reducing the risk of unknown problems in the product. To reduce the risk, make sure every team member understands what his or her testing role is, use a wide variety of testing techniques, and make the testing as concurrent as possible with the development.

As you define how each team member will test the product, consider the testing continuum. The developers will perform much of the testing from the leftmost side (unit testing) through integration testing. If you have a release engineer or testers who can write great smoke tests, it might be worth having those people write smoke tests.

13.5 Define Every Team Member's Testing Role

It's too easy for developers to think their job is restricted to designing and writing code. They don't see a need for testing along the way. If you don't care how good the code is, I can write all the code you need. In an afternoon. With one hand tied behind my back. But would that code work? Not a chance.

I bet you care whether the code works. And I bet your developers do too. Too many developers are unaware that when they write code they also write defects. The way to write fewer defects is to have continuous review of the work products and to find the defects faster.

If everyone is testing all the time, why do you need system testing? System testing helps the team see the problems that don't appear until the system is built with all the pieces. Without system testing, it takes a tremendous amount of team discipline to continue all the other testing activities. How much risk can you take? Is your team ready to accept the responsibility for finding all their own problems? Not many teams are.

Managing a Project with (Virtually) No System Testing

Big Cheese Manager called the project team together. "We need a new release with these new features in four months. Make it happen."

The team got together and as a rough estimate suspected they had eight months of work. They had no idea how to finish the project in four months with the people they had.

The project manager begged for more developers—no extra people were available. He begged for more testers—no testers were available. He returned to the project team and said, "We have to change what we're doing, because we aren't getting more people."

The developers decided that they would code review all the code and write automated unit tests for all the code. The single tester maintained the automated regression tests that already existed for the product.

At first, the developers wrote unit tests after the code. But every so often, the developers forgot to write all the tests, which they discovered during code reviews. The developers decided to try TDD.

The project team was able to deliver a product in five months (not the four that the Big Cheese had promised). And, they all spent time developing more automated system tests post-release.

The product won an award and generated enough revenue to prevent layoffs. This project team continued their TDD and code review practices.

The reason this team succeeded was because the developers were orthodox about their testing and review practices. (And there was no GUI for the product. A product with any significant GUI would have been quite difficult to develop and test with just developer testing.) If the developers had relaxed their practices at all, they would not have succeeded.

System testing is still necessary. If your project team cannot match the rigor that these developers used, you will need system testing. If you have a system with a substantial GUI, you will need system testing. And if you want to reduce overall technical risk, you'll need system testing.

Can Your Testers Do the Job?

Testing a complex system is just as difficult as creating one. Just creating unit tests that test each path or object individually is not sufficient testing for a complex system. You might also need product experts to test the system. Sometimes you need people who understand the design of the system, even if they don't have any coding background. Sometimes you need fabulous exploratory testers, people who want to see how they can break the software. And, sometimes you need testers who can develop maintainable automated tests. The larger the system, the more likely the system will hang around for more years than anyone can believe, and well-designed, well-developed automated regression tests that don't require much maintenance can save you money.

If you think that testers exist only to find defects in the code, you're not receiving the full value of your testers, and any new testers you hire won't be able to keep up with the developers. You'll have a second-class test group. Take a moment to take the survey in Figure 13.2, on the next page.

	Yes	No
Are your testers routinely excluded from requirements or design meetings?		
Do your tests resort to eavesdropping to hear information about the product?		
Are your testers' requests for tools postponed or ignored?		
Are product testability requirements postponed or ignored?		
Is the testers' per-person training budget significantly less than the developers' budget?		
Are all your testers interchangeable, i.e., they have such similar skills it doesn't matter who works on which projects?		
For non-agile projects: Do your testers work with developers on the code only after the product is built, either because they're not brought into the project early enough to work with requirements and design or because they don't know enough about requirements and design to supply feedback?		
For agile projects: Do your testers work only with the product owner to develop tests, because they don't understand the internals of the product enough to work with the developers to help build more complex tests?		

Figure 13.2: ARE YOUR TESTERS SECOND-CLASS?

If you answered "yes" to even half of the questions in Figure 13.2, your testers are second-class. They are excluded from key discussions and prevented from obtaining the tools and product expertise they need to do their jobs. The project team probably doesn't do it intentionally. Usually, the testers don't know enough about the technical side of testing, they don't have the knowledge or skills to test the product adequately, and management is afraid to "waste" money hiring people who have other expertise, because the managers can't perceive an adequate return on their investment.

But if you're serious about saving time and money on your project and if you're serious about managing technical risk, you need first-class testers.

First-class testers are sufficiently creative to assess the design and architecture of the system before the code is written. While the code is under construction, first-class testers design and implement their testing harnesses, both automated and manual, creating tests that stress the system in ways the developers do not expect. First-class testers can measure what they've tested, assess the risk of what they've tested, and know whether they've tested enough of the system to help you understand the risks of product release. First-class testers keep up with developers, assuming the developers are using continuous integration and not checking in a week's worth (or more) of code at one time.

First-class testers have a peer relationship with developers. They work as partners, not as adversaries. Great testers alter the way the developers create the product.

When the testers understand the product and find problems early, the developers tend to be more interested in creating a product with fewer defects for the testers to find. Why? Because the testers are their peers, and peer recognition is a significant motivator for developers and other technical staff.

When testers develop appropriate tests that detect more problems early, the developers have more flexibility in choosing how and when to fix them. When testers can't detect problems early, the developers are faced with the dilemma of having to choose which one or two of ten significant problems found in the last scheduled week of the project they should fix. No matter what they choose, the developers will be unhappy with their result.

You might think that because developers want to be proud of their products, they would look for problems early and fix them early. Many of the developers I've met do. However, the developers are not testers, looking at the big picture of the whole system. Developers usually can't see their own defects, so they can't detect all the problems in their work products. And, the larger and more complex the system, the less likely the developers will see their defects.

When testers help developers see their problems early, the developers are more likely to include the testers in other requirements and design discussions. The developers are more likely to build testability into the product by defining APIs or other hooks for testing.

Testers need to know about or have the ability to learn about these kinds of testing: boundary condition testing, equivalence partitioning, combinatorial testing, exploratory testing, and testing the product from end-to-end, not just testing requirement-by-requirement.[1] You can train people on test techniques if they have the ability to understand the product design or look into the code and read it. You can't train people on these test techniques if they don't have the ability to understand product architecture and design or the ability to read code. They need one or the other. Both is even better.

First-class testers do more than find and report defects; they supply information about the product to the entire organization. Sometimes that information includes test results, defect reports, or data about the system's performance. Sometimes, the information is feedback about requirements or design. The more information your testers provide to the developers, the requirements people, the writers, and anyone else involved in product development, the more valuable they are. Properly done, testing will reduce your cost to market, the risks of releasing with outrageous defects, and the cost of ongoing maintenance.

If your testers are not first-class testers, you will need to manage the risks of finding too many defects too late in the project. Try using short iterations, with test-driven development. Hire someone who can help develop automated system-level tests, and use the testers you have for exploratory testing. And think about what you will do for the next project. You have a project team who will take too long to complete their work.

13.6 What's the Right Developer-to-Tester Ratio?

It doesn't matter whether I teach, coach, or assess projects. Almost everyone has this question: "How many testers do we need?" The short answer is enough to be able to assess the state of the product.[2]

Testing is another technique for managing risk—the risk that the product you're developing somehow won't meet the customers' needs or the risk that you can't get enough testing done to assess the product state. Developers can (and should) certainly perform some testing, but developers are blind to the defects they create.

---

1. For more information about testing techniques, see [CK02].
2. See http://www.jrothman.com/Papers/ItDepends.html.

Too often, managers are looking for some kind of industry standards to justify their claims, so they can influence their senior managers. There are some resources available, including [CS98] and the software engineering FAQ.[3] These resources discuss developer-to-tester ratios from 1:1.5 to 10:1, including organizations, such as Microsoft, that have ratios that are 1:1 [CS98]. With such a wide variability, you can't just choose someone else's ratios, you have to analyze your situation and derive an appropriate number of testers for your situation. That analysis needs to consider the following:

- The requirements, product size, and complexity of the product. The more complex the product, the more complex the testing.

- How your organization develops products, and your customers' tolerance for defects and ship delays. The more serial your life cycle, the more testers you will need unless the developers are highly proactive about finding defects.

- Your development and test staff's abilities and responsibilities and when they are assigned to the project.

Since these issues are different for every organization, you and your organization have to analyze the choices you're making for products, process, and people. You might be able to apply the same analysis again, as a rule of thumb on future projects, if you continue to make the same choices and if your products and processes don't change.

How Product Risks Affects the Ratio

Product complexity affects the number of testers. The more complex the product, the more testing you need. Testing is not necessarily testers. Some testing can be automated and easily done by developers. But seeing how the whole system works together is best done by professional testers.

Figure 13.3, on the next page is one way to look at product complexity.

You might have other product risks. I've seen problems with systems that had outgrown their architecture—it was close to impossible to add more features without causing problems in the system. As you assess your product, place an *X* in each column where you think you have risk. The more *X*s, the more testing you'll need.

---

3. See http://www.faqs.org/faqs/software-eng/testing-faq/.

Product Risk	In Your System?
Large system	
Complex, real-time	
No well-defined API	
Data-dependent GUI	

Figure 13.3: POTENTIAL AREAS OF PRODUCT RISK

How Project and Process Risks Affects the Ratio

The more serial the life cycle, the more testers you will need. That's because even if the project team has been reviewing documents, the developers have not been receiving feedback on the code (because it's not built yet). The team will need more eyes and more time at the end to see how the whole system works together.

The more the team uses feedback as the product is under development, such as test-driven development, unit testing, pair programming, reviews, or inspections, the fewer testers you will need. The less the team uses these practices, the more testers you will need because the developers have not obtained feedback about their code.

The more the developers have used inch-pepples (see Section 8.10, *Use Inch-Pebbles*, on page 158) and the more they implement by feature (see Section 9.3, *Implement by Feature, Not by Architecture*, on page 170), the more they understand what they're doing. The more the developers understand what they've done and what they have yet to complete, the fewer testers you need.

If you're using a serial lifecycle, several project and process risks will demand you add more testers, as in Figure 13.4, on the facing page. Put an *X* next to any technique in this chart that you are *not* regularly using. The more *X*s, the more testers you'll need.

How People and Their Capabilities Affect the Ratio

The more capable your developers, the fewer testers you need. The more capable your testers, the fewer testers you need. If you hire developers who don't test their work or if you hire all one kind of tester and they can't test the product in depth, you will need more testers.

Not only can one developer impact the number of testers needed, but also variation in abilities is a key issue for determining the number of testers needed. DeMarco and Lister [DL99] discovered significant variation in technical team members' capabilities during their coding war games.

Productivity does not always correlate positively with experience. Good developers and testers are not always the oldest ones or the ones with the most experience. Productivity has much more to do with self-discipline and understanding, as well as solution-space domain expertise. There is considerable variation in people's abilities.

Project and Process Risks	Place an X in this column if you don't reliably do these on your project
We consistently define and manage our requirements.	
We know how to evaluate the product architecture as the project proceeds.	
We evaluate each feature's design.	
We implement by feature.	
We have and use a unit test infrastructure for automated unit testing.	
We have a test infrastructure for automated system testing.	
We maintain a daily build rhythm.	
We always review open defects in a cross-functional team to assess impact.	
We have and use a daily build and smoke test.	

Figure 13.4: POTENTIAL PROJECT AND PROCESS RISKS

People Risks	In your project?
Our developers don't have a lot of experience with this kind of product.	
Our testers don't have a lot of experience with this kind of product.	
We haven't built feedback into the development team's practices.	
The people on the test team have limited testing ability and provide developers with limited feedback.	

Figure 13.5: POTENTIAL AREAS OF PEOPLE RISK

Consider the people risks in Figure 13.5. The more *X*s, the more testers you'll need.

I've worked on projects where we had ratios of one developer to one tester, and we didn't have enough testing. I've worked on projects where we had ratios of six developers to one tester, and we had enough testing. There is no one right ratio.

But you can ask yourself and the project team these questions:

- How do I estimate the effort needed to test this product *here*?
- What kinds of testing do we need for this product?
- How many of what kinds of testers will it take to do that work here?
- How do I know how many testers it will take to keep up with development for this project?

Review your product attributes. Add up your *X*s, and see how risky your project is. Then review how your team develops the project. Can you check off any of the proactive defect-finding activities? If so, that reduces the risk of insufficient testing. Then look at the pressures on your project.

Do you have substantial pressure to ship by a certain date, or are your customers intolerant of shipped defects? That increases the risk and implies you should have more testers.

Then review the team's capabilities on the project. Do your developers know how to create product in a low-defect way? Do they understand the product? How flexible are your testers? Can they change how they test according to where in the project they are and the kind of product they're testing? If you can't check off any of the people attributes here, you have substantial risk and will need more people.

There is no One Right Answer for the developer-to-tester ratio. Analyze the problem before you can give an answer. It all depends—and what it really depends on is the analysis you perform of the risks and trade-offs.

13.7 Make the Testing Concurrent with Development

Since testing illuminates the risks in a project, the sooner everyone sees those risks, the better. In a serial life cycle, bring the testers in during requirements. Ask for their feedback about product requirements. In an iterative life cycle, ask the testers to help evaluate prototypes. In an incremental life cycle, have the testers start testing features as soon as there are any to test. And in an agile life cycle, make sure the testers work with both the developers to develop the technology-facing tests and with the product owners to develop customer-facing tests.[4]

13.8 Define a Test Strategy for Your Project

If you have a test manager or a test lead, defining the strategy is that person's job. You'll need to review it and make sure you agree with that person's assessment of the risks.

Decide whether you need a formal system test phase for your product. If you work in a regulated industry and you use an agile life cycle, you can integrate formal system test into every iteration. You'll need to explain to your auditors how you're working. In any other life cycle, you'll need some system-level testing at the end, because that's where the integration occurs. Only you know how formal you need that last testing part to be.

---

4. See http://www.testing.com/cgi-bin/blog/2003/08/21#agile-testing-project-1.

13.9 System Test Strategy Template

Here's a system test strategy template:

- Product revision and overview
- Product history
- Features to be tested
- Features not to be tested
- Configurations included and excluded
- Environmental requirements
- System test approach
- System test entry criteria
- System test exit criteria
- Test deliverables
- Other documents referenced

Product Revision and Overview

Describe the product and revision designator. Describe briefly how the product works. Reference other documents as needed.

Product History

Include a short history of previous revisions of this product that is three to four sentences. Include defect history. (The defect history will indicate the level of technical debt.)

Features to Be Tested

List all features to be tested. Organize the list in the way that makes most sense: by user features or by architectural area. If you can reference a requirements document, do so, but don't list all the requirements here.

Features Not to Be tested

If you know of features you don't have to test, list them here. This might make sense only for small point releases.

Configurations Included and Excluded

List the hardware and software options you will be testing and not testing in this project. If it makes sense, use a matrix to show what's being tested and what's excluded.

Environmental Requirements

Note the specific test environment the testers need. They might need an electrically isolated network, access to a very large server, special firmware, or specific software.

System Test Approach

Explain how you will make sure the testing occurs when it needs to occur. If you plan to use a different life cycle than the developers are using, this is the place to mention that. If you plan to use combinatorial testing as a way to cover the myriad of configurations, explain that here. This is the place to mention your milestones to the rest of the project team.

System Test Entry Criteria

The system must meet these criteria before the product can start formal system test. Especially if you're working in any life cycle other than the agile life cycles, it's too easy for the project team think they've met their milestones. Then they arrive at system test and realize the product doesn't work. If you provide the minimum criteria of what the product has to do to work as the system test entry criteria, the testers won't think they're in formal system test when they're not. (They can still test; it's just not formal system test.) Make the system test entry criteria SMART, as you did in Section 2.3, *Release Criteria*, on page 21.

System Test Exit Criteria

The system must meet these criteria before the product can end formal system test. Your system test exit criteria might be your release criteria (see Section 2.3, *Release Criteria*, on page 21) if you plan to release as soon as system test is over. (Some organizations have an additional user acceptance test step before release.)

Test Deliverables

If you keep artifacts from testing, such as logs, automated tests, plans, or metrics, itemize them here.

Other Documents Referenced

You might need to reference requirements or other specifications in the strategy.

13.10 There's a Difference Between QA and Test

I'm not talking about integrating QA into the project. QA means *quality assurance*, which is a process improvement and process measurement activity. Although many testing groups are called QA, they are not. They are test groups.

Isn't this just a word problem? Why am I so concerned about this?

Process improvement is a management activity. It's possible to have a QA manager who performs the process measurement and manages the testing. But it's much more likely that the person titled QA manager manages the testing only. Titles with an incorrect meaning lull senior management into thinking they have covered that activity—such as process improvement and measurement—when they haven't. That doesn't help anyone in the organization.

You need to be able to tell the difference between testers and QA staff. The key to the distinction is that QA team members have the ability to change the product development process.

You know you're working with a QA group when the QA group or manager has the following:

- The authority and cash to provide training for developers (or writers or testers or release engineers or business analysts—anyone in product development) who need it
- The authority to settle customer complaints or to drive the handling of customer complaints, especially in the ranking of requirements for the next release of the product
- The ability and authority to fix defects
- The ability and authority to either write or rewrite the user manuals
- The ability to study customer needs and design the product accordingly
- The ability to measure the product development process over several projects, compare results, and explain those results—and not be fired for it
- The ability to study the current product development process and the authority to change it

The QA manager or group might not directly perform this work; they have the ability to staff and schedule the work.

QA manager and QA engineer are important roles. Unfortunately, organizations are more willing to provide the titles rather than the authority and responsibility people with these titles deserve.

Testing is an honorable, creative profession. Great testers are just as rare as great developers. And, they're just as necessary for a successful project. Don't be fooled by titles.

Remember This

- If you plan to integrate testing into the project, you will.
- Use test-driven development to improve the design of the product as well as improve the code.
- Consider a continuum of testing approaches for the project.

Chapter 14

Managing Programs

You might be saying to yourself, "Fine, JR. I can do this kind of project management for my simple projects. But I don't manage simple projects anymore. I manage bundles of projects that all have to release at the same time. Or, there's a strategic reason for a series of projects. This is a logistical nightmare. Got any ideas for those projects?"

Sure I do. What you're describing is a program, and your job is *program management*.

14.1   When Your Project Is a Program

Here's a useful definition of program management:[1]

Program management:
> Coordinating several subprojects or a series of projects to meet some specific business objectives.

Project management is tactical. The project manager's role is to complete this project, without regard to other projects underway. But the program manager's role is more strategic. Because the program manager coordinates several subprojects or a series of projects, the program manager must continually review the strategic business objectives of the program to make sure each project follows those objectives. And, if objectives change, the program manager decides (with the relevant project managers) what to change in the projects. The project manager will decide how to change.

---

1.   © 2007 R. Max Wideman, http://www.maxwideman.com; reproduced with permission.

Here's an example. Let's assume you're the program manager for a new online business. Your site will allow people to buy and sell tangible products and software. You might find it easiest to organize the project into several subprojects such as buying tangible products, buying software, selling tangible products, and selling software. In addition, you might need to have marketing literature and a sales plan available at the same time to be able to market the product to both buyers and sellers. All of those projects are part of a program with a common objective: the successful launch of this new site.

Imagine the subprojects are making progress. Assume that midway through your development, the buyer subprojects are working, but you're having trouble calculating taxes on the seller subprojects. Your lawyers can't decide who is liable to pay the taxes where—in which state or country. And, the performance of some of the scenarios for buying software is not fast enough.

The program manager makes the decision (along with corporate management) about whether to hold up the entire program until lawyers understand the tax implications or whether it's worth releasing just the buying part of the site and adding the selling part later. If you're one of the buying project managers, you don't care what the program manager decides, unless that decision changes how you integrate your project with the whole program.

Program managers might decide on the interdependencies between projects when they manage strategically. Some of those interdependencies are deliverables. Most often, those interdependencies are how to allocate people and money among the project portfolio. To manage the people and money allocation, see Chapter 16, *Managing the Project Portfolio*, on page 307.

14.2 Organizing Multiple Related Projects into One Release

Managing a program is similar to—but bigger than—managing a project. Especially when you're trying to bring people and deliverables across the organization (and not just across the technical organization) together, you'll need influencing and negotiation skills. But the first thing you need is a plan.

I've use a template similar to this program plan in a variety of situations where I wanted to make sure the entire program was focused on the deliverable and how to make their part of the deliverable work.

Here's a program plan template:

- Overview
- Features
- Program requirements
- Program goals
- Market evaluation and marketing plan
- Sales plan
- ROI and product lifetime
- Schedule overview
- Staffing curve
- Training plan
- Service/support plan
- Other plans

Overview

Provide a brief overview of the product. Why are you developing the product? What purpose will the product have in the business scheme of the company?

Features

Discuss the significant features of the program—the high-level product requirements and goals. Include internationalization issues. If you're working on several models of a product, explain what differentiates each model or where people can learn about that differentiation.

Program Requirements

Just as a project can have requirements and goals, so can a program.

Program Goals

These are more likely to be corporate goals.

Market Evaluation and Marketing Plan

Include the estimated product lifetime, revenue curve over lifetime, estimated support cost, and the cost of doing nothing.

Sales Plan

Answer these kinds of questions: expected sales cycle, expected sales path, and so on.

ROI and Product Lifetime

Include estimated program costs, estimated current and future costs without this program, estimated future costs after the program, and estimated ROI.

Schedule Overview

Block out the major milestones in the schedule. If you have demos or trade shows, note those. I like to add the risk of making those dates.

Staffing Curve

If you are competing for scarce people and capital resources across the organization, define those needs now. Estimate the total number people required.

Training Plan

Whether you need to train internal or external people, note that here.

Service/Support Plan

If you have service/support issues, note them here.

Other Plans

Your program might need an operations plan, hardware plan, deployment plan, and more. Add those issues into the program plan somewhere.

Developing your program plan will help you recognize the risks. You'll find it easier to manage risks if you have a separate program risk list. I find that my first-draft program plans tend to be about five pages long, and my initial risk list is a couple of pages long. As the program becomes clearer, the plan is longer, and the program risk list becomes shorter. Some of the risks migrate to the projects; some are addressed in the program and subprojects.

14.3 Organizing Multiple Related Projects Over Time

With multiple related projects over time, one of the hardest things to do is track which requirement is going into which release. Using an agile life cycle will make your life infinitely easier, because the product will be potentially releasable at the end of any iteration. Then it becomes a business decision about what to release when.

If you can't use an agile life cycle, try release trains to deal with the actual releasing and a backlog of product requirements for managing the continual change of requirements in *future* releases.

OK, I'll come clean. A release train is a three-month iteration. And this backlog is what agile life cycles use, except that they tend to have smaller chunks to consider because the customer or customer surrogate can see the product at all times. What I'm actually telling you is to use agile practices, except you'll have more risk because the timeboxes are longer.

Organize Multiple Releases of a Product into Release Trains

Release trains[2] are a way to organize features into a quarterly timebox so you can time periodic multiple releases of the product.

If you're a project manager who knows you will be releasing products periodically, you can use release trains. And, if you're a program manager, you can use release trains to manage the strategy of which features you release when.

Release trains decouple releases from projects. The train is a quarterly plan to ship products, generally on the same day of the same month in a quarter (such as the tenth of the second month). Completed projects, which can be as small as one feature, would be eligible to be loaded on the train and be shipped. Incomplete projects are not shipped. To make release trains work, it's easier to divide work into smaller projects.

If you have the schedule game problem discussed in Section 6.11, *We Gotta Have It; We're Toast Without It*, on page 110, release trains can help. Release trains change conditions in only one dimension for a given project. Instead of having to cram lots of features into one release, you can organize concurrent projects to achieve all the "gottas."

Some project managers have used release trains to separate the work of adding more features and improving performance. You can group the features and performance work into separate chunks of work and then schedule a release for each chunk. Start the releases at the same time so you're still working on the same product, just with different deliverables at different times.

With release trains, you schedule a large number of independent pieces. Release trains allow you to manage several incremental projects concurrently. As each piece is ready, they are loaded onto the train and

---

2. See http://www.jrothman.com/weblog/2003/08/release-trains-help-manage-resources.html.

released. The slower pieces don't prevent the faster ones from being part of the product or from shipping. If you need to change which pieces release first, you have more flexibility.

Making Release Trains Work for You

Release trains aren't difficult, but you need some project and program conditions to make them work.

- The program manager must work with the people who define the project portfolio; see Section 16.1, *Build the Portfolio of All Projects*, on page 307. The program manager manages the overall product release criteria, the project managers, and whatever corporate-level issues need managing to make each release successful. The program manager determines whether something is going to miss a particular train and whether it should be postponed until the next train. Anything that misses a train returns to the product backlog (see Section 16.6, *Build a Product Backlog*, on page 313). The program manager helps each project maintain its cohesion and reduces coupling between projects.

- Project managers manage each project; program managers manage the trains. Each project is a significant effort so requires at minimum a technical lead and more likely a project manager to make sure the developers and testers (and the other necessary staff) estimate and deliver their work on time. The project manager has to ensure the developers do no more than necessary. YAGNI (which stands for *you aren't going to need it*) isn't just for agile projects; it's for all projects [JAH02]. The project managers have to be technical enough to understand the inevitable trade-offs and discussions of what's in and what's out.

- You'll need great SCM, both in the tool and how the release engineers use the tool. You might need as many as four simultaneous code lines (one for every release train in a year), and the developers still need to manage to build exactly the sources they need. The release engineers will have to merge the code lines into the main-line too, in case you need to make a patch separate from the next release. (Avoid that, unless the lack of a patch means corporate death.)

- Everyone (developers, testers, project managers, and any other project staff) needs good estimation skills, so you can meet your projected release date for each train.

- The team will need enough automated tests for regression testing. A release train is a combination of an iterative life cycle, with increments for each release. You're guaranteed to change the same modules again and again. If you don't have enough automated tests (sorry, I don't have a number I can give you), you won't be able to release on schedule.

You'll need all of these to create successful release trains.

Release trains help you manage all your resources, because you can group similarly sized or similar-impact projects together into one program. Because there's one program manager whose job is to satisfy the execs or other corporate stakeholders, one project doesn't "win" over another project. The suboptimization that can occur at the project level can't occur in the program, or the program doesn't allow the train to release on time.

Organize Multiple Releases of a Product Without Release Trains

If you don't want to use agile life cycles or release trains, you will find it difficult to manage multiple releases. I don't know how to make serial or iterative life cycles work—and still meet the desired release dates. If you don't have release dates you are supposed to meet, maybe you can make the other life cycles work. But unless you're using some sort of incremental or agile life cycle, the sequence of releases falls apart quickly. The risks of not being able to release anything are too high. You just don't have enough feedback built into the projects and therefore the program.

14.4 Managing Project Managers

Whether you're managing a program to bring many subprojects together in one release or releases over time, you'll be managing project managers.

When you're managing project managers, make sure to manage by deliverable. Also, consider managing by exception. That is, assume people are responsible and handling problems until they tell you they aren't. You'll need to build trust with your project managers and make sure you understand what they're doing. See [RD05] for more details.

There's always a problem when you manage by exception—that of overly optimistic project managers or those who are not measuring their projects enough. You'll need to review their project dashboards with them in order to make sure they are making progress. Review their risk lists to see whether they are managing their risks.

Encourage your project managers to use agile or incremental life cycles so everyone can see frequent feedback. Don't rely on forecasting—or allow your project managers to do so; rely on feedback.

If you're stuck with a serial life cycle for the program and you're not willing or able to work with the project managers to use timeboxes or incremental delivery, good luck. You'll need it.

Obtaining Status from Project Managers

It's even more important as a program manager to avoid serial status program team meetings. You'll have enough problems to solve as a group. Don't waste time obtaining everyone's status. And since you're bringing together many deliverables from across the organization, your managers might want to see a Gantt chart. You need a program/project coordinator person, someone to manage the Gantt. You can still start with yellow stickies (and I recommend you do), but you will be reporting status to people who want to see Gantts. You need someone who can play with the scheduling tool while you do the hard job of managing the program.

Tip: Manage Cross-Program Schedule Changes with Stickies

If you need to change the program's schedule, use stickies so everyone can see who's doing what when. You might be able to use a Gantt chart for verifying program progress. But using a Gantt to change the schedule is not enough. Make the schedule a Big Visible Chart. Manage it that way.

You can still ask your project managers to ask their people to develop inch-pebbles. Your job, along with your project managers, is to develop the schedule of handoffs so everyone can see the interdependencies. The project managers manage how their team members achieve those deliverables. Your job is too look for obstacles and remove them.

Ask your project managers to send you a status report once a week, outlining their progress toward their deliverables. If your project managers are using an agile life cycle, all you need to see is their velocity charts (Figure 11.1, on page 205) and their iteration contents charts (Figure 11.2, on page 207)

If some of your project managers are using an incremental life cycle, they can't provide you with those charts until they start developing and testing. Make sure they timebox the precoding parts of their projects so you can see delivered value as early as possible.

Review the project managers' risks lists with them weekly, or as often as they need you to do so. Monitoring their risk lists will provide you the information you require to remove obstacles across the organization and to manage by exception so you're not micromanaging. You'll also have the information you need for your risk list.

Once you've started collecting status, you can create a program dashboard.

14.5 Creating a Program Dashboard

If you're managing a program, you'll want to see all the data for the projects. You might need to collect some of that data into one program dashboard.

Measurements for Interdependent Projects

The measurements in your project dashboard (see Chapter 11, *Creating and Using a Project Dashboard*, on page 201) are the ones you'll need, because you're organizing people's efforts across the organization to create one deliverable. You might need to integrate several subprojects' measurements to create a program dashboard you can use. One program manager used a storyboard-like mechanism to describe his program's progress.

Storyboards to Describe Program Status
by Eric, senior program manager

I'm managing a large program. We have seven subprojects, of which three are hardware that we're integrating into the product. To show progress, I decided pictures and a storyboard might be the right approach.

I commandeered a wall in my hallway. Our project teams were all over the building, so I figured anywhere I put the pictures was OK, as long as they were in one place.

We drew ten pictures at the beginning of the project, to show where we wanted to be at the end of each iteration. (We used timeboxed iterations.) The pictures weren't beautiful, but they conveyed where we wanted the state of the product at the end of each iteration. We put those pictures about halfway up the wall, labeled "Planned Progress."

As we finished each iteration, we took pictures of the product, in whatever state it was in. Some of those pictures weren't too clear to people who didn't understand the internals too well, so we annotated the pictures. We labeled those pictures as "Actual Progress." We put the actuals above the planned pictures. Below all the pictures were the velocity charts and iteration content charts for each subproject. If you looked at the top line, you could see what we had actually done. You could see where we hoped to be at the end of each iteration, and you could see the charts below.

We finished the third iteration and realized we had underestimated the time to integrate some of the hardware. We reestimated and put a sticky at the beginning of the fourth iteration, saying, "Understood integration here." A bunch of managers asked me about that, but once I explained, they understood. Since that happened on most of our projects, they weren't surprised. They were surprised to hear about it as early as they did.

By the time we finished the eighth iteration, marketing decided to drop a couple of features from the next iteration—a surprise to all of us. But because they had seen the product as it evolved, and could see each iteration's progress, they realized these features just weren't important.

We didn't quite make the ten iterations—we had a last shorter iteration to finish the work we hadn't finished in the tenth iteration. But we were able to end the eleventh iteration early.

Showing progress with pictures made our progress visible to the rest of the organization.

Measurements for a Series of Projects

Aside from the measurements in Chapter 11, *Creating and Using a Project Dashboard*, on page 201, make sure you perform retrospectives (see Section 15.4, *Plan for a Retrospective*, on page 300) to know what you want to measure in the future. For example, ROI might be an ongoing measurement, as well as cost to fix a defect or cost to support a release. If your projects have trouble meeting their schedules, first examine the life cycle each is using, and then consider using the schedule charts (see Figure 11.6, on page 213). If the projects are using agile life cycles, review their velocity charts (see Figure 11.1, on page 205).

 ### Remember This

- Program management incorporates a strategic view of the product, not just a tactical perspective.
- Make sure you can see visible progress from all the project teams.
- Determine which measurements make sense for your program.

Chapter 15

Completing a Project

You might need to perform several activities to complete the project: requesting an early release, conducting a beta test, and shepherding the project through to actual completion. And whatever else you need to do to end a project, don't forget the retrospective.

15.1 Managing Requests for Early Release

If you've been using an agile life cycle (and keeping up with the testing as you proceed), you don't have to worry about a request for early release—the software is always releasable at the end of an iteration. Customers might not want to pay for it if it doesn't have enough features, but making the product releasable is not an issue.

For other life cycles, you need to know far enough in advance that there will be a request for an early release. Look back at your most recent project or, in a large organization, at other people's most recent projects. Did they have requests for early releases? If so, chances are good that you will too.

To manage early releases, it's OK to cheat. Sure, you're supposed to be using a serial life cycle, but nothing during the coding phase says that you can't implement by feature, do continuous integration, and test each feature as it's done. Does it matter whether you've turned your serial life cycle into a staged-delivery life cycle? Only you know the answer to that question. But in all the organizations I've assessed, the answer has been a resounding "no!"

If cheating doesn't work in your project because the developers can't implement by feature, you can still ask the developers to use continuous integration and the testers to start testing by feature.

If those alternatives won't work for your project, you'll need to plan for two endings for your project. The first ending will be the early release. The second ending will be your actual release. This alternative is expensive. Avoid this by talking with the project team and explaining that they will go nuts-o if you really have to do this. (People dislike the Crossing the Desert Syndrome; see Appendix B, on page 335.)

15.2 Managing Beta Releases

You have several decisions to make with beta releases: how many releases do you anticipate, how finished does the product have to be, and who are the customers who will use the beta releases? And of course, all the answers to these questions depend on the beta duration and purpose.

Try organizing the beta into a subproject. If you're using an agile life cycle, estimate in the release plan which iteration you'll use to start beta—and update the release plan as you know more. If you're using any other life cycle, estimate when you'll start beta, and update that estimate as you proceed.

Here's my beta test template:

- Beta purpose
- Beta customer selection
- Beta entry criteria
- Beta exit criteria
- Overall beta schedule

Beta Purpose

Briefly describe the product version, why you want a beta test, what benefits accrue to the company, and so on.

Beta Customer Selection

This includes how will you select beta customers, the initial customer list, and who is responsible for customer paperwork.

Beta Entry Criteria

This is milestone criteria so you know you're ready for beta test. This is similar to release criteria or system test entry/exit criteria.

Beta Exit Criteria

This is milestone criteria so you know you're ready to end beta test. How will you know you've reached the end of the beta period? If you need customer references, make sure asking for those references is part of the beta schedule.

Overall Beta Schedule

Define who the beta coordinator is, or assign a person for each week. Define who will answer beta customer phone calls and email. Here's an example schedule overview.

Week	General Task
Week 1	Verify installation with customers.
Week 2	Make sure customers have tried features 3 and 4. Ask about performance.
Week 3	Start asking for references.

15.3 When You Know You Can't Meet the Release Date

Despite your best efforts, you realize somewhere toward the end of the project that you're not going to meet the release criteria in the desired schedule. In that case, it's time to determine what you have left to do and replan the rest of the project.

First, verify that the project's release criteria are still valid. Can you do any less? (See Section 5.3, *How Little Can You Do?*, on page 78.) Do you need to do more? Remember, the release criteria are the few minimal criteria that make the release useful to customers.

Next, decide how long you need to finish the minimal required set of features. If the team has not been developing by feature, integrating and testing as they proceed, it's time to start. The more you can help people develop, integrate, and test feature by feature, the less time you'll need for the slip.

"Take No Small Slips"

(The title of this section is from Peter Fagg, as quoted by Fred Brooks.)

You need to know how far behind the project team is. If you have been implementing by feature and have measured velocity, learn what's keeping people from finishing their work. Chances are good that they are multitasking or are being interrupted with questions from other projects. Once you're late, you can work with the team and the rest of the organization to make sure they stay focused on this project. You and the team can derive a new schedule fairly easily.

But if the team has not been implementing by feature, you don't have data about how quickly the team can work and what's left to do. In that case, you need to slip the release date enough so the team can finish their work.

No matter what, do not take a small slip. Small slips lead to Crossing the Desert Syndrome (see Appendix B, on page 335). If you've ever worked on a project that slipped a week every week, you know how awful that is. People need an aggressive schedule, not an impossible schedule.

Committing to a New Date

Once it's clear you're not going to meet the original schedule, you need to replan. You're not going to take any small slips, because you know how disastrous that can be. How do you arrive at a new schedule to which the project team can commit?

First decide whether you need to commit to a new date. Have you already implemented the most valuable features? Can you declare victory and finish this project? Do so, if you can.

But if you do need to finish the features you've started, it's time to replan.

Invite everyone on the project to a replanning meeting. (If you're running a program, ask the independent groups to plan independently and bring their dates. If you have only interdependent groups, invite everyone.) Ask everyone to use sticky schedule (see Section 4.3, *Basic Sticky Scheduling*, on page 56) to generate their task lists. Wherever possible, estimate using inch-pepples (see Section 5.8, *Estimating Using Inch-Pebbles Wherever Possible*, on page 83).

Crossing the Desert Syndrome Can Kill Your Project

Everyone has put in tons of overtime. Tempers are frayed. You're not sure of the last time Frederick showered. But you've made beta. You still have to reach the end of the project.

When people focus on an interim milestone, they lose track of where the project is headed. They work too many hours, turning a project that won't meet its schedule into a death march.

When you realize the project is not going to meet the desired date—whether that date is an interim milestone or a release, it's time to replan and reschedule. You might need to remove some features from the list. You might decide to drop some reliability or performance goal. And you might decide to slip the interim and release dates.

Your choices will depend on what success means to your project and who your customers are. If you use your success and release criteria, you can still make a good decision. Your management might not like the decision, but it will be the best decision you can make.

Whatever you do, don't allow the project team to exclusively focus on an intermediate milestone. They will. And you will have to deal with Crossing the Desert Syndrome. Not fun.

After you've defined the tasks, it's time to estimate. If you really want people to commit to a definite date, separate the sizing (how big the task is) from the duration (how long the task will take); see Section 5.1, *Separate Sizing and Duration During Estimation*, on page 71.

People will resist sizing some of the tasks. "We've been working on that driver for weeks. We don't know what's wrong. I'm not giving a date." This is where understanding the problem you're trying to solve is helpful. You might be able to help develop some questions to know when a particular task is stuck or done. And if you've been implementing by feature all along, you might have some historic data from this project to use for estimation.

At some point, you'll have estimations of durations. Add them up, and see where the project looks like it will end. Apply some intelligence to the estimate. Do you have people who are multitasking on other projects? Increase the estimate. Do you have people who have never

> ### Slipping a Week Each Week Is Hell
>
> Early in my career, I was on a project that slipped a week every week for four weeks. At the end of those four weeks, the entire project team was frustrated. We had no idea when this hell would ever end.
>
> The project manager gave up. "I don't know how to estimate when we'll be done. Everything we've done for that device driver just hasn't worked. How can I know when it will be done?"
>
> We'd slipped into the 90% Done schedule game (see Section 6.14, *90% Done*, on page 115). And because we were at the end of the release, the pressure was very high to finish *now*.
>
> We decided that we needed to change who worked on what. The problems need fresh eyes. Once we did a reassignment and a short Delphi estimation (see Section 5.1, *Delphi and Wideband Delphi Estimation*, on page 64), we developed a new schedule. We thought it would take another three weeks. We decided we would commit to six weeks.
>
> We finished in four weeks. Even though we had fresh eyes on the problems, some of the problems were quite difficult to solve. And if we had maintained the three-week estimation, we would have been down in the morale dumps again, wondering whether there was a way to end this project.

received feedback on their estimates now, and you're not sure you trust their current estimates? Explain, "Tom, you've just started to receive feedback on your estimates. You've improved since the start of the project. Are you willing to bet your paycheck on this date?" (See Section 5.1, *When You Don't Trust the Team's Estimate*, on page 64 for more details.) Don't ask people to bet their paychecks; use that as a gauge of how good your new estimate is.

When you add up the durations, make sure that the sum of the time estimates is no more than a few weeks out; otherwise, your risk is quite high. (After all, your estimates until now have helped you into this pickle. Don't trust the same kind of estimate to get you out of the pickle.)

At the end of the project, people want it to be over. And they want to tell anyone with *manager* in their title how quickly the project will be over. You aren't really betting Tom's paycheck; you are asking him to consider the ramifications personally. This will help you derive a better estimate—one that the team is much more likely to meet. And at the end of the project, if you need to slip, this more conservative estimate will allow the team to finish properly, instead of rushing and increasing technical debt (see Appendix B, on page 335).

Estimating System Test Time

The final system test includes several steps: testing the product, finding defects, and verifying defects. Your first step is to separate these tasks when you estimate the duration of final system test.

If you do test-driven development and have integrated system testing into an iteration, there is rarely even an iteration's worth of at-the-end testing. If you're new to agile development, you might need to plan for one iteration at the end for final system test and customer acceptance test. Once the team has more experience with finishing features in an iteration, they can plan better.

But if your team is not using test-driven development and if the testers are not able to find problems until the GUI has settled down, you will need more system test time at the end of the project than you might want. And that time will be difficult to predict.[1]

The more serial your life cycle is, the more final testing time you will need. The more incremental your life cycle is, the less final testing time you need and the more interim regression testing you will need. By incremental, I mean continuous integration, TDD, and testing during development.

Here's the question you want to be able to answer: How long will one cycle of "complete" testing take? It's not possible to do "complete" testing, so your version of complete is the tests you planned to run and any other exploratory tests or other tests you need to run in one cycle of testing to provide enough information about the product under test. I realize that's vague and depends on each project. I don't know how to be more explicit because this is a project-by-project estimate. If your developers work to reduce the defects as they proceed by adding unit and integration tests, the cycle time can decrease a bit from the first cycle to the last—because the testers know how to set up the tests better and the product has fewer defects, which allows the testing to proceed faster.

---

1. See http://www.stickyminds.com/s.asp?F=S8918_COL_2.

> ### ☇ Joe Asks...
> #### Can't the Developers Fix As the Testers Test?
>
> They can. And I hope they do. But if you're in the position of managing a project where the developers didn't continuously integrate, use TDD, or review each other's work products, they are going to be slower at fixing the defects than you want.
>
> Only you and the project team know how concurrent the development and testing can be.

Once you know how long a cycle of testing takes, estimate how long it will take the developers to fix the problems. Start with this data: the number of problems found per cycle in the last project, your gut feel for how many more/less you should find per cycle in this project, and cost-to-fix-a-defect data prior to release. I once worked on a project where in the previous release we found 200 problems in the first test cycle. It took the developers half a person-day each to fix the problems, and we had ten developers. Our initial estimate was ten working days to fix problems—at the end of the first testing cycle. That's a long time. It was agonizing—we thought we'd never finish fixing problems. (Hint: collect this data, and use it at your retrospective to help people choose alternative practices for the next project; see Section 15.4, *Plan for a Retrospective*, on page 300.)

You have an estimate of the test cycle duration and a first guess at how long it will take to fix the defects exposed by that testing. All you need to do is know how many cycles of testing you need.

Each product and release is unique and will require its own number of testing cycles. The more proactive about looking for defects and the more incremental the developers are, the fewer cycles you'll need. The less proactive and the more serial the developers are, the more cycles you need. I've heard numbers that range from three or eight or thirty cycles of testing.

The way to talk about testing cycles, especially with people who want the testing done three months ago, is to supply a time per cycle and an estimate of the number of cycles. "It will take us six days per cycle for testing. I estimate three days between test cycles for all the problems to be fixed—that's a total of nine days per test-and-fix cycle. Right now, I think we need four cycles, a total of 36 days, the better part of two months, assuming everyone stays on the project. We'll have to reevaluate as we proceed."

Managing the System Testing When You Don't Have Enough Time

You've made your case for more testing time. And your sponsor says "no." Now what?

Consider timeboxing as an approach to manage your time constraints. Imagine that you've planned for three months of testing. And your management says they want to release in six weeks. Here's how to work with the testers or test manager to timebox the testing:

1. Review the original test plan. The testers had some idea of what and how they had planned to test. Make it clear to your management and other stakeholders that the testers are not going to accomplish everything in the original plan, and determine what you can complete.

2. Start by defining the testing plan of attack in the first week. Define how you'll discover what pieces of the product you will attempt to test and how you'll test them. You might choose exploratory testing for discovering what to test, and you might need combinatorial test techniques for how you'll test. At the end of this week, you will have a ranked list of what you'll test in the product and how you'll test it. Consider testing by value, that is, first testing the most valuable parts of the product, not necessarily the riskiest. See Section 9.3, *Implement the Highest-Value Features First*, on page 172.

   Part of defining your attack plan is to explain the three major risks of timeboxing testing: first, you might find something critical during testing that the developers won't have time to fix; second, you might miss something critical that the customers will find significant; and third, you might encounter a blocking defect that will prevent you from testing a particular area. Everyone must understand that the test team won't know everything about the product, and the organization could be releasing a product different from the one everyone anticipated.

3. During the next three weeks, develop tests and continue to refine the test plan. Develop tests and test for specific work flows (or

areas of the product) one at a time, according to your ranked list. You don't sit around waiting for something to test; instead, you test a workflow or piece of the product from beginning to end before starting a new workflow or product area. For example, if you are testing a banking system, you might test from opening a specific account type to verifying the account is in the database and is active. You don't test just opening different kind of accounts; you test one specific kind of account from beginning to end. In other words, if you are testing a biomedical device, you test that the device can accept a specific input, perform the computation, and generate the expected output—just one specific input. Again, you don't test all inputs and all outputs; you test each end-to-end result serially. (This is testing by feature.)

As you're refining the test plan, you're confirming scope as you proceed. Every time you realize there's something else you can't test, you list that piece in the not-to-test category and assign a risk to not testing it. As you complete testing, you update the test reports with your completed plans and tests.

4. Evaluate your progress at the end of every week of testing, and report test data. (Think of this as an end-of-iteration review meeting.) If you can verify fixes as you test, plan to continue testing and verifying through the fifth week. If not, plan on completing the testing—as far as you can go—in the fourth week.

5. You're now at the fifth week. If you haven't been able to verify fixes yet, this is the time to do so. As you verify fixes, you'll perform whatever regression tests you have created to make sure the fixes didn't break anything. If this takes you the full two weeks, you're done. If you have another week, you can attack more features, employing the end-to-end testing you've done before.

6. In the sixth week, you verify the last of the fixes and report on your progress and what you know and don't know about the product.

I'm certainly not recommending you utilize only six weeks for testing on a project. The time you need for testing depends on what's in the project and how well the product is built. But, if you're ever caught in a pickle, where you don't have enough time to test everything, use timeboxing to help you evaluate how little you can do and still deliver a valuable result to the organization.

Joe Asks...

Why Is System Test Taking So Long?

A long system test period at the end of a the project is a result of not integrating testing into the project as the project proceeded; see Chapter 13, *Integrating Testing into the Project*, on page 255. You might have had good reasons for not integrating testing into the project earlier—but you will need to plan for more testing now, at the end of the project.

15.4 Shepherding the Project to Completion

Assuming you're on track, now all you have to do is finish the project.

Managing the End Game

Your project looks like it will be on time (or close). The testers are keeping up with the developers. You're tracking the release criteria, and it looks like you'll meet all the criteria at the desired release date. Is there anything else you need to do?

Keep gathering data about defects, and make sure you don't play the promotion/demotion defect game just to meet the release date. If you choose to take on more technical debt (see Appendix B, on page 335) in your project to meet the date, fine. But make that a conscious decision.

If you've been steering the project, your only remaining tasks are planning for the retrospective and a celebration.

Avoiding the Promoting/Demoting Defects Game

Every morning at 9 a.m., the product manager (Tim), the software project manager (Dan), and the program manager (Sue) gathered in a room to do "defect triage." It was their job to assess each defect and make sure the necessary ones were fixed in the release.

Dan started the discussion by passing around the current list of known open defects and the defect trend chart. "We found ten more defects yesterday. We fixed only three. We now have 547 open defects, and we're two weeks from the date. We are not in good shape."

Sue said, "Let's see about that." She and Tim reviewed the defects and start circling the high-priority defects. "None of these is really high. We can wait and fix them in a point release next month. And these marked High severity—they're not really high either. Make all of those Medium." Sue and Tim conferred for another minute or so. "And these Medium priority and severity—we can make them Low. We have only one open High severity. You can fix that by the end of next week, right?"

Dan sat there, stupefied for a moment. He recovered. "Maybe I haven't been clear. We're finding more defects than we can fix in a day or a week. You can call those Low priority or severity, but our customers will know they're not Low, and they'll be angry. Then you'll put more pressure on me to do a point release in less than four weeks. Is the problem that we need to meet this date?"

Tim nodded. "We really can't miss this date."

Dan replied, "OK, here's what we'll do. Instead of changing priorities and severities, let's deliver a set of release notes with a section called *known problems*. We'll rank them and let our customers know when we'll fix them. How does that sound to you?"

The three of them discussed Dan's idea, and they agreed to the known problems instead of changing the severities and priorities of the open defects. Another defect demotion game averted!

Plan for a Retrospective

Always conduct a retrospective at the end of a project. Even if you have been conducting interim retrospectives (see Section 8.2, *Conduct Interim Retrospectives*, on page 144), make sure you hold a retrospective at the end of the project. Although trading off facilitators during the project might work for interim retrospectives, find someone else to facilitate the final retrospective. You and the entire project team are too close to the deliverables and the work to facilitate the retrospective yourselves.

A retrospective is not a "lessons learned" gripe session. And it's not a post-mortem, because let's hope no one died while making this product. It is a structured meeting, designed to look back at how the project proceeded, what people learned, and how they felt about working on that project. A well-designed and facilitated retrospective can save you weeks of work on your next project.

Derby and Larsen [DL06] have a five-step approach to the retrospective:

1. Set the stage.
2. Gather data.
3. Generate insights.
4. Decide what to do.
5. Close the retrospective.

If you've managed a project of three months or more, I strongly recommend you spend an entire day reflecting and learning about the previous project—especially if many of these same people will be working together on the next project. And yes, that's an entire day for everyone who worked on the project. Longer projects need even long retrospectives.

A day might seem like a lot of time to spend, especially if you had a project of more than twenty people and more than one site. It's possible to organize smaller retrospective by teams, gathering all the teams at one site together. But the more you break the teams apart, the less useful data you will gather that could benefit the entire project or program.

But you have a large or a multisite project. How do you do a retrospective with everyone on the project?

Carefully. But you still need to do it, assuming you want to harvest the learnings from the project. First see whether you can bring everyone together to do a retrospective at one site—a separate site from any one team's site [Ker01]. Use the same technique as you used for the interim retrospectives in order to facilitate a retrospective in each location or with each team, and ask the managers to solve cross-team problems. Have each team select someone to represent their learnings, and have those selected representatives do a sharing/learning and look at cross-site problems (that aren't management problems).

Another alternative is to do a virtual retrospective with all the teams. Set up a webcam so everyone can see each team's room. Use a wiki (because multiple people can write to it and everyone can read it) to gather information. Have multiple conference call lines available for people to call in for small group work. Use Cardmeeting.com for people to cluster and group ideas.[2]

---

2. From a private conversation with Esther Derby and Diana Larsen.

Remember, some of the problems will be between the people at different sites. Managers can't solve those problems. You'll need to bring the people together in one physical location to address those problems.

Plan for a Celebration

People need rituals. Just as there was a kickoff for the project, make sure you celebrate the end of a project too.

Parties or celebrations don't have to be expensive or include everyone's families. Some of the best post-project celebrations I've attended were some beer, wine, and cold cuts at the end of the day that the master went to the duplicator. One of my clients has developers and testers from many countries, and they celebrate by each bringing in some native food to share. The company provides the (nonalcoholic) drinks and cookies and ice cream for dessert. One small project team decided to celebrate by playing laser tag for an afternoon.

Celebrations have to fit the people on the project. If you want to acknowledge the project team's participation in a larger setting, that's fine. But that's not the project's celebration of completion.

If you're comfortable with giving a little speech at the celebration, it's nice to recap everyone's participation on the project. One of my speeches went something like this (with the names changed).

"I've gathered you all here for ice cream and cookies to celebrate Release 4.1. We did a great job. I know we gave appreciations at the retrospective already. I have just a few additional acknowledgments.

"Jared, your sense of humor kept us going. MaryAnn, somehow you kept me on the straight-and-narrow for my meeting agendas and minutes. Patrick, I'm amazed that I can tell the mood you're in by the way you type on the keyboard—it's a great warning sign for me when I'll be interrupting you. Bill, you do find the most amazing defects. Next time, you're reviewing my project documents, OK? Cyrus, you have the nicest handwriting. When we do our sticky scheduling next time, can you please write my stickies?

"Let's not forget people who weren't officially on our project. Although Cindy wasn't on our project, she helped me stay organized—thank you, Cindy, for your admin support and for making sure I had my plane tickets on time.

> \\/ Joe Asks...
>
> **Does a Failed Project Deserve a Celebration?**
>
> Of course. At least to celebrate the fact that project is over.
>
> Before you decide the project was a failure, arrange for a retrospective. I find that too often management—the sponsors, senior management, or even the project manager—has failed the project. Sometimes, the sponsor changes overall project goals partway through the project. Sometimes the organization demands a phase-gate life cycle but wants the project to adapt to changes as if the project were using agile development. Sometimes, the project manager gathered no measurements, so the project team had no idea where they were. Projects "fail" for lots of reasons; few of those reasons are because of the technical staff's inability to perform the technical work.

"That's it. Let's enjoy our desserts now and bask in the glory of having completed work we can be proud of. We did a great job."

That's it. Make a point of saying something nice to each person. Avoid saying, "Nice job, everyone." That's a thankless thank you. When you say something specific to each person, they feel as if you've paid attention to their work throughout the project—which you have.

If you do decide to make a speech that's more than the "Let's celebrate the release. We did a great job," write it down and practice. You can even use your notes. Your actions—preparing for the speech—are one more indication to your team that you care about them as human beings. If you work with these people again, they will remember that and respond with trust and respect.

15.5 Canceling a Project

Canceling a project is one way to end a project. And it can be quite difficult for everyone involved. One developer was so enamored of a project that even after he was laid off from the company, he returned on his own time to complete the project! You might think he was a giving, helpful person—and you'd be right. But his continued work on the project, even for "free," cost the company time in support of his "free" work.

If your company has canceled a project, then work to stop the project.[3] Here are some ways to make sure the work stops:

1. First, explain to the people on the project why you're canceling the project and what happens to them. They want to know what work they'll be doing now.

2. Appreciate each person for the work they performed on this project. If you have a small project team, use the meeting at which you cancel the project to appreciate what each person has done [RD05]. For a larger team or a program team, ask the subproject managers or technical leads to appreciate the members of their teams.

3. Give people time to clean up their work before starting on their new work. That means checking in the code that's checked out with comments that explain the state of the code, noting on a design which alternatives were under discussion, or noting which tests were or were not completed. Cleaning up work is not the same as finishing up work, so I recommend this step take less than a day to perform. If you're using an agile life cycle, this stop might take a few minutes or an hour. For other life cycles, timebox this to one day.

4. Cancel all periodic meetings associated with this project. Once people clear their schedules of these project-related meetings, they will see other time they have available for new work.

5. Assign someone to handle the inevitable questions about the canceled project, preferably someone high up in management. If a technical person has the project information, he or she might start working on it again. If a manager is assigned to be the point person, the manager is less likely to start working on the project.

6. If you're canceling a project that's had even one week of work, take the time to perform a project retrospective and see what people learned from this project.

7. Start people on their new project as soon as they've cleaned up their work.

---

3. See http://www.jrothman.com/Newsletter/kill-cancelled-projects.htm.

Canceling a project might not be fun. But if you cancel the project cleanly, you won't have to do it again—and you'll be helping the company move forward to the next project in the queue.

 ## Remember This

- Avoid Crossing the Desert Syndrome caused by focusing on interim milestones.

- Always plan for a retrospective at the end of the project even if you do interim retrospectives.

- If you have to cancel a project, cancel it. No halfway cancellations.

Chapter 16

Managing the Project Portfolio

If this is a book about managing projects, why is there a chapter about managing the project portfolio? When I work with project managers, they say things such as "My management can't decide which project they want first." Or, they say, "My management wants everything now." Or, they say, "My management makes decisions about projects so late that I start the project late." Or, they say, "I can't keep people just on *my* project; they're multitasking all over the place."

Managing the portfolio, or helping your management to manage the portfolio, might be a survival skill for you. If your management defines its corporate (or unit) strategy and tells you which project to do when, skip this chapter. But if your management doesn't always make timely decisions, this chapter can help.

Project portfolio management consists of three parts: building the list of projects [RD05], evaluating each of them, and making the decisions about which projects to fund and staff. Once you have a portfolio, you can manage it by keeping a running product backlog [Sch04] for each product. The backlog allows you to start and end smaller, more frequent projects, increasing throughput.

16.1 Build the Portfolio of All Projects

Not every organization knows which projects are active, which projects are supposed to be active, or which projects are planned for when. The first step is to build the portfolio of projects.

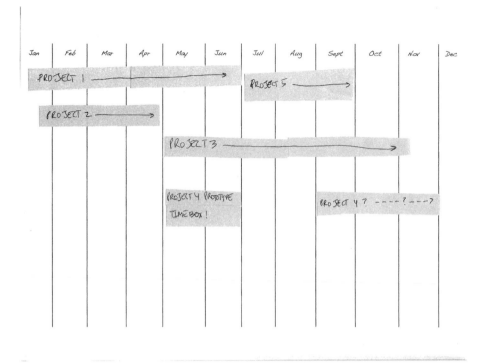

Figure 16.1: PROJECT PORTFOLIO

Gather the list of all the projects in your department. Note when management thinks the projects have started or are planned to start and when they are supposed to end. Organize them in a grid, month by month.[1] If you used stickies on the wall, it would look something like Figure 16.1. Yes, you can certainly use a spreadsheet or a grid and make the portfolio look nicer. But if you want to be able to change it, use the most low-tech tool you can so you have the flexibility to change it easily.

Once you have a portfolio, you can evaluate the projects, both qualitatively and quantitatively.

---

1. See http://www.jrothman.com/weblog/2006/03/courage-required.html.

16.2   Evaluate the Projects

If you have some idea of start and end dates—even wished-for start and end dates—you can start evaluating the projects. You'll want both qualitative and quantitative evaluation.

Qualitatively Evaluate the Projects

Ask these questions for qualitative evaluation[2]:

- How does this project fit in with all the others?
- What is the strategic reason for this project?
- Is there a tactical gain from completing this project?
- To make this project successful, are we ready to adequately fund it?
- To make this project successful, are we ready to adequately staff it?
- Do we know what success looks like for this project?

If you can't determine an answer for all these questions, it's time to ask whether the project should be in the portfolio. Sometimes, companies keep projects they can't adequately staff in the portfolio, but decide *when* to start them so the projects are not inadequately staffed for the entire duration.

Quantitatively Evaluate the Projects

Here are questions to ask for quantitative evaluation:

- When will we see any monetary return from this project?
- What's the expected revenue curve for this project?
- What's the expected customer acquisition curve for this project?
- When will we see retention of current customers from this project?
- What's the expected customer growth curve?
- When will we see reduction in operating costs from this project?
- What's the expected operating cost curve?

Many of my clients find these questions adequate in making decisions about the portfolio, but if your management wants more data, refer to [Coh06] where there is a great section on determining the monetary value of projects.

---

2.   See http://www.jrothman.com/Papers/Cutter/Projectportfolio101.html.

After evaluating the projects, you can make decisions about them. Being able to make decisions about the possible projects in the portfolio is not easy. But, that's why senior management is paid the big bucks, right? And, not making a decision about the projects is also a decision—and one that's more costly than making a decision that's reversible.

16.3 Decide Which Projects to Fund Now

The qualitative and quantitative questions allow you to have a conversation about which projects to fund now and which projects to fund later. It will be clear from the questions and their answers that some projects should be funded now. And some should be funded only if the company has more money than they know what to do with. But your managers might run into trouble deciding among some projects—which really should be funded now and which should be funded later—and when could you change those decisions?

Here's where using agile life cycles (see Section A.4, *Agile Life Cycles*, on page 331) and building (and using) a product backlog (see Section 16.6, *Build a Product Backlog*, on page 313) can really help. If you develop in iterations and always develop the highest priority requirements first, you can change priorities as often as you finish an iteration. (I'm not recommending that you do so but that you could.)

16.4 Rank-Order the Portfolio

You have your evaluated project list, so you can rank-order the projects. If you know which ones you want first, second, third, and so on, you can staff them in that order.

Ranking projects is similar to ranking the project drivers (see Section 1.4, *Decide on a Driver for Your Project*, on page 7). At some point, one project *is* more important than the others. If your management is having trouble deciding, list all the projects in a spreadsheet. Across the columns, ask the questions. Meet with your managers, and facilitate their discussion about the answers to those questions. Once they're done, you have a ranked list of projects. You know where your project fits. Once you have a ranked portfolio, you can deal with the problems of starting the projects faster.

Joe Asks...

How do I Decide When Two Projects Really Are the Same Priority?

Here's a common organizational problem. You have two projects, each with a different focus, that you want to fund at the same time. You don't have enough people to staff two different projects. The projects are not similar enough to be part of one program. Now what?

It's time to go back to the corporate mission. If you have two different projects, each that requires the same staff, your senior management needs to articulate their mission. Once they decide on a mission, the decision will be clear.

16.5 Start Projects Faster

Typically, long start-up times are a problem of decision making, life-cycle choice, and requirements definition. As a project manager, you might not be able to solve all of these problems. But if you can identify them and point people to the causes and possible solutions, you might be able to start your projects earlier.

Project Decisions Take Too Long to Make

If it seems as if your projects never get started, your management might have a problem with decision making. Make sure your decision making includes all of these steps:

1. Defining the desired outcome, such as ranking the projects in order, so everyone knows the relative importance of each project.

2. Establishing the boundaries around the decision, such as chartering analysis of the projects and including who will make the final decision. If you have one person who will decide when to start and staff projects, you need to work with only that person. But if you have a committee, what happens when one person on that committee thinks he or she can veto a decision? Knowing who will make the decision is key to generating a quick decision.

3. Identifying the options so that the group can make a decision. I've met managers who didn't want to select an alternative (do this project *or* that project), so they refused to make a decision to ratify that alternative. The Rule of Three [Wei85] helps people realize there isn't just one alternative but that with multiple ways to approach the decision, it might be possible to realize what everyone wants. One management team, after years of not being able to make decisions about determining the relative importance of any project, realized they didn't have to decide on one or the other, but they did have to decide when to finish each project. That freed them to allow intermittent prototyping on several projects simultaneously but to assign staff full-time to only one project.

4. Selecting from among options, including identifying the decision criteria about how you (or your management) will make the decision. It's not always easy to choose from among projects. See Section 16.2, *Qualitatively Evaluate the Projects*, on page 309 and Section 16.2, *Quantitatively Evaluate the Projects*, on page 309 for questions to ask about how to evaluate those projects.

5. Implementing the decision. Even if you've managed to rank the projects, determine the boundaries around the decision, identify the options, and select an option, if no one says, "Yes, start this project!" it won't start. And then two or three weeks later, you're surprised when a new project lands in your lap. If you find yourself surprised by projects and feeling as if you are late before you even start, work with your management to help you know when project decisions are being discussed. You don't have to attend the meeting; you need to know the outcome of the meeting.

Senior management teams might have trouble determining the strategic outcome they desire. You might see this as an inability to decide among projects. You might even see the schedule games discussed in Section 6.6, *Pants on Fire*, on page 99 and Section 6.7, *Split Focus*, on page 101.

This might occur because some management teams have trouble defining the boundaries around their decisions. Some management teams have trouble identifying the options. More teams have trouble selecting from among the options and might try to partially fund all the projects, thinking that some progress on all projects is better than funding some projects and not funding others.

If your management has trouble deciding which project to start when, you can help. Try the pairwise comparison technique (see Section 8.3, *Rank the Requirements*, on page 145): looking at these two projects, which project do you want more than the other? Compare all the projects to each other, and you'll end with a relative ranking of all the projects.

16.6 Manage the Demand for New Features with a Product Backlog

Part of managing when you'll start which project is managing the demand for new features. If you fall prey to any of the schedule games (especially the one discussed in Section 6.11, *We Gotta Have It; We're Toast Without It*, on page 110), it's time to offer your management the opportunity to manage the demand for new features on a regular basis.

Build a Product Backlog

There are two parts to building a product backlog: what you'll accomplish in *this* release and what you'll list for a future release.

A running list of requirements requests—a product backlog—is different from managing the requirements of the *current* release. When you commit to some number of requirements for the current release, your customers are depending on you to deliver them. And, whether you're protecting the iteration from any changes or the release from too many changes, your customers will have some pent-up demand for the next set of features. A running list separates the current release's requirements from future releases.

The product backlog is a release-by-release ranked list of requirements (or things that could become requirements in the future) [Sch04].

These "requirements" don't have to be fully formed and valid requirements. They can be user stories or a promise to talk about the requirement later. But the word needs to mean something to the developers. Figure 16.2, on the following page, is what a quarterly list might look like. Few things on this list look like requirements, except for the named defects. Note the dark line in Q1. Everything above the line is needed in Q1. Everything below the line is negotiable for Q1. If the project team can't understand it or finish it for Q1, those "requirements" will be addressed for Q2.

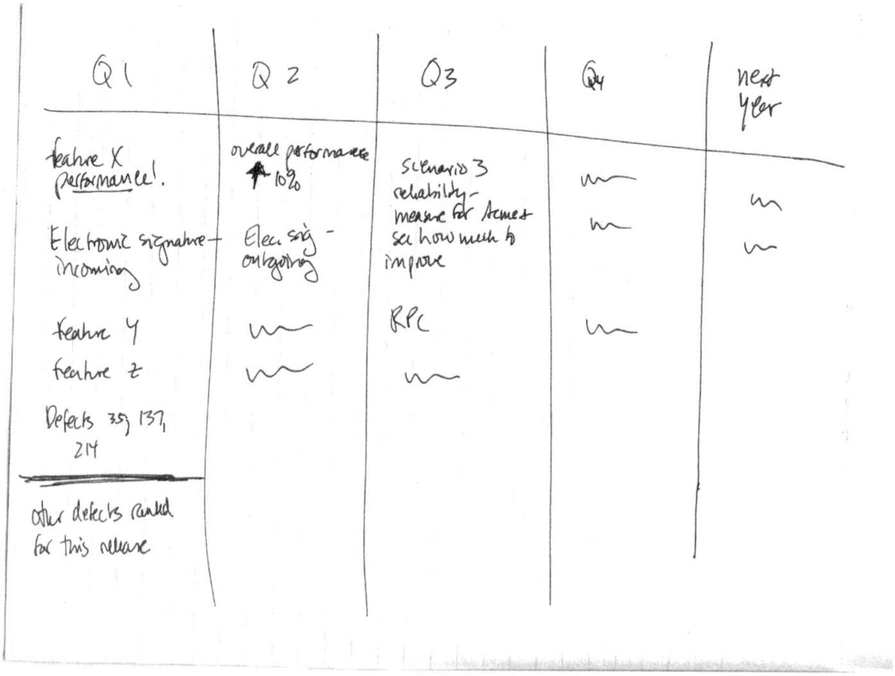

Figure 16.2: PROJECT PORTFOLIO

You might find it helpful to keep a product backlog (some people call these backlogs *product road maps*) at several levels. The extended view is four to six quarters of information. Expect that to change relatively frequently. The midrange view is three to nine months. Again, you'd expect the information past the current quarter to change frequently. The short view is zero to three months. Depending on your life cycle, you can either expect change or manage change.

If you're using an agile life cycle, you don't care how often people change features past the current iteration you're in. The only thing you need to do as a project manager is to protect the contents of the *current* iteration from change. Anything can be moved around past the current iteration. Only the size and duration might cause your sponsors or managers to change their minds about what could be in which iteration. Use planning poker to quickly estimate the size of a number of items in the backlog (see Section 5.1, *Planning Poker*, on page 72).

If you're using an incremental life cycle, especially one where you time-box requirements and architecture work, you can accept change once you've started developing chunks, even if the chunks aren't all the same duration. Then your sponsors and managers can make decisions based on size, duration, and the availability of certain people.

If you're using an iterative or serial life cycle, you can use a quarterly backlog as long as you keep your releases relatively short or you modify your life cycle to produce chunks during the prototype or coding phases.

Manage the Product Backlog

You manage the product backlog by discussing it periodically, either as a program team or as a management team, depending on how your organization works. (If you have a product owner or product manager, that person might decide what's in the product backlog or facilitate the discussion of the backlog.) During the discussion, you allow reranking of all the features in the backlog as often as necessary. For an agile life cycle, that means you review and rerank the product backlog before the next iteration starts in order to finalize the backlog for the iteration.

If you're using a serial life cycle but managing to implement by feature and keeping the duration of the release to three to six months, you probably want to discuss the product backlog every month or so. Before planning the next release, discuss as often as you want, and decide before the release starts what's above the line.

You can change the ranking of the items in the product backlog at any time. You protect only an iteration's backlog contents. Once you've started an iteration, you don't change the contents of the backlog for *this* iteration; any future iteration or release can be changed at any time.

16.7 Troubleshoot Portfolio Management

You've tried. You generated the list of projects and a quarterly backlog for each product. And you still have two projects that your managers rank #1. You have a limited number of people. You don't really want them all to work on both projects at the same time, but you don't see another option. It's time to see whether you can put a price or value on the multitasking that people will have to do.

Managing Multiproject Multitasking

In Section 5.4, *Estimating with Multitasking*, on page 78, I told you not to allow multitasking. If you really want speed, don't allow multitasking. But speed isn't the only variable. Sometimes multitasking can benefit the organization.

Let me be clear. The more multiproject multitasking you allow (or even worse, encourage), the longer your projects will take. But sometimes, because of revenue concerns, customer experience, or the ability to keep a particular customer, your company will ask you to change project priority. If you make decisions with thought and understand the trade-offs, you can manage the multitasking. You won't obtain the benefit of finishing the project you shift people from. But you will obtain the benefit of completing a different project.

Say you're managing a program that won't be released to the customers for another two months. You're making progress, and you're on track to meet your deadline. Imagine that one of your developers is needed for a Crucial Fix to an already-existing customer. You know that losing that developer will prevent you from meeting your deadline. As a project manager, you don't want to let this person move to the Crucial Fix. But as a relatively senior manager in the company, you realize that turning a happy customer into an unhappy customer is a Bad Idea. What do you do?

As long as you don't bounce any members of the project team back and forth (as in Section 6.6, *Pants on Fire*, on page 99) between projects incurring cognitive overload,[3] look at the relative value of each piece of work. You might decide that keeping your already-existing customer happy is the highest priority. (Your context might not be about customers; it could be about revenue.) You might decide that finishing the program on time is the highest priority. But whatever you do, decide. Asking the developer to work part-time on both programs is a guarantee that nothing will get done fast.

Convincing Management That Context Switching Is a Bad Idea

Managers, especially senior managers, don't believe context switching wastes time because all they do is context switch. Senior managers frequently have several projects in the air, most of them waiting for input from other people. But that's not how technical projects work. Most

---

3. See http://seattletimes.nwsource.com/pacificnw/2004/1128/cover.html.

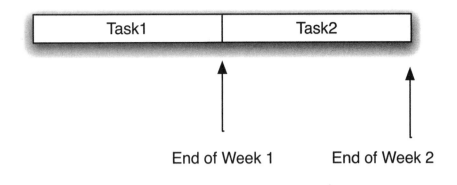

Figure 16.3: TWO TASKS, NO MULTITASKING

of the time, technical people are not in wait states but can continue to work productively on projects. Senior managers don't understand or remember that the work technical people perform is substantively different from the work they perform.

To reach managers and convince them that context switching is a bad idea, make sure you speak their language. First, set the stage by explaining the cost of multitasking technical work. Next, make sure you've developed a project portfolio, so you and your manager can discuss the relative priority of each project. Once you do understand not just the cost but also the value, block out the work, and keep your management apprised of the status.

Explain the Cost of Multitasking Technical Work

Managers expect to work on several projects and be in wait states for several of them. And, managers typically have assistants to help manage the projects, work on the projects, and monitor the manager's time. But technical staff don't have assistants. They feel the costs of multitasking much more strongly than a manager will.

In Figure 16.3, you can see a picture of two tasks, each of which takes a week to complete. If you work on one task at a time until it's complete, Task 1 finishes at the end of week 1. Task 2 finishes at the end of week 2.

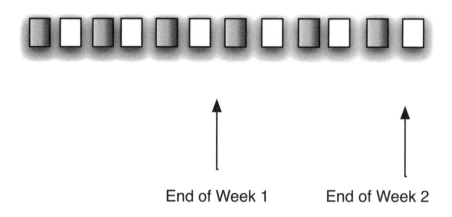

End of Week 1   End of Week 2

Figure 16.4: Two tasks with multitasking

But consider Figure 16.4, which happens when multitasking. Assume that Alice, the person assigned to these two tasks, is working on Task 1 for an entire day and Task 2 the next day. And, let's assume Alice has no other interruptions.

The earliest Alice can complete any task is near the end of week 2, when Alice completes task 1. Sometime early in week 3, Alice completes task 2.

The more tasks Alice has (questions, other projects, whatever), the longer it will take Alice to finish anything. That's because Alice incurs costs each time she switches tasks. The costs for your developers include the following:

- Stopping the work you're doing. The stopping cost is the time it takes to mark your place, save your work, and so on. You haven't stopped thinking about what you're doing, but when you stop to take a phone call or answer a question, there's a stopping cost. If you're in flow, this is surprisingly high.

- Swapping out what you're working on. The swapping out is the act of clearing your mind of the work you had been doing so you have room to swap in the new work. If you were in flow or concentrating deeply, this can take anywhere from five minutes to thirty minutes. Sometimes, it can take even longer.

- Swapping in the new task. Swapping in depends on the complexity of the work and how long it has been since you last touched the task. The more complex and the longer the time since you last touched the task and the more people you have to talk to, the longer it takes.

- Waiting for someone else to stop what they're doing to talk to you about your new task. There's a multiplicative effect of waiting for other people to be available when you have to pick up a new task.

- Swapping the original task back in. Depending on how complex that task is, it can take a few seconds to an hour to wrap your head around what you were doing. (And from a project management point of view, this is when the defects creep in—because it's so hard to remember all the little details you had when you stopped.)

Once you've articulated the cost of multitasking, make sure you understand the relative priority of each project. Review your project portfolio with your manager. If you ask the qualitative and quantitative questions, do you still receive the same answers? If so, then nothing has changed, and your manager will agree to not staff the new work. But maybe things have changed, and it is appropriate to change priorities for now. Develop an agreement with your manager for how long you need to move people from one project to another and when you'll revisit the decision. Then make sure you're using an incremental or agile approach to the project so you have the maximum flexibility.

How to Say No to Multitasking

You and your manager recognize that the desired work does not have more value than the current work—at least not now. And either you or your manager is having trouble saying no to more work.

Sometimes it's politically incorrect to say no. Sometimes you feel like a heel because you want to say no. And there are some organizations in which it's not just politically incorrect—it's career suicide. You have many ways to say no to more work, without actually using the word *no*. I've used these and found them effective. Find some ways that work for you. Otherwise, you'll constantly be in the schedule game discussed in Section 6.12, *We Can't Say No*, on page 112.

"Not right now" and offer a new date. You can say, "I can't fit that in right now, but the team can start in April. Here's when we could start, and here's when we could finish." That helps your management see your other priorities and helps them see what you could stop doing if you really need to start this new work.

"Here's what I'm doing—what should I stop doing?" A caution here: make sure to say this nicely. If you say this sarcastically, you are not helping yourself.

As you show your manager (or your manager's manager) the list of the all the work, explain the priorities. "We're doing this project for Laura. Tom and Betty are doing that project for Sidney. And, we have that project for Allen. My team can't do more—there just aren't any more people. Which project do you want us to stop?"

Build a product backlog with your manager. Sometimes, managers ask you to do more work because they don't know or can't depend on any work getting out of your group. In that case, you can move to timeboxed iterations and build a product backlog with your manager to discuss what the manager will see out of your group and when. See Section 16.6, *Build a Product Backlog*, on page 313.

Prioritize the work with a project portfolio. If a more senior manager asks you to do one more thing, causing multitasking, try this conversation. "Jim, I know you have five or six ongoing projects now. But it will take us longer to do the work if we multitask. And the feedback I have from the product managers is that this release is really important. Let's prioritize the work with a project portfolio so I understand your priorities."

Take your product backlog, and break the work into iterations or relatively short releases (no more than three months). You can plan a project portfolio of what you'll do when for which project. I've used a technique of moving to one- or two-week iterations to finish pieces of work for each project. You don't have to try to do each project simultaneously; even moving to one-week iterations and finishing some work for a given project is better than multitasking.

These are the risks/consequences of the request. Try pointing out the business risks of the multitasking request. "John, we can do that. And if we do that, the writers will be behind for this release because the developers were off working on that other project. I don't know if you remember from last year, but Very Big Customer called our Big Cheese to explain that the undocumented workflow cost them tons of money and time. I'm concerned we'll do that again. Is that a chance we can take?"

"When do you need this" Sometimes, the manager is asking you to add more work to your portfolio, not actually start it now. It's worth asking, "When do you need this? I can put it on the backlog for the next iteration." If it's an entirely new project, asking when the organization needs it means you can respond, "I can slot it in here, after Ron finishes this project. OK?"

If you try all of these, and your sponsor still doesn't accept "no," you are headed for project failure. In that case, consider whether it's time for you to leave. See Section 7.7, *Know When It's Time to Leave*, on page 134.

 ## Remember This

- Use a product backlog, no matter what life cycle you're using.
- Develop a project portfolio to obtain a visual perspective on all the projects, in process and planned.
- Learn how to say no.

More Detailed Information About Life Cycles

A.1 Serial Life Cycle: Waterfall or Phase-Gate

If your project has little technical risk, little schedule risk, a stable project team, and no requirements risk, then consider a serial life cycle. That means if you're doing a short, small-number-of-people project where the requirements are clear (such as a fix to a previous release), this life cycle might be just what you want. See Chapter 11, *Creating and Using a Project Dashboard*, on page 201 for ideas about how to measure a serial lifecycle project so you gain insight as to the real state of the project.

Apparent Risks Addressed by Serial Life Cycles

The following are the apparent risks addressed by serial life cycles:

- Feature set
- Knowing what to do when
- Cost risk

Serial life cycles optimize for the feature set. That's because the requirements are defined at the beginning of the project in a serial life cycle.

In a serial life cycle, it's clear from the schedule what phase you are supposed to be in, so creating a project schedule at the beginning of the project is easy. (Creating one that's useful is more than difficult—it's usually impossible.) Even in stage-gate life cycles with sign-offs that

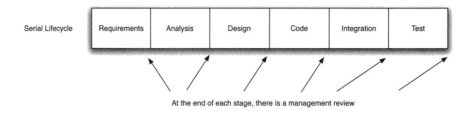

At the end of each stage, there is a management review

Figure A.1: Gantt-like picture of a serial life cycle

allow one phase to start before the previous one is complete, it's possible to know at a glance where the project is supposed to be. And, because the project team spends time at the beginning of the project generating requirements, it's possible to schedule which features to work on when at the *beginning* of the project.

If you use a serial life cycle, make sure you use deliverable-based planning (as discussed in Section 4.3, *Deliverable-Based Planning*, on page 60), where the deliverables are the milestones, not phase ends. If you use phase ends as major milestones, without the rollup of the deliverables behind those milestones, you might not discover until the testing phase that your project is late.

Serial life cycles have a undeserved reputation for managing cost, because it's possible to incorporate management reviews and reestimations into the project plan. In reality, it's easier to manage costs with any other life cycle, because it's easier to measure and see the project's progress.

If you look at the original paper [Roy70], the waterfall life cycle was intended to be an iterative approach with feedback loops. Royce recommended that the team iterate on the analysis for the project and then to implement, not to try to obtain all the requirements perform the analysis up front.

Risks Hidden by Serial Life Cycles

Although people think the serial life cycles expose the following risks, in reality the life cycle hides the risk until too late:

- Architectural risk. Many successful technical people believe that they need to do a full definition of the architecture at the beginning

Who Still Uses Waterfall?

Given the growing popularity of agile practices and life cycles, some of my colleagues have been saying "No one uses waterfall." But plenty of projects still do.

I know of some successful projects that use serial life cycles with feedback. Those project managers use the major milestones as opportunities to gather feedback on the project. Not only do they obtain feedback from their management teams through management review, but some of the PMs also conduct interim retrospectives (see Section 8.2, *Conduct Interim Retrospectives*, on page 144). Their projects aren't as short as they could be, but they do release software their customers want to use. Some successful PMs use a waterfall life cycle.

But too many project managers who use serial life cycles don't take the opportunity to replan at every major milestone or phase. If you must use a serial life cycle, make sure you manage the risks of not seeing the product grow as you proceed.

of the project. And they believe that providing that definition will reduce architectural risk.

The problem with architectural definition up front (what the agile community calls *big design up front*) is that you can't actually tell how the architecture will work until the developers implement some of the features. And because the architecture is defined by components, people tend to develop components, and they don't learn until integration that the architecture is not going to work.

- Testing risk. Some organizations believe that because the serial life cycle has a testing piece after the development piece, the testers should not start testing until the code is done or partway through coding. Nothing could be more wrong.

The formal part of final system testing is after coding, but if you must use a serial life cycle, integrate testing and the testers at the beginning of the project. See Chapter 13, *Integrating Testing into the Project*, on page 255 for ideas. Testing is not just testing code: it's verifying requirements with requirements reviews and inspections; it's verifying architecture with architecture reviews and so on. Any work product can be "tested"—it's just not code-based testing.

If you're developing a product in a regulated industry, you will need a formal validation step—a part of the project that can trace the requirements through the project's process and that delivers test logs and other artifacts that explain how well the requirements were met. Don't confuse verification (testing the product as you proceed to make sure the system works) with validation (testing the process to make sure the product was developed in the correct manner.) For verification, you want testers to work with developers as closely as possible. For validation, you might need more of an audit function. See Section 13.10, *There's a Difference Between QA and Test*, on page 276 for more discussion of what you could obtain from a QA group.

A serial life cycle withholds feedback from developers until they start coding, which is why there is so much schedule risk in serial life cycles. Testing that late takes longer. Make that extra time part of the schedule. If you require that the developers and testers test all work products and ideas, the developers will have more feedback than is otherwise built into this life cycle.

- Schedule risk. A serial lifecycle project with more than a few people and more than a few weeks has little chance of meeting its desired project schedule. The primary reason is lack of feedback to the developers. Because no one can adequately test ideas until the ideas have been codified, the developers don't know whether they have pursued an inadequate architecture until the coding part of the project. In addition to lack of developer feedback, too often the testers are still testing the last product, so they start the project late. And, if the developers run into trouble, project sponsors are too likely to remove time from the testing part of the project in order to meet the desired date. The lack of testers or testing reduces feedback to the developers, which prevents the developers from being proactive, which causes the project to slip or causes more defects, or both.

When to Replan with Serial Life Cycles

Take advantage of every phase milestone to replan the rest of the project. Even if you have not used rolling-wave planning before, consider it even with a phase-gate or waterfall life cycle (see Section 5.6, *Using Rolling-Wave Scheduling*, on page 80). With rolling-wave planning, you have an opportunity to replan each week, or as long as your planning

Serial Life Cycles Seduce with Forecasting

Serial life cycles are seductive. When you create a Gantt chart that looks like you know when events are going to occur, you're forecasting. You're looking into a crystal ball and hoping you see the future.

But projects are full of risk. Your carefully crafted schedule falls apart as soon as people start to work on the project. Because of the risks, the schedule is the one way the project will not unfold. And, you can't see it.

When meteorologists forecast the weather, they gather data about the actual weather to improve their forecasts. But project managers using serial life cycles can't gather project or product data until the coding phase of the project—too far along to know that the project has been off schedule since the second week.

If you must use a serial life cycle, beware that the forecasting you and the team will perform, based on your estimates and documents, might have no basis in reality. And, you won't know that until very late in the project.

timebox is. Even if you take advantage of replanning only at a phase end, that will help you steer the project in a more reasonable direction.

A.2 Iterative Life Cycle: Spiral, Evolutionary Prototyping, Unified Process

If you have customers who want to work with you and you can manage the project team's prototyping, these life cycles are useful when you need to see the effects of a variety of features on the total product. The spiral life cycle (see Figure A.2, on the next page) is helpful when you want to prototype large pieces of the system and then engineer/finish the product development. Evolutionary prototyping (see Figure A.3, on the following page) can be helpful if you have more technical risk with integration than you think a spiral life cycle can handle. The Unified Process (of which RUP, the Rational Unified Process, is the most famous), shown in Figure A.4, on page 329, can be particularly useful because the iteration timeboxing and integration helps manage the schedule risk.

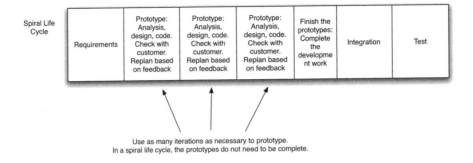

Figure A.2: GANTT-LIKE PICTURE OF SPIRAL LIFE CYCLE

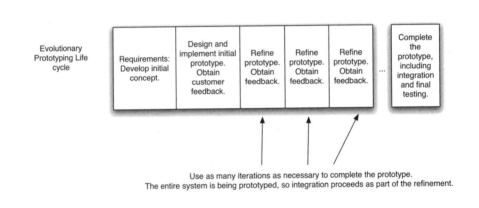

Figure A.3: GANTT-LIKE PICTURE OF EVOLUTIONARY PROTOTYPING LIFE CYCLE

Risks Addressed by an Iterative Life Cycle

These are the risks addressed by an iterative life cycle:

- Frequently changing requirements. Because you prototype a piece at a time, it's easy to absorb additional or changed requirements.

- Technical (architectural or design) risks. By prototyping early, the team settles on an architecture or design that they know works.

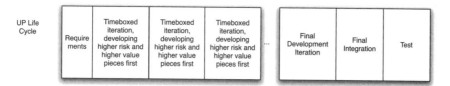

Each timebox (2-6 weeks) delivers completed functionality, including the testing of that functionality.
Many successful UP projects include full system-level integration during each timebox.
Use as many timeboxes as necessary to complete the number of iterations needed for the project.
Requirements can change/evolve during the project and are addressed during each iteration.
By attempting to implement the high-risk and high-value requirements first, the consequences of changing requirements are reduced.

Figure A.4: GANTT-LIKE PICTURE OF UNIFIED PROCESS LIFE CYCLE

Risks Exposed by an Iterative life Cycle

These are the risks exposed by an iterative life cycle:

- Schedule. In a true spiral or evolutionary prototyping life cycle, *finishing* the project can be difficult, especially if the team enjoys prototyping and prototypes for a long time. For the UP, finishing can be difficult if the team has not kept to the timeboxes or completed each iteration's work within the timebox.

- Cost risk. These life cycles assume the team will implement the riskiest parts of the product first, not necessarily the most valuable parts of the product. Sometimes the most risky parts are the most valuable, but not always. See Section 9.3, *Implement the Highest-Value Features First*, on page 172.

Iterative Life Cycles Differ from Agile Life Cycles

Iterative life cycles are different from the agile life cycles in these ways:

- The agile life cycles have one- to four- week timeboxes—the same iteration duration throughout the entire project. Strictly iterative life cycles have no standard limit on their timeboxes; some iterations could be two weeks, some five weeks, some three weeks, or whatever works for your project. (Some teams implement the RUP with timeboxes of a standard size.)

- Agile life cycles strive for completed features at the end of an iteration and will change what they plan for the next iteration based on what they completed during the previous iteration. The iterative life cycles do not necessarily complete a feature during an iteration; it's possible that the goal of an iteration is to develop a prototype, not completed, tested, and reviewed code.

When to Replan with the Iterative Life Cycles

Replanning is most effective at the end of an iteration in preparation for the next iteration. If you find you need to plan in the middle of an iteration, your iterations might be too long, or the team might be trying to fit too much into an iteration.

As you replan, consider when you want to encourage the developers to complete prototypes into releasable code. One part of replanning might be mixing this life cycle with either incremental life cycles or with agile life cycles so you obtain the benefit of the prototypes early in the project and the benefit of completed features later in the project.

A.3 Incremental Life Cycle: Staged Delivery, Design to Schedule

Incremental life cycles (see Figure A.5, on the next page) shine when you don't have continuous access to the customer and you can create feature teams to implement by feature. Incremental life cycles work even better if you have cross-functional teams so you can *complete* the feature with the cross-functional team. They work less well if the feature teams don't finish all the necessary work for a feature (including testing and documentation) even when the feature team is collocated. One of the ways to organize teams for incremental life cycles is to acquire the scarce resources (people, machines, whatever) and implement those features that require the scarce resources early in the project. If the feature team doesn't complete their work when the scarce resource is assigned to the project, they might not be able to complete the project.

Risks Addressed by an Incremental Life Cycle

The following are the risks addressed by an incremental life cycle:

- Schedule risk. As the team builds, tests, and integrates features, you can gather data about the team's real progress, which decreases schedule risk.

- Project team changes. If someone leaves the project, the leaving tends to affect just one of the cross-functional teams, not the entire project team.

- Requirements changes, as long as they don't change the underlying product architecture.

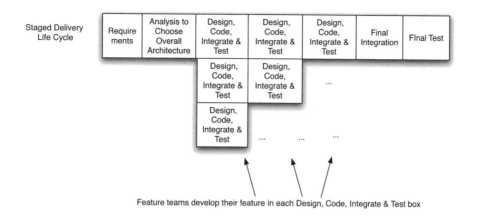

Feature teams develop their feature in each Design, Code, Integrate & Test box

Figure A.5: GANTT-LIKE PICTURE OF AN INCREMENTAL LIFE CYCLE

Risks Exposed by an Incremental Life Cycle

The following are the risks exposed by an incremental life cycle:

- Architectural risk. If the team guesses wrong about which features to implement first, a later feature could change the architecture.

- Requirements changes. Since features are completed as the team proceeds, if someone wants to change a previously developed feature, the team will need to do more work.

When to Replan with an Incremental Life Cycle

It makes sense to replan after each feature is implemented. Incremental life cycles lend themselves well to rolling-wave (see Section 5.6, *Using Rolling-Wave Scheduling*, on page 80), so the amount of total project replanning is minimal.

A.4 Agile Life Cycles

Agile life cycles (see Figure A.6, on the next page) handle schedule, technical, requirements, and cost risks the best. They plan to complete features—most often the most valuable features—within a short time-boxed iteration. These life cycles require frequent access to the customer or customer surrogate. (In one-week iterations, the customer needs to be available for questions every day.) As long as the team

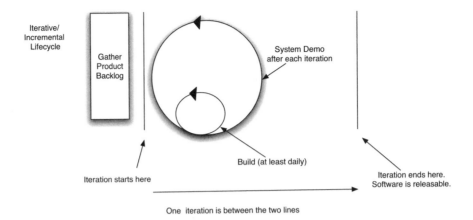

Figure A.6: GANTT-LIKE PICTURE OF AN AGILE LIFE CYCLE

members are not multitasked onto several projects, leave in the middle of a timebox, and can commit to completing features, the team is likely to succeed with this life cycle.

When I work with teams exploring the idea of moving to an agile life cycle, one of their stumbling blocks is this: "We need to know how to break things apart and estimate well. We don't do that now. We can't go to agile, can we?" The answer is yes—as long as you gather the data for velocity charts and the team understands they will need to learn to break things into small pieces. Test-driven development (as discussed in Section 13.3, *TDD Is the Easiest Way to Integrate Testing into Your Project*, on page 257) can help team members learn to think in smaller pieces.

Risks Addressed by Agile Life Cycles

The following are the risks addressed by agile life cycles:

- Schedule risk. Because you never plan for more than an iteration's worth of work, it's easy to replan a schedule or see what you really need to meet the schedule.

- Project team changes. As long as the project team doesn't change *within* the iteration, the team is more resilient against personnel changes.

- Requirements changes. Sure, if you have a requirements change that modifies the architecture, that's an issue, but that's an issue for any life cycle. Because the agile life cycles manage requirements changes with a living backlog, it's easier to talk about the cost and the value of each of those changes.

- Cost risk. Because the product owner can rerank the requirements before the next iteration (see Section 16.6, *Manage the Product Backlog*, on page 315) and because the iterations are relatively short, the project can end much sooner than management or the product owner might otherwise plan.

For agile life cycles, the PM's job is to protect the contents of the iteration and to protect the state of the people working on the project. The requirements continue to evolve for the project *outside* the iteration, before the next iteration starts. You can always add or remove features, but the contents for any given iteration are protected.

In addition to the iteration's content, the PM protects the iteration's staffing. All people on the project must be fully committed to this project—and this project alone—during an iteration. What about interruptions? No interruptions until after the iteration. Yes, you can stop an iteration at any time, work on interruptions, and replan the next iteration. For more on how to handle interruptions, see Section 8.11, *Manage Interruptions*, on page 159. (And if you can't protect the people during an iteration because these people are a scarce resource, see Section 5.5, *Scheduling People to Multitask by Design*, on page 79.)

Risks Exposed by Agile Life Cycles

If you need to manage schedule, cost, requirements, and technical risk, the agile life cycles are best. The agile life cycles will expose the risk that your management can't decide which projects are ranked at which priority. And, they expose the risk that the people who need to decide about requirements can't decide. And, if your management isn't willing to protect the people and the contents of the iteration, you won't be able to maintain the life cycle—and that's true for any life cycle.

Because there's so much more discipline in an agile life cycle, a work environment that does not support the life cycle becomes much more obvious. And that's a risk to the long-term retention of the people on your project. (If you or your management isn't consistent with what you say and what you do, people will flip the bozo bit [RD05] on you and eventually leave.)

Consider an Agile Life Cycle When...

The more risks you have, the more an agile life cycle and agile practices will help. Scrum [Sch04] is a project management framework. You need to be ready to protect an iteration's worth of work and to protect the people working on the project from being yanked off to work on another project. Since the agile life cycles have short iterations, you could always try three iteration's worth of work and see how it goes and then plan the rest of the project. (I recommend you try three iterations worth of work because it might take you and the team that long to find your natural rhythm.)

When to Replan with an Agile Life Cycle

Replan at the beginning of an iteration. Plan to reorganize the product backlog (not this iteration's contents) continuously.

Agile Life Cycles Are Based on Feedback

Agile life cycles use feedback to provide the project team information about the true state of the project. You don't need a crystal ball to know what's going on—you can see and touch and measure and feel what's happening.

These are the only life cycles based on feedback from beginning to end. If you have a project that's highly risky, consider an agile life cycle so you can obtain feedback about the project from day 1.

Appendix B

Glossary of Terms

Critical path:

The critical path is the longest serial chain of dependent tasks. It is the shortest time it will take you to complete the project.

Crossing the Desert Syndrome:

This is the feeling that you'll never be done. It occurs when the team has focused all their attention and time on trying to meet an intermediate milestone. Once they meet that milestone, they still have the rest of the project to do. Just when you think you're at the oasis, you realize you're not even close.[1]

Inch-pebbles:

Inch-pebbles are one-to-two day tasks that are either done or not done.

Life cycle:

This is the way your organize the project and shepherd it through to completion.

Parking lot:

This is a place to put issues you don't want to lose but don't necessarily want to address at this time.

Product owner:

This is the person who makes decisions about what goes into the product and when. This is also the person who manages the product backlog.

---

1. I first heard this from Jack Nevison of Oak Associates.

Program management:

    Project management means coordinating several subprojects or a series of projects to meet some specific business objectives.

Project:

    A project is a novel undertaking or systematic process to create a new product or service, the delivery of which signals completion. Projects involve risk and are typically constrained by limited resources.[2]

Project manager:

    This is the person whose job it is to articulate and communicate what *done* means and to guide the project team to done. By *done*, I mean a product that meets the needs of the organization developing the product and the customers who will use the product.

Product:

    This is the set of deliverables that results from the project.

Rolling-wave planning:

    This is detailed scheduling for a fixed period of time. Ongoing planning maintains the timebox.

Spike:

    A spike is a timeboxed task to gain information about other work. In XP, the work in the timebox is thrown away [Coh06].

Technical debt:

    Technical debt is the work you owe your product that the project team didn't complete in a previous releases. It can be any kind of work the project team didn't accomplish in previous releases: design debt, code redesign or refactoring debt, testing debt, or writing debt.

Work breakdown structure:

    The work breakdown structure (WBS) is the organization of tasks, showing their dependencies, durations, and owner. The higher level the WBS (and the earlier in the project), the less you know. Expect to evolve the WBS as you proceed.

---

2. © 2007 R. Max Wideman, http://www.maxwideman.com; reproduced with permission.

Appendix C

Bibliography

[Aus96]   Robert D. Austin. *Measuring and Managing Performance in Organizations.* Dorset House Publishing, New York, 1996.

[BB96]   Tony Buzan and Barry Buzan. *The Mind Map Book: How to Use Radiant Thinking to Maximize Your Brain's Untapped Potential.* Plume, New York, NY, 1996.

[BF01]   Kent Beck and Martin Fowler. *Planning Extreme Programming.* Addison-Wesley, Reading, MA, 2001.

[Bro95]   Frederick P. Brooks, Jr. *The Mythical Man Month: Essays on Software Engineering.* Addison-Wesley, Reading, MA, anniversary edition, 1995.

[BWe01]   James Bullock, Gerald M. Weinberg, and Marie Benesh eds. *Roundtable on Project Management: A SHAPE Forum Dialogue.* Dorset House Publishing, New York, 2001.

[CB91]   Allen R. Cohen and David L. Bradford. *Influence without Authority.* John Wiley & Sons, New York, 1991.

[CK02]   Bret Pettichord Cem Kaner, James Bach. *Lessons Learned in Software Testing: A Context-Driven Approach.* John Wiley & Sons, New York, NY, 2002.

[Coc01]   Alistair Cockburn. *Agile Software Development.* Addison Wesley Longman, Reading, MA, 2001.

[Coc04]   Alistair Cockburn. *Crystal Clear: A Human-Powered Methodology for Small Teams.* Addison Wesley Longman, Reading, MA, 2004.

[Coh06]   Mike Cohn. *Agile Estimating and Planning.* Prentice Hall, Englewood Cliffs, NJ, 2006.

[Cov91]   Stephen R. Covey. *Principle-Centered Leadership.* Summit Books, New York, 1991.

[CS98]   Michael A. Cusamano and Richard W. Selby. *Microsoft Secrets.* Touchstone, New York, 1998.

[DeM86]   Tom DeMarco. *Controlling Software Projects: Management, Measurement, Estimation.* Prentice Hall, Englewood Cliffs, NJ, 1986.

[DeM97]   Tom DeMarco. *The Deadline.* Dorset House, New York, 1997.

[DeM01]   Tom DeMarco. *Slack: Getting Past Burnout, Busywork, and the Myth of Total Efficiency.* Broadway Books, New York, 2001.

[DL99]   Tom Demarco and Timothy Lister. *Peopleware: Productive Projects and Teams.* Dorset House, New York, NY, second edition, 1999.

[DL03]   Tom Demarco and Timothy Lister. *Waltzing with Bears: Managing Risk on Software Projects.* Dorset House, New York, NY, 2003.

[DL06]   Esther Derby and Diana Larsen. *Agile Retrospectives: Making Good Teams Great.* The Pragmatic Programmers, LLC, Raleigh, NC, and Dallas, TX, 2006.

[Gol97]   Eliyahu Goldratt. *Critical Chain.* North River Press, Great Barrington, MA, 1997.

[Gol04]   Eliyahu Goldratt. *The Goal, 3rd ed.* North River Press, Great Barrington, MA, 2004.

[Gra92]   Robert B. Grady. *Practical Software Metrics for Project Management and Process Improvement.* Prentice Hall, Englewood Cliffs, NJ, 1992.

[GW89]   Donald C. Gause and Gerald M. Weinberg. *Exploring Requirements: Quality Before Design.* Dorset House, New York, 1989.

[Hal07]   Payson Hall. Exploring project priorities. *stickyminds.com*, 2007. http://www.stickyminds.com/s.asp?F=S11953_COL_2.

[HT03]   Andy Hunt and Dave Thomas. The art of enbugging. *IEEE Software*, 10(1):10–11, 2003.

[JAH02]   Ron Jeffries, Ann Anderson, and Chet Hendrickson. *Extreme Programming Installed.* Addison-Wesley, Reading, MA, 2002.

[Ker01]   Norman L. Kerth. *Project Retrospectives: A Handbook for Team Reviews.* Dorset House, New York, 2001.

[Koh93]   Alfie Kohn. *Punished by Rewards: The Trouble with Gold Stars, Incentive PLans, A's, Praise, and Other Bribes.* Houghton Mifflin Company, Boston, 1993.

[KS99]   Jon R. Katzenbach and Douglas K. Smith. *The Wisdom of Team: Creating the High-Performance Organization.* Harper-Collins Publishers, New York, 1999.

[McC96]   Steve McConnell. *Rapid Development: Taming Wild Software Schedules.* Microsoft Press, Redmond, WA, 1996.

[McC06]   Steve McConnell. *Software Estimation: Demystifying the Black Art.* Microsoft Press, Redmond, WA, 2006.

[Mey93]   Christopher Meyer. *Fast Cycle Time: How to Align Purpose, Strategy, and Structure for Speed.* The Free Press, New York, 1993.

[Moo91]   Geoffrey A. Moore. *Crossing the Chasm.* Harper Business, New York, NY, 1991.

[MP06]   Mary and Tom Poppendieck. *Implementing Lean Software Development: From Concept to Cash.* Addison-Wesley, Reading, MA, 2006.

[Phi04]   Dwayne Phillips. *The Software Project Manager's Handbook: Principles that work at work, 2nd ed.* IEEE/Wiley, Hoboken, NJ, 2004.

[RBS00]   ed. R. Brian Stanfield. *The Art of Focused Conversation, 100 Ways to access Group Wisdom in the Workplace.* New Society Publishers, Gabriola Island, BC, Canada, 2000.

[RD05]   Johanna Rothman and Esther Derby. *Behind Closed Doors: Secrets of Great Management.* The Pragmatic Programmers, LLC, Raleigh, NC, and Dallas, TX, 2005.

[RG05]   Jared Richardson and Will Gwaltney. *Ship It! A Practical Guide to Successful Software Projects*. The Pragmatic Programmers, LLC, Raleigh, NC, and Dallas, TX, 2005.

[Rot98]   Johanna Rothman. Defining and managing project focus. *American Programmer*, 11(2):19–23, 1998.   http://www. jrothman.com/Papers/aparticle.html.

[Rot99]   Johanna Rothman. How to use inch-pebbles when you think you can't. *American Programmer*, 12(5):24–29, 1999. http://www.jrothman.com/Papers/Howinch-pebbles.html.

[Rot02a]   Johanna Rothman. Release criteria: Is this software done? *STQE*, 4(2):30–35, 2002.

[Rot02b]   Johanna Rothman. What does success look like? *Stickyminds.com*, 2002. http://www.stickyminds.com/se/S3181.asp.

[Rot04a]   Johanna Rothman. Got good rhythm? *Software Development Magazine*, 12(6), 2004. http://www.drdobbs.com/dept/architect/184415151.

[Rot04b]   Johanna Rothman. *Hiring the Best Knowledge Workers, Techies, and Nerds: The Secrets and Science of Hiring Technical People*. Dorset House, New York, 2004.

[Roy70]   Winston W. Royce. Managing the development of large software systems. *Proceedings, IEEE WECON*, pages 1–9, August 1970.

[Sch04]   Ken Schwaber. *Agile Project Management with Scrum*. Microsoft Press, Redmond, WA, 2004.

[SH06a]   Venkat Subramaniam and Andy Hunt. *Practices of an Agile Developer*. The Pragmatic Programmers, LLC, Raleigh, NC, and Dallas, TX, 2006.

[SH06b]   Venkat Subramaniam and Andy Hunt. *Practices of an Agile Developer: Working in the Real World*. The Pragmatic Programmers, LLC, Raleigh, NC, and Dallas, TX, 2006.

[SR98]   Preston G. Smith and Donald G. Reinertson. *Developing Products in Half the Time: New Rules, New Tools, second ed.* John Wiley & Sons, New York, NY, 1998.

[TCKO00]   Stephanie Teasley, Lisa Covi, M. S. Krishnan, and Judith S. Olson. How does radical collocation help a team succeed? *Proceedings of CSCW'00*, pages 339–346, 2000.

[Wei85]   Gerald M. Weinberg. *The Secrets of Consulting*. Dorset House, New York, 1985.

[Wei92]   Gerald M. Weinberg. *Quality Software Management: Volume 1, Systems Thinking*. Dorset House Publishing, Inc., New York, 1992.

[Wei94]   Gerald M. Weinberg. *Quality Software Management, Volume 3: Congruent Action*. Dorset House, New York, 1994.

[Wei97]   Gerald M. Weinberg. *Quality Software Management: Volume 4, Anticipating Change*. Dorset House Publishing, Inc., New York, 1997.

[Wie00]   Karl Wiegers. Stop promising miracles. *Software Development*, 8(2), 2000.

[Wie05]   Karl Wiegers. *Project Initiation Handbook*. Process Impact, Clackamas, OR, 2005.

[WJ77]   Bruce W.Tuckman and Mary Ann C. Jensen. Stages of small group development revisited. *Group and Organizational Studies*, 2:419– 427, 1977.

[WJC00]   Robert Wysocki, Robert Beck Jr., and David B. Crane. *Effective Project Management, second edition*. John Wiley & Sons, New York, NY, 2000.

[WK02]   Laurie Williams and Robert Kessler. *Pair Programming Illuminated*. Addison-Wesley, Reading, MA, 2002.

[You99]   Edward Yourdon. *Death March: The Complete Software Developer's Guide to Surviving âĂŸMission Impossible' Projects*. Prentice Hall, Englewood Cliffs, NJ, 1999.

Index

A Pragmatic Career

Welcome to the Pragmatic Community. We hope you've enjoyed this title.

If you've enjoyed this book by Johanna Rothman, and want to advance your management career, you'll be interested in seeing what happens *Behind Closed Doors*. And see how you can lead you team to success by using *Agile Retrospectives*.

Behind Closed Doors

You can learn to be a better manager—even a great manager—with this guide. You'll find powerful tips covering:

• Delegating effectively • Using feedback and goal-setting • Developing influence • Handling one-on-one meetings • Coaching and mentoring
• Deciding what work to do-and what not to do
• . . . and more!

Behind Closed Doors Secrets of Great Management
Johanna Rothman and Esther Derby
(192 pages) ISBN: 0-9766940-2-6. $24.95
http://pragmaticprogrammer.com/titles/rdbcd

Agile Retrospectives

Mine the experience of your software development team continually throughout the life of the project. Rather than waiting until the end of the project—as with a traditional retrospective, when it's too late to help—agile retrospectives help you adjust to change *today*.

The tools and recipes in this book will help you uncover and solve hidden (and not-so-hidden) problems with your technology, your methodology, and those difficult "people issues" on your team.

Agile Retrospectives: Making Good Teams Great
Esther Derby and Diana Larsen
(170 pages) ISBN: 0-9776166-4-9. $29.95
http://pragmaticprogrammer.com/titles/dlret

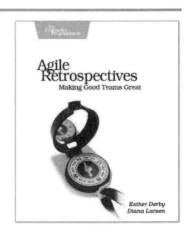

Competitive Edge

Need to get software out the door? Then you want to see how to *Ship It!* with less fuss and more features. And every developer can benefit from the *Practices of an Agile Developer*.

Ship It!

Page after page of solid advice, all tried and tested in the real world. This book offers a collection of tips that show you what tools a successful team has to use, and how to use them well. You'll get quick, easy-to-follow advice on modern techniques and when they should be applied. **You need this book if:** • You're frustrated at lack of progress on your project. • You want to make yourself and your team more valuable. • You've looked at methodologies such as Extreme Programming (XP) and felt they were too, well, extreme. • You've looked at the Rational Unified Process (RUP) or CMM/I methods and cringed at the learning curve and costs. • **You need to get software out the door without excuses**

Ship It! A Practical Guide to Successful Software Projects
Jared Richardson and Will Gwaltney
(200 pages) ISBN: 0-9745140-4-7. $29.95
http://pragmaticprogrammer.com/titles/prj

Practices of an Agile Developer

Agility is all about using feedback to respond to change. Learn how to apply the principles of agility throughout the software development process • Establish and maintain an agile working environment • Deliver what users really want • Use personal agile techniques for better coding and debugging • Use effective collaborative techniques for better teamwork • Move to an agile approach

Practices of an Agile Developer: Working in the Real World
Venkat Subramaniam and Andy Hunt
(189 pages) ISBN: 0-9745140-8-X. $29.95
http://pragmaticprogrammer.com/titles/pad

Cutting Edge

Now that you've finished your project, are you sure that it's ready for the real world? Are you truly ready to *Release It!* in this crazy world?

Interested in Ruby on Rails, but don't want to learn another framework from scratch? You don't have to! *Rails for Java Programmers* leverages you and your team's knowledge of Java to quickly learn the Rails environment.

Release It!

Whether it's in Java, .NET, or Ruby on Rails, getting your application ready to ship is only half the battle. Did you design your system to survive a sudden rush of visitors from Digg or Slashdot? Or an influx of real world customers from 100 different countries? Are you ready for a world filled with flakey networks, tangled databases, and impatient users?

If you're a developer and don't want to be on call at 3AM for the rest of your life, this book will help.

Design and Deploy Production-Ready Software
Michael T. Nygard
(368 pages) ISBN: 0-9787392-1-3. $34.95
http://pragmaticprogrammer.com/titles/mnee

Rails for Java Developers

Enterprise Java developers already have most of the skills needed to create Rails applications. They just need a guide which shows how their Java knowledge maps to the Rails world. That's what this book does. It covers: • The Ruby language • Building MVC Applications • Unit and Functional Testing • Security • Project Automation • Configuration • Web Services This book is the fast track for Java programmers who are learning or evaluating Ruby on Rails.

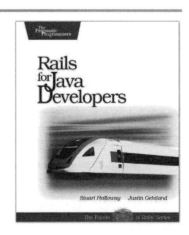

Rails for Java Developers
Stuart Halloway and Justin Gehtland
(300 pages) ISBN: 0-9776166-9-X. $34.95
http://pragmaticprogrammer.com/titles/fr_r4j

Facets of Ruby Series

If you're serious about Ruby, you need the definitive reference to the language. The Pick-axe: *Programming Ruby: The Pragmatic Programmer's Guide, Second Edition*. This is *the* definitive guide for all Ruby programmers. And you'll need a good text editor, too. On the Mac, we recommend TextMate.

Programming Ruby (The Pickaxe)

The Pickaxe book, named for the tool on the cover, is the definitive reference to this highly-regarded language. • Up-to-date and expanded for Ruby version 1.8 • Complete documentation of all the built-in classes, modules, and methods • Complete descriptions of all ninety-eight standard libraries • 200+ pages of new content in this edition • Learn more about Ruby's web tools, unit testing, and programming philosophy

Programming Ruby: The Pragmatic Programmer's Guide, 2nd Edition
Dave Thomas with Chad Fowler and Andy Hunt
(864 pages) ISBN: 0-9745140-5-5. $44.95
http://pragmaticprogrammer.com/titles/ruby

TextMate

If you're coding Ruby or Rails on a Mac, then you owe it to yourself to get the TextMate editor. And, once you're using TextMate, you owe it to yourself to pick up this book. It's packed with information which will help you automate all your editing tasks, saving you time to concentrate on the important stuff. Use snippets to insert boilerplate code and refactorings to move stuff around. Learn how to write your own extensions to customize it to the way you work.

TextMate: Power Editing for the Mac
James Edward Gray II
(200 pages) ISBN: 0-9787392-3-X. $29.95
http://pragmaticprogrammer.com/titles/textmate

The Pragmatic Bookshelf

The Pragmatic Bookshelf features books written by developers for developers. The titles continue the well-known Pragmatic Programmer style, and continue to garner awards and rave reviews. As development gets more and more difficult, the Pragmatic Programmers will be there with more titles and products to help you stay on top of your game.

Visit Us Online

Manage It! Home Page
http://pragmaticprogrammer.com/titles/jrpm
Source code from this book, errata, and other resources. Come give us feedback, too!

Register for Updates
http://pragmaticprogrammer.com/updates
Be notified when updates and new books become available.

Join the Community
http://pragmaticprogrammer.com/community
Read our weblogs, join our online discussions, participate in our mailing list, interact with our wiki, and benefit from the experience of other Pragmatic Programmers.

New and Noteworthy
http://pragmaticprogrammer.com/news
Check out the latest pragmatic developments in the news.

Save on the PDF

Save PDF version of this book. Owning the paper version of this book entitles you to purchase the PDF version at a terrific discount. The PDF is great for carrying around on your laptop. It's hyperlinked, has color, and is fully searchable.

Buy it now at pragmaticprogrammer.com/coupon.

Contact Us

Phone Orders:	1-800-699-PROG (+1 919 847 3884)
Online Orders:	www.pragmaticprogrammer.com/catalog
Customer Service:	orders@pragmaticprogrammer.com
Non-English Versions:	translations@pragmaticprogrammer.com
Pragmatic Teaching:	academic@pragmaticprogrammer.com
Author Proposals:	proposals@pragmaticprogrammer.com